CREWE TO CARLISLE

CREWE
TO
CARLISLE

BRIAN REED

LONDON

IAN ALLAN

First published 1969

S.B.N. 7110 0057 3

Published in the United Kingdom by Ian Allan Ltd, Shepperton Surrey, and printed by The Press at Coombelands Ltd, Addlestone, Weybridge, Surrey

Contents

Summary of Tables

To
The Archivist of British Railways Board
and his Staff,
every member of which at London and York
has withstood many a seven-hour session
1967-68

No one but he who has to collect them (the facts), can have any notion of the extreme difficulty which is occasionally experienced in obtaining a correct knowledge of the slightest matter. We have frequently found in the course of our labours, that out of five or six accounts already published of a subject not one was correct; and we have spent days in search of a little information, which we previously supposed was known to everyone concerned with it, and yet, to our surprise, no one could furnish it.—E. C. and W. Osborne, in the preface to *Osborne's Guide to the Grand Junction Railway*, 1838.

I

The Grand Junction Tail

THE PROMISCUOUS begetting of the 141 miles of route from Crewe to Carlisle (Fig. 1a) is still evident today in the mile posts. Not in strict accordance with the original limits of any one of the eight companies concerned (Fig. 1b), nor of any combination of them, they are in four series: (*a*) Euston to Golborne junction; (*b*) Golborne junction to Preston; (*c*) Preston to Lancaster; and (*d*) Lancaster to Carlisle. Each series begins on the main line at zero except (*b*), the starting point of which is at the old Parkside junction on the Liverpool & Manchester Railway. The final series begins at Lancaster Castle station and not at No. 1 signalbox, where the old Lancaster & Carlisle Railway joined the Lancaster & Preston Junction Railway. The 188 m.p. from Euston is located a few yards north of Golborne Junction signalbox, and some quarter of a mile on is No. 1 m.p. from Parkside. Moreover, the bridges are also numbered separately, e.g. from 1 to 93 reading from Preston northward; and from Lancaster (Castle) another series beginning at No. 1 extends to Carlisle.

All this is in the tradition of the old Grand Junction Railway. That company's mileposts were ordered to be on the west side of the line (that is, the present down side), but Liverpool was to be the zero point though 15 miles away from the nearest point on the G.J.R. There was also a proposal to put another set of posts, numbered from Birmingham, on what is the present up side; but this does not seem to have been accomplished. If it had, both sets of posts would have been 'wrong side.' The mileposts for most of the history of the G.J.R. section have actually been on the down side, and have had London as the zero point since the formation of the L.N.W.R. and the construction of the Trent Valley line.

First public suggestion for a railway from Lancashire through Carlisle to Glasgow seems to have been made in 1835, at a time when no railway was in operation north of Wigan, though one was in the early stages of construction between that town and Preston. By 1841 a railway 'undivided in its interests and management' from Lancaster to Edinburgh and Glasgow had become the avowed aim of all interested parties in the various localities; but as practical politics the railways down the backbone of Lancashire had to be built piecemeal. To get a true idea of the origin and fortunes of the Crewe–Carlisle division of the West Coast Route, a review of nearly a dozen separate railways is needed; and through the story of the 55 miles and four railways from Wigan to Oxenholme drifts again and again the sitting tenant — the Lancaster Canal Company.

For ease in reading and reference, these railways and the abbreviations of their titles may be listed as:

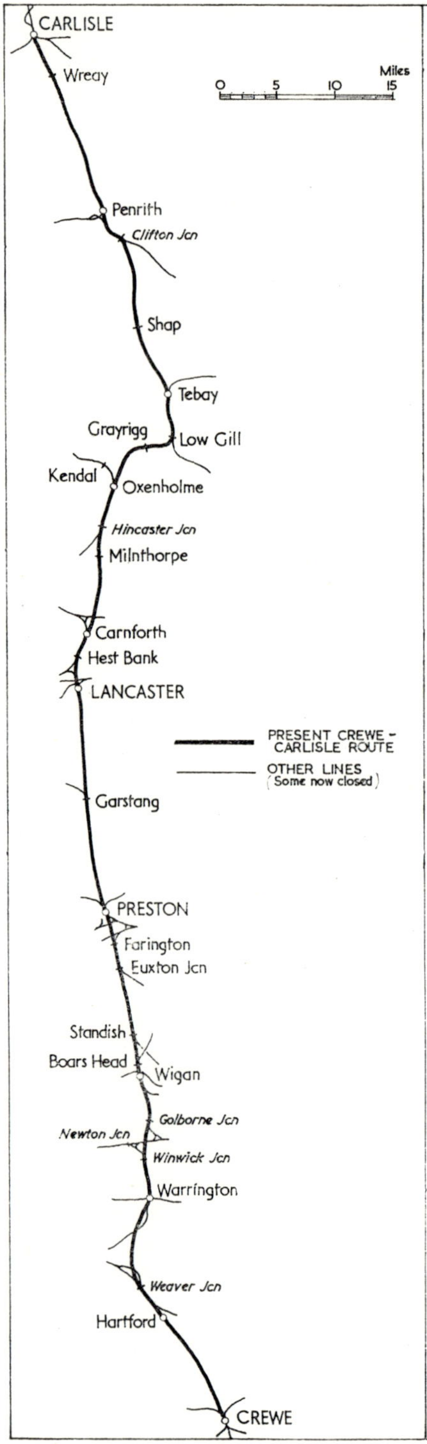

1a Crewe to Carlisle, present line

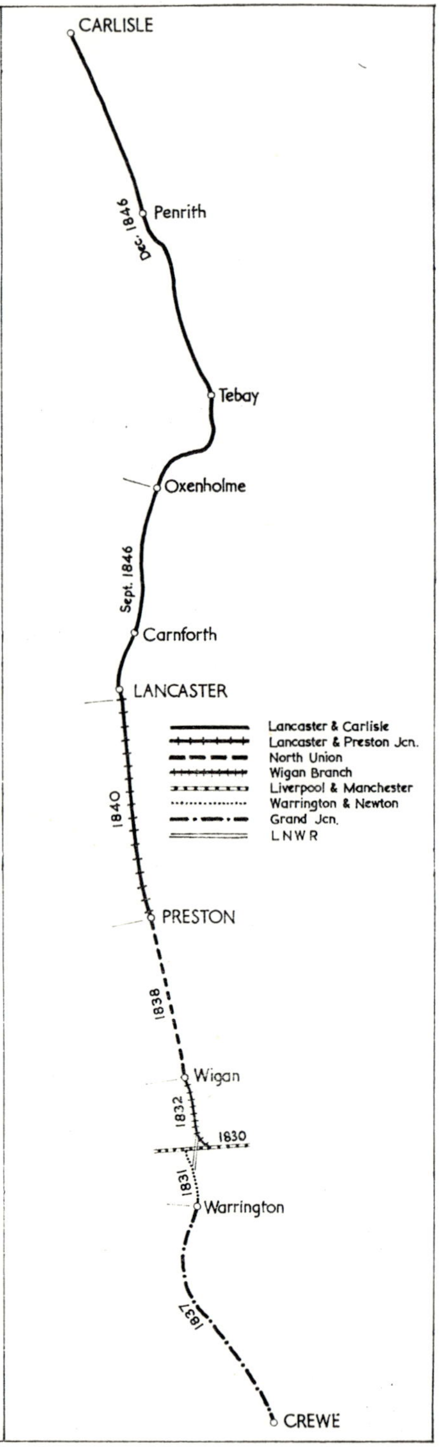

1b Crewe to Carlisle, original ownership

G.J.R.	—	Grand Junction Railway
L. & M.	—	Liverpool & Manchester Railway
W. & N.	—	Warrington & Newton Railway
W.B.	—	Wigan Branch Railway
N.U.	—	North Union Railway
B. & P.	—	Bolton & Preston Railway
P. & W.	—	Preston & Wyre Railway
L. & P.	—	Lancaster & Preston Junction Railway
L. & C.	—	Lancaster & Carlisle Railway
K. & W.	—	Kendal & Windermere Railway
N.W.R.	—	'Little' North Western Railway
M. & C.	—	Maryport & Carlisle Railway
N. & C.	—	Newcastle & Carlisle Railway
Caley	—	Caledonian Railway
L.C.C.	—	Lancaster Canal Company
L.N.W.R.	—	London & North-Western Railway
L.Y.R.	—	Lancashire & Yorkshire Railway

The section immediately north of Crewe was no beginning of a great trunk line to the north; rather was it the tail end of another from the south, for the Crewe–Warrington length was the last part of the original G.J.R. scheme, which began at Birmingham. This tail in no sense wagged the dog; on the contrary, the dog did a good deal of tail-wagging as the tail grew gradually for another 120 miles to the north. The G.J.R. was incorporated on May 6, 1833 (Act 3 & 4 Wm. 4, cap. 34), and its 78 mile main line from Birmingham to Warrington, and then on to join with the L. & M. at Newton Junction, was opened on July 4, 1837, without any of the ceremonies and magnificent cold collations usual on such occasions. Several accounts have stated this was due partly to John Moss, the chairman, and Charles Lawrence, the vice-chairman, having witnessed the accident to Huskisson seven years before and having been much affected by it; but the real reason may have been that though Victoria was on the throne, William IV had not been buried. He died on June 20, but the funeral was not until July 8 and so official mourning would still be the rule on July 4. Goods traffic on the G.J.R. did not begin until February 1838.

Apart from Dutton and Vale Royal viaducts, and the smaller bridge over the River Mersey and the Mersey & Irwell Navigation, the original tail had no engineering features or works of particular interest. Weaver flying junction was a later addition, coming well after through communication with Scotland had been established; so was the complete realignment south of Warrington, and the extensive Crewe avoiding lines. The original rails were 62 lb. a yd., with sleepers at 3 ft. 8 in. centres, and chairs weighed 21 lb. apiece.

Dutton viaduct, over the River Weaver and the Weaver canal, has 20 arches of 65 ft. span and a maximum height of 65 ft., but the ships folding their sails under the bridge come no more. David McIntosh's price for erection was £54,440 "with the piers sunk down to solid substance," and the bridge took two years to build. Credit for it has been given variously to George Stephenson and Joseph Locke individually; both of them participated. Stephenson was chief engineer of the company at the beginning; he approved the design and specification, and it was on his insistence that the piers were carried down further than Locke had been willing to accept; but he ceased his connection with the G.J.R. before the viaduct was fairly put in hand, and Locke supervised the construction. It was the largest viaduct for which he had then been responsible. Before the contract was placed Jesse Hartley, the Liverpool docks engineer, was invited by the board to give his opinion as a result of marginal notes he had scribbled on a copy of the specification shown to him; but no alteration to the design approved by Stephenson was made after Hartley's views were obtained.

Vale Royal is a smaller viaduct, of five 63 ft. spans up to 60 ft. high, but it is stated to have cost £40,000 and kept up to 700 men busy for two years. Like Dutton, it spans the River Weaver, and all the stone for it came down, and up, the Weaver and the canal in flat barges. The Weaver Navigation in those days was often referred to as *Miss Weaver, the Cheshire heiress,* because of the large profits it made—a feature shared by those other canals, mainly the Lancaster canal and the Bridgewater network, that cut across what came to be the Crewe to Carlisle main-line railway.

Original G.J.R. stations on the tail section were Crewe, Coppenhall (2 miles), Minshull Vernon (4¾ miles), Winsford (7¼ miles), Hartford (11¾ miles), Acton (14¼ miles), Preston Brook (18½ miles), Moore (21 miles) and Warrington (24 miles). Short-distance fares out of Crewe at first were on a zonal basis, Coppenhall, Minshull Vernon and Winsford all being 1s. 6d. first class and 1s. 0d. second. Further out, every fare was on a mileage basis, from 2s. 6d. and 1s. 6d. to Hartford up to 5s. 0d. and 3s. 6d. to Warrington. By mail train the fare from Crewe to Warrington was 6s. 0d.; a gentleman's carriage was 16s. and a horse 8s. Fare from Crewe to Liverpool or Manchester was 9s. 6d. first, 7s. second and 11s. mail. Coppenhall station was closed in September 1840.

The G.J.R. was to join the existing Warrington & Newton Railway at Warrington. In W. & N. days there was no intermediate station between Warrington and Newton Junction to the north; but a stopping place was put in at Winwick by the G.J.R. immediately after the opening from Birmingham, though it does not appear in that company's early time sheets or fares lists. Probably there was no station building; and the only operating record of it is that a signal pole was placed at Winwick quay, and that the mixed trains were directed to stop at it if the flag was hoisted. The station was closed before the end of 1840.

Though Crewe in the first three years from the opening of the G.J.R. was a small station, it was considered 'first class', and all trains stopped there for the omnibus and carriage connections to Sandbach and Nantwich. There was also a shed with accommodation for one engine, always held in steam as a spare and to act as pilot up to Whitmore; but there was only one crossover between up and down tracks, opposite the engine shed (Fig. 2a). Six passenger trains a day in each direction stopped at

Crewe between 8.32 and 21.04 during the first year or so of working; but times varied, and in the winter of 1838–39 there were six trains a day in each direction over a span from 5.02 to 20.02.

A feature of early G.J.R. timetables was the centring of the column of place names, with the down-train times reading downwards on one side and the up-train times reading upwards on the other side. This has been the basis of many Continental timetables, but the system never caught on in England. The public timetable of 1837–38, until the opening of the London & Birmingham Railway (adjusted to 24-hr. time), is given in Table Ia. On Sundays only the four first-class trains ran, but with the addition of second-class coaches; they stopped only at the first-class stations. On weekdays the trains did not wait for time at the smaller stations if they happened to be early, but went off as soon as station business was concluded. There were no by-laws on the G.J.R. in early years, and in 1839 the company stated it "found no inconvenience from the want of them."

Practice in regard to ticket issue and regulation was also unusual. As given to a Select Committee of the Commons on the state of railway communication: "Persons paying at Liverpool are furnished with tickets which are collected at the top of the tunnel about a mile out. At Birmingham they are collected when the bell rings, after the passengers have taken

2a Crewe station layout, 1839

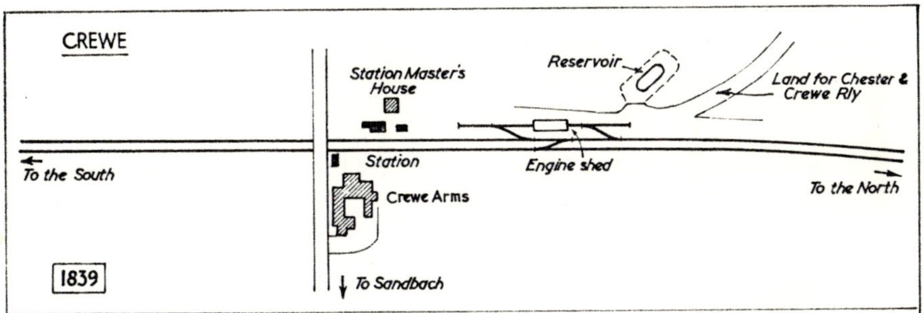

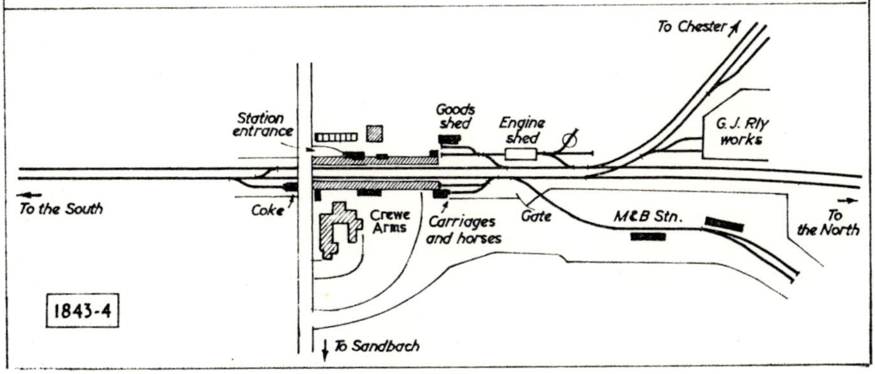

2b Crewe station layout, 1843–44

their seats, immediately before starting; at the other stations immediately after they have taken their seats. The company would prefer to be subject to the little frauds now existing rather than annoy honest passengers with stringent regulations."

A few months after the inauguration of the service from Birmingham to Lancashire came a G.J.R. announcement: "The first class Trains consist of coaches carrying six inside, and of mails carrying four inside, one compartment of which is convertible into a bed carriage, if required. The mixed trains consist of both first and second class coaches, the latter affording complete protection from the weather, and differing only from the First Class in having no lining, cushions or divisions of the compartments. Both kinds have seats on the roof for the accommodation of those who prefer riding outside." Fortunately for the outside passengers the G.J.R. had no tunnels except one of 200 yd. near Wednesbury, and another of under 100 yd. near Preston Brook up to which the electrification masts and catenary were taken when the Crewe–Liverpool line was converted; but through G.J.R. trains to Liverpool did have to go down into that port through a much longer tunnel on the L. & M. Original fares between Birmingham and Liverpool or Manchester were £1 1s. first class with six inside, £1 5s. with four inside; and, after the night mail started in September 1838, £2 for the bed carriage in the mail coach. After the opening of the L. & B. on September 17, 1838, the G.J.R. service was altered (Table Ib), and most trains then connected with L. & B. trains. Through bookings from Liverpool and Manchester at first were given only to London and not to any other L. & B. station, and then only for first class passengers. The fare in a through coach was £2 11s. by the day trains with six inside, or £2 13s. with four inside; by the night trains the fares were £2 13s. 6d. with six inside and £2 15s. 6d. with four inside.

Charles Greville made an early trip on the G.J.R. Under date July 18, 1837, he wrote: "I started at five o'clock on Sunday evening (from London by coach), got to Birmingham at half-past five on Monday morning, and got upon the railroad at half-past seven. Nothing can be more comfortable than the vehicle in which I was put, a sort of chariot with two places, and there is nothing disagreeable about it but the occasional whiffs of stinking air which it is impossible to exclude altogether. The first sensation is a slight degree of nervousness and a feel of being run away with, but a sense of security soon supervenes, and the velocity is delightful . . ."

When the line was opened, additional to "a very neat house for the clerk of the station" at Crewe (it was actually a spacious house considering the humble position of the occupants), there was erected by Lord Crewe a "convenient and lofty brick house, built in the modern Gothic style for an inn." This inn was at first run by a private lessee; not until 1864 did the railway take a 40-year lease at £225 a year. With enlargements and modernisation the inn remains to this day as the Crewe Arms Hotel, but is once again in private hands. While it was in the hands of its first lessee, Sam Sidney recorded (1851) with appreciation: "Parties passing

. . . will find very fair accommodation . . . and often, about one o'clock, a fine hot joint of grass-fed beef of magnificent dimensions."

One wet Saturday night in September 1848, Queen Victoria and her suite stayed at the Crewe Arms on no notice at all; though Bowen Cooke stated (*Round the Works of Our Great Railways*), that the Queen sent word shortly in advance of her approach. Travelling south from Scotland, the Queen decided to break the tedious journey at Crewe and, if suitable accommodation could be found, to stay over-night with her party of 30. The contemporary account reads: "Mr. Edwards (the lessee) met the Queen and Prince Albert at the top of the steps from the platform. He bore a silver candlestick and wax candle, and preceded the Royal pair to the foot of the staircase leading to a drawing room upstairs . . . Sir George Grey and Mr. Anson inspected the rooms, and the convenience the house contained being considered ample for the wants of the party, the decision of Her Majesty was made known to Mr. Edwards and dinner ordered for 8.30 . . . The Queen's room contained a really noble four-post bedstead elegantly hung . . . the beds were supplied with linen brought in the Royal train . . . During the night Mr. Winby (the stationmaster) took every precaution that Her Majesty's slumber should not be disturbed by the shrieking of railway whistles and rattling of the railway trains in his bustling station . . . even on Saturday night when traffic is less busy than usual there are eight or ten trains through."

It was of the continuation of this journey next day that Francis Trevithick gave his celebrated account of the trip to London. Writing some 30 years afterwards he said it was about 1846, but it seems that it was on this journey of September 1848 that the Royal train rolled over a section where the rails had been lifted a foot high to pack in some ballast, and the engine kept time to the next station with a bent driving axle and broken bearing brasses.

Many writers have stated there was nothing at all at Crewe until the G.J.R. put a station there; but in 1838 Freeling stated it had 295 inhabitants. Perhaps mistakes have arisen in regard to parishes, for much of the present-day Crewe lies within the boundaries of the old parishes of Church Coppenhall and Monks Coppenhall. Gilbert Stoker, Central assistant district superintendent of the L.N.W.R. at the end of last century, wrote that Coppenhall village had 140 inhabitants at the time the railway arrived, and that the collection of houses known as Crewe, in another parish, had only 20 persons. This is probably correct, as the G.J.R. schedule of lands shows the 'township of Crewe in the parish of Barthomley', and that the land required by the railway was occupied by Wm. Emberton (barn, cowhouse, fold, stackyard, house and garden), John Sherratt (garden), Wm. Beech (cottage and garden), and George Thornhill (cottage and garden). The division between the two parishes was the Crewe–Sandbach road. Possibly the station was named out of respect to Lord Crewe, and to avoid confusion, for there was another station scarcely two miles north, and named Coppenhall.

Crewe station, the beginning of the works, and the first railway houses were built mainly on fields attached to Oak farm. From 1840 the farmhouse had the Chester & Crewe Railway running more or less through its front garden until it disappeared altogether. This property, according to accounts of the 1840–50 period, had been bought by a Nantwich lawyer, Richard Edleston, in the early 1830s at £35 an acre; later his trustees (he died in 1839) sold much of it to the G.J.R. at prices reputed to have gone up to £500 an acre. The Edleston family today is commemorated in Crewe by the name of one of the main streets.

Crewe as an operating centre dates from the arrival of the Chester & Crewe Railway in 1840 and of the Manchester & Birmingham Railway in 1842; and an operating feature possibly was frequent derailments of the light wagons if the statement of W. L. Steel (*History of the L.N.W.R.*) is true that the G.J.R. gauge was 4 ft. 8½ in., that of the Chester & Crewe 4 ft. 8¾ in., and that of the M. & B. 4ft. 9 in. There was little exactitude in those days; tolerances approached the 'Doncaster sixteenth', and probably the gauge of all three just approximated to 4 ft. 9 in., and not one of the three railways used the remarkable L. & M. rail section with the inner side shaved off to match the tyre profile.

The incoming of the two railways just mentioned quickly brought an enlargement of the station facilities, as shown in Fig. 2b; and there was a complete metamorphosis in 1845/46 to cater for the increasing traffic on the G.J.R. and L.N.W.R. resulting from the extension of the railway system to Lancaster, Carlisle and Scotland, and from the increment of traffic on the Manchester and Chester lines. From that date there were two through tracks between the two platform lines; and the two long platforms were covered by roofs supported on cast iron columns which are reported to have had carved oak figures at the tops; a clock was centred on the overbridge. In 1854 the station was described by Bradshaw as "a huge ganglion of iron arteries presenting to the uninitiated eye an apparently hopeless mass of confusion, with the diverging tramroads crossing and intersecting at every point, until, seen from this height (the overbridge), the line appears to resemble the maze of Rosamund's bower." The extent of this genial exaggeration is obvious from Tait's prints of 1848 (Plate I); Tait was an accurate illustrator. In 1867 what amounted practically to a new station was built, and substantial further improvements were made in 1878; but before this, in 1861, the first Bessemer-steel rails ever laid were put in at Crewe station.

The rise of Crewe town began with the opening of the G.J.R. works in March 1843, after construction spread over two years. But though Crewe was a first class station, then a junction of growing importance, and, from 1843, the site of a considerable and expanding locomotive and carriage works, it was not an important locomotive running station. Up to 1851 only the barest handful of engines was stabled there. In that year Arthur and George Holmes were given a £2,886 contract to erect a shed to stable 16 engines; this was the beginning of Crewe North depot. Not until 1865/66 was a large shed built. Only after the fusion of the old Northern and Southern divisions of the L.N.W.R., under Ramsbottom, did Crewe start to become a principal main-line engine-changing point, in place of Stafford, and by 1880 around 150 locomotives of passenger and freight types were stabled, all at the north end. Crewe South shed was not established until 1896, and can be regarded as the first stage in the complete remodelling of the whole Crewe area between 1896 and 1906. From that time Crewe North depot had a concentration of passenger engines and Crewe South took the freight locomotives.

The Crewe spare engine, the brand-new *Charon* at the time, was in trouble early on, though in the section immediately south of Crewe, and not on the Warrington tail. Early in the foggy morning of February 11, 1841, a 20-wagon southbound freight from Manchester, headed by No. 8 *Wildfire*, an old 2–2–2 from Robt. Stephenson's works which had hauled the first northbound train out of Birmingham on the opening day in 1837, had difficulty in surmounting the bank up to Whitmore, and panted to a halt near the top. There it was run into by the following freight, a 50-wagon train from Liverpool, double-headed by Stephenson 2–2–2 no. 65 *Charon* and no. 67 *Briareus*, a Tayleur 0–4–2. Recorded death roll was one man and 50 fat pigs. According to W. L. Steel, writing in 1913-14, *Wildfire* had run 11,865 miles in the first 89 days from the G.J.R. opening, and its fellow Stephenson engines *Scorpion* and *Shark* had run 11,137 and 10,018 miles respectively in the same period.

From its arrival at Crewe in 1842 the Manchester & Birmingham Railway for some years had its own station against the Manchester junction, with an approach road round the back of the Crewe Arms, approximately where the dock platform can still be seen. Across the single connecting track between the two stations was a gate, and this was unlocked by the one employee at the M. & B. station when any stock transfer had to be made. Apart from through coaches between Manchester and Birmingham, there was from an early date a through Manchester–Chester carriage; and a curious through train working was from Manchester (London Road) to Liverpool (Lime Street) via Crewe and Warrington. This latter service had an equally curious composite operating on it, consisting of a first class covered centre portion with an open second class trough at each end. Chester trains always used the G.J.R. station at Crewe, as the C. & C. was taken over by the G.J.R. under 3 & 4 Vict., cap. 69, of May 19, 1840, before it was opened to traffic on October 1. The Chester & Crewe had the distinction of being the first railway authorised in Queen Victoria's reign, the Act of Incorporation 7 Wm. 4 & 1 Vict., cap. 63, being dated June 30, 1837; the Manchester & Birmingham Railway incorporating Act was given Royal Assent the same day, but was cap. 69.

For some years the G.J.R. platforms at Crewe were entirely north of the bridge carrying the Nantwich–Sandbach road over the railway. Not more than one-quarter of the present station is north of this bridge, and all extensions in length have been southward; longest platform face is 1,476 ft. Similarly, the enormous enlargements of Crewe station up to 1906 were all to the west side, and swallowed up the house built for the first stationmaster, Capt. Winby, a retired sea-dog who, said Stoker 70 years ago: "brought to his new duties the sense of discipline acquired in the rough school in which he had been brought up, and was endowed with a native humour." The bridge carrying the Sandbach road over the station was first widened and rebuilt in 1847 at the end of the station renewal scheme, and the work was done by Charles Tayleur and his then partner, G. S. Sanderson, the iron coming from the Bank Quay foundry and not from Vulcan.

Of the intermediate stations on the G.J.R. line from Crewe to Warrington, Hartford and Preston Brook also were omnibus termini. From the former buses ran to Northwich, Knutsford, Tarporley and Chester; from Preston Brook there was a bus service to Runcorn. Hartford station was not finished in time for the opening of the railway, though the stationmaster appointed had already been dismissed as unsuitable; but the board minuted on August 16, 1837, that as soon as the station was sufficiently complete the 8.00 train ex-Warrington for Liverpool and Manchester should begin at Hartford at 7.30. This was a local train, extra to those shown in Tables Ia and Ib. Hartford station had a crossover and two short sidings, one off each track; from Preston Brook station a siding led to the Duke of Bridgewater's canal, and at Acton was a small coal depot. Otherwise the intermediate stations were without form and void.

From Warrington itself, though the trains ran on north to Newton and then east and west to Manchester and Liverpool, coaches started in 1838 at 10.00 for Carlisle and Edinburgh, and at 10.30 (mail) for Glasgow and Edinburgh. They gave no convenient connection off express trains, for the night mail from the south, leaving Birmingham at 3.00 from September 1838, was due into Warrington at 6.24; the next train in was the 6.00 slow from Birmingham due in at 10.14. Nor was the connection any better in the reverse direction, for the Glasgow mail was due in at 15.00 and the next first class train to the south was at 18.50.

Warrington was in trouble almost at once, for *Centaur* broke its axle there on August 15, 1837, and there was a long delay to traffic that annoyed the board. Early operation at Warrington was bound up with that at Newton Junction a few miles to the north, and often called Warrington Junction. More about the layout at both stations is given in the next chapter. The G.J.R. was to make an end-on connection with the existing W. & N.; and though a memorial from some inhabitants of Warrington asked the G.J.R. to project its line more through the town, the directors felt there was insufficient inducement for a change from the proposed connection on the Bank Quay line of rail. Later they may have wished there had been, for great trouble came with the turnpike trust about the bridge over the road at Bank Quay; this was not settled without a law case, of which the G.J.R. got the worst. The W. & N. had been wiser in its time; its Act gave it power to terminate "within 20 yd. of the north side of the Turnpike Road," and so it was saved all trouble with turnpike trusts, which in early days formed, with canals, the "vested interests." According to plans, the W. & N. was to fork at Jockey Lane on the northern outskirts of Warrington, one branch going to Bank Quay (of which Bank Key was an alternative spelling at the time) and the other to Dallum Lane, nearer the centre of the town The latter was the local station for trains to and from Newton from 1831 to 1839, and for a time it had the major facilities. The short branch to Bank Quay was not opened at the beginning of the W. & N., but was in operation by the beginning of 1835. At the simple station first provided at Bank Quay, J. R. Chorley, treasurer of the G.J.R., had one of his toes taken off when he slipped trying to get into a moving train in 1839.

Table Ia—G.J.R. Timetables, Crewe to Merseyside, 1837-38

1st class	Mixed	1st class	1st class	Mixed	1st class	Stations	1st class	Mixed	1st class	1st class	Mixed	1st class
7.00	8.30	11.30	14.30	16.30	19.00	dep. Birmingham arr.	11.30	14.00	16.30	19.30	22.00	23.30
9.24	11.29	13.54	16.54	19.29	21.24	*Crewe*	8.32	10.53	13.32	16.32	18.53	20.32
	11.40			19.40		Coppenhall		10.43			18.43	
	11.48			19.48		Minshull Vernon		10.32			18.32	
	11.57			19.57		Winsford		10.26			18.26	
9.59	12.07	14.29	17.29	20.07	21.59	*Hartford*	7.58	10.10	12.58	15.58	18.10	19.58
	12.18			20.18		Acton		10.00			18.00	
	12.31			20.31		Preston Brook		9.46			17.46	
	12.36			20.36		Moore		9.33			17.33	
10.36	12.44	15.06	18.06	20.44	22.36	*Warrington*	7.20	9.25	12.20	15.20	17.25	19.20
	13.02			21.02		Newton Junction		9.10			17.10	
11.45	13.45	16.15	19.15	21.45	23.45	arr. Liverpool dep.	6.30	8.30	11.30	14.30	16.30	18.30
11.45	13.45	16.15	19.15	21.45	23.45	arr. Manchester dep.	6.30	8.30	11.30	14.30	16.30	18.30

Station names in italics are those of first-class stations.

Table Ib—G.J.R. Timetables, Crewe to Merseyside, 1838-39

1st class	Mixed	1st class	1st class	Mixed	1st class		Stations		1st class	Mixed	1st class	1st class	Mixed	1st class
3.00	6.00	11.30	14.30	16.00	17.00	dep.	Birmingham	arr.	7.45	12.00	14.00	16.15	22.00	22.45
5.14	8.59	13.44	16.44	18.59	19.14		*Crewe*		5.02	8.53	11.17	13.32	18.53	20.02
	9.10			19.10			Coppenhall			8.43			18.43	
	9.18			19.18			Minshull Vernon			8.32			18.32	
	9.27			19.27			Winsford			8.26			18.26	
5.49	9.37	14.19	17.19	19.37	19.49		*Hartford*		4.28	8.10	10.43	12.58	18.10	19.28
	9.48			19.48			Acton			8.00			18.00	
	10.01			20.01			Preston Brook			7.46			17.46	
	10.06			20.06			Moore			7.33			17.33	
6.24	10.14	14.54	17.54	20.14	20.24		*Warrington*		3.50	7.25	10.05	12.20	17.25	18.50
	10.32			20.32			Newton Junction			7.10			17.10	
7.30	11.15	16.00	19.00	21.15	21.30	arr.	Liverpool	dep.	3.00[1]	6.30	9.15	11.30	16.30	18.00
7.30	11.15	16.00	19.00	21.15	21.30	arr.	Manchester	dep.	3.00	6.30	9.15	11.30	16.30	18.00

(1) Edge Hill station, London connections at Birmingham off all up trains except 16.30 mixed from September 1838

II

Warrington & Newton Railway

ON SEPTEMBER 15, 1830, the west-east Liverpool & Manchester Railway was opened officially and Huskisson killed in the process. Already another railway to join the L. & M. was under construction, the Warrington & Newton Railway, incorporated on May 14, 1829, by 10 Geo. 4, cap. 37, for a railway to run from Newton to Dallum Lane in Warrington, with two collateral branches making a Y on the outskirts of the latter town (Fig. 3), and to have a share capital of £53,000 plus borrowing powers of £20,000. Soon afterwards, on June 4, the first general meeting was held, but it was adjourned until the December, when it was resumed with the avowed object of carrying the Act into execution! Among the original shareholders of the W. & N. were George Stephenson, Joseph Sandars (one of the 'fathers' of the L. & M.), Joseph Locke, Benjamin Hick and Edward Pease.

Already the railway had begun with a certain amount of internal friction, for two rival meetings had been held in Warrington on the same day, July 7, 1828, each with the purpose of promoting a railway. Wisely the parties got together, had a joint meeting on August 4, and thereafter combined. In due time, when the W. & N. came to an end, it did so after further friction, this time external, with its potentially powerful neighbour the Grand Junction Railway, by which it was swallowed.

The line was laid out by Robert Stephenson, and even before the end of 1829 he mentioned in a letter that the company had ideas of promoting an extension from Warrington to Sandbach, 22 miles, as a step towards the eventual link-up by rail with Birmingham. At the end of 1830 a Bill was proposed for the extension of the line south from Warrington Bank Quay to the then intended railway from Merseyside to Birmingham at Norton or Preston-on-the-Hill, in Cheshire, near the junction of the Trent & Mersey and Bridgewater canals. This idea came to nothing, mainly because of the abandonment of the projected railway from Birkenhead to Norton or Chorlton (Cheshire), which was to link up with a second section running thence to Birmingham.

An advantage of this W. & N. project had been the link-up with the Midlands by way of both canal and railway; and it is interesting to record that the link-up canal, the Trent & Mersey, which got its Act 200 years ago, had also been granted a supplementary Act (42 Geo. 3, cap. 25) on April 15, 1802, for making several railways to connect with the canal as it passed through the Potteries. Steam locomotive enthusiasts today will feel a glow that among the commissioners of the canal appointed in 1802 was Sir Nigel Bowyer Gresley, Bt.; but the very cockles of their hearts will be warmed to learn that so long ago as September 1182, according to a pipe roll of 28 Henry II, Nigel Gresley of Drakelow had been paid £4 16s. by Ralph Fitzbernard.

Despite the shortness of the W. & N. line Robert Stephenson could not lay out the trace just as he wanted. James Scott Walker recorded in 1832 that those who saw the great horizontal curves might be inclined to blame the engineer, but that the real opposition was from "certain influential persons who to protect a pheasant preserve or some such object have not hesitated to divert a great public work from its just and natural direction." There may well be truth in this; certainly Lord Lilford and the Rector of Winwick ensured in the Act of May 14, 1829, that no locomotive should be allowed along the railway within the townships of Burtonwood and Winwick or on any adjacent ground belonging to those two gentlemen if it was considered by them to be a nuisance or annoyance from the noise or smoke or from any other cause connected with the machinery. The company thus began in a quandary, for something like half the line passed over land within those restrictions.

The two collateral branches at Warrington were to divert at Jockey Lane from the main line to the Dallum Lane station, engine shed and goods shed. One was to go s.s.w. to Bank Quay, and the other s.e. to Cockhedge field. The second one was never built. The point of junction at Jockey Lane is marked today by Dallam Lane Sidings signalbox on the

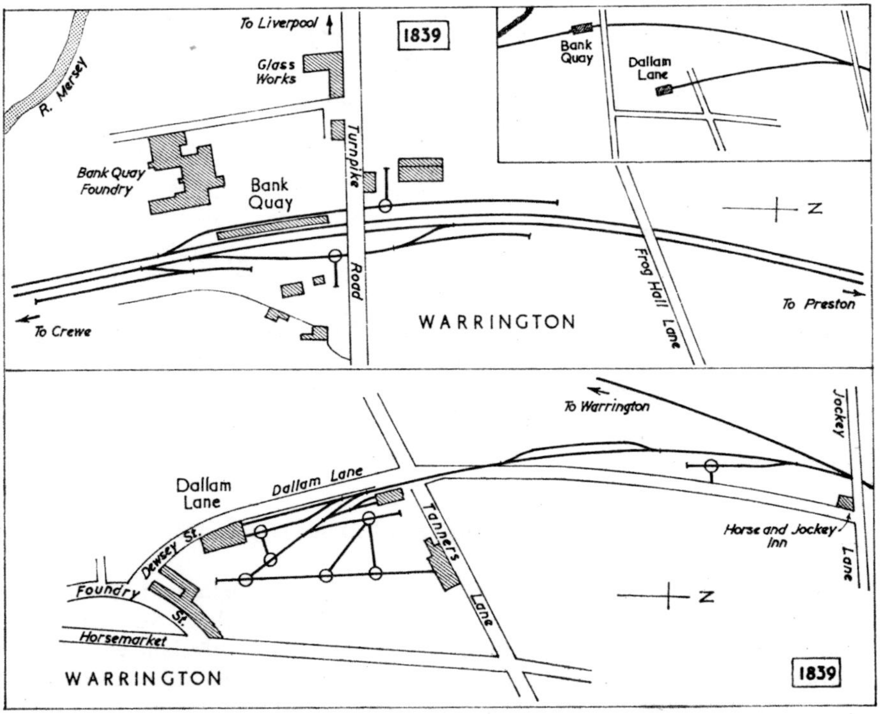

3 Warrington layout, 1839

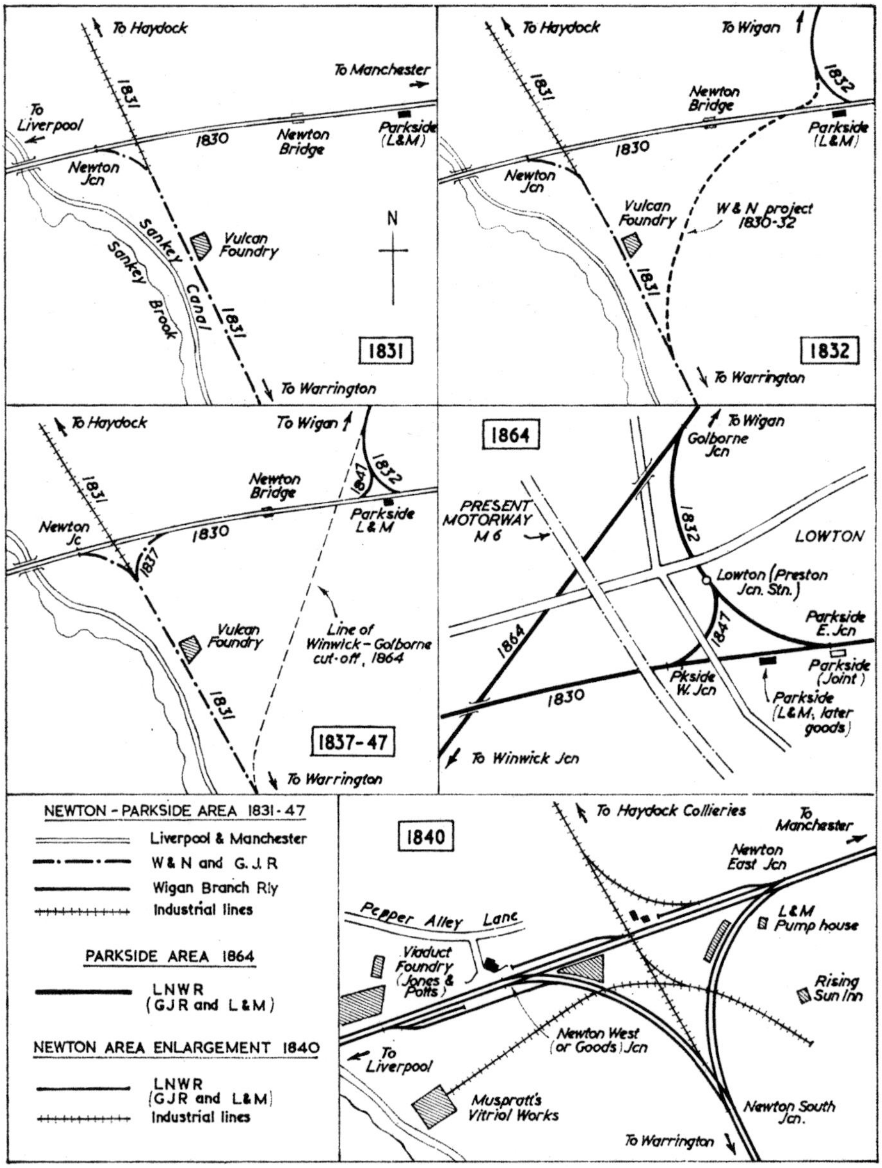

4 Quintuple diagram of Newton and Parkside layouts, 1831–1864

down side of the main line. Today the spelling is Dallam throughout; in the old days it varied. The Act says Dallum; Robert Stephenson's Parliamentary plans show Dallam. The track was lightly laid with fish-bellied rails; and as the kyanising process had not then been fully developed, many of the sleepers were of untreated larch, and long before 1840 had to be renewed because of decay; though Joseph Locke in his evidence for the Great Western Railway Bill in 1835 referred to the W. & N. and said the sleepers were better than stone blocks for embankments. As described in 1838, about three years after its purchase by the G.J.R., the W. & N. had been a wretched undertaking. Nevertheless, it had paid up to 2½ per cent dividend; and the G.J.R. calculated on getting a net profit of £1,000 a year out of it.

The W. & N. was to join the L. & M. at Newton, some 15 miles from Liverpool (Edge Hill). The original scheme was for a junction facing the Liverpool direction; but on May 29, 1830, a year before any part was opened, a further Act (11 Geo. 4, cap. 57) was obtained to construct a branch leading into the L. & M. in the Manchester direction between Newton and Parkside, and to connect with the Wigan Branch Railway (Fig. 4). This Act gave further borrowing powers of £20,000; more important, it also repealed the veto on steam locomotives through Burtonwood and Winwick, as recent experiments had proved to both ermine and cloth that the use of properly-constructed steam locomotives could be admitted. Presumably the experiments were the Rainhill trials, the operation of contractors' locomotives on the L. & M., and the working of the *Lancashire Witch* on the Bolton & Leigh. Clause 11 of this Act also empowered the tenants of Burtonwood farm to use the railway as a footpath in times of flood; possibly they have this right today.

The whole purpose of the branch line as given in the second Act was to unite with the W.B. and open up a through line between Wigan and Warrington, and to give direct communication to the south from the Manchester direction. The original plan was for a line close to the existing Winwick–Golborne main-line cut-off, but to make a junction with the L. & M. close to Parkside, and so almost straight on to the proposed Parkside west curve of the W.B. in order to get to Wigan. This line is shown as a project in the map of the area in Henry Booth's celebrated book *An Account of the Liverpool & Manchester Railway*, published in 1830 before the September ceremonial opening of that line, and just at the time the W. & N. got its second Act and the W.B. its first one. As roughly surveyed by Robert Stephenson the branch to the L. & M. was to be about 1½ miles long and was to have a total rise of 49 ft. to the L. & M.; estimated construction cost was £7,008.

Both the W. & N. and W.B. were short of money, and each hoped the other would stand all or part of the cost; but only a fortnight before the W. & N. 'main' line was opened, the W.B., following talks between the two companies, had to write regretfully that it did not have enough funds to proceed on the proposed line of junction. After further discussion, the W.B. said that if the W. & N. was prepared to make the line from near Warrington to near Golborne, the W.B. would pay for the bridge over the road at Golborne. The W. & N. was unable to undertake this; and so, because of the poor finances of two small lines, the whole communication chain in the area was upset, resulting in reversals or train-changes at Newton for Manchester and Wigan, and again at Parkside for Wigan. This projected line was resurveyed by Locke for the G.J.R. in 1837, but he stated it would be expensive to construct, though little more than

$1\frac{3}{4}$ miles long, and the G.J.R. abandoned the idea, a most regrettable decision, as the Anglo-Scottish main line was by then far forward in the thoughts of all those directly concerned.

The W. & N. was opened between Warrington and the south end of Newton at the beginning of June 1831 to cater for the Haydock Park races, and passenger trains ran daily after that. Research among contemporary documents and journals by Mr. E. Craven has brought this to light. Hitherto the opening date has been considered as July 25, 1831, but that was the date the Newton west curve, and so the line throughout, was opened. On that date the directors travelled in a special train to Newton to meet there some directors and officials of the L. & M. who had come in a special from Liverpool; the two parties then went by the special to Warrington for suitable refreshment. There were four trains each way on weekdays, connecting with L. & M. trains, but no trains ran on Sundays at first. Local fares, Warrington to Newton were 1s. 6d. first and 1s. second for the $4\frac{1}{2}$ miles; from Warrington to either Liverpool or Manchester the fares were 4s. 6d. first and 3s. 6d. second.

Dallum Lane (Fig. 3) was the original Warrington station; the short branch from Jockey Lane to Bank Quay authorised by the first Act was not built at once by the W. & N., but had been completed by the early part of 1835, though the exact date of its opening cannot be determined. At first it was used only for coal and freight traffic. From the completion of the G.J.R. in 1837 through north and south trains used Bank Quay; but until around 1839 Dallum Lane was used for local passenger and freight trains. After that, the roles of the two branches were reversed. Warrington plans of 1840 show that by then the Dallum Lane branch was being used for goods only. The site of the Dallum Lane ensemble remains more or less clear today. The yard is a coal depot and stabling area for lorries. The original two-storey red-brick station building, exactly in the position shown by the G.J.R. track plans of 1839/40, is in the possession of Suttons, the carriers, and the ends still show evidence of the inlet for trains at the outer end and an arched doorway for passengers at the 'town' end. The most delightful feature is a much more modern, though now obsolete, level-crossing type of gate shutting in some 30 yd. of track right against the end of the Three Pigeons public house, though the 50 to 60 yd. of track remaining in the area are not fish-bellied rails. It has been surmised that the Three Pigeons, erected as a public house shortly before the railway, may have served by the good offices of the then landlord, as a booking office for the W. &. N. This seems unlikely; it is at the outer end of the whole station area, and with Warrington as it was in 1831–37 most passengers would come in at the town end from Bewsey Lane and Foundry Lane, and not along Tanner's Lane; and the station building would be of ample size to provide booking accommodation and a waiting room. The Dallam Lane branch no longer exists right through. The Three Pigeons-station area is an island of ghostly memories, and with the adjacent part of Dallam Lane still a narrow thoroughfare.

The branch was the scene of an accident in December 1841. The

G.J.R. engine *Eagle* has been sent round from Bank Quay to collect a goods train at Dallam Lane; after admitting the engine to the branch the pointsman at Jockey Lane forgot to reset the points for the main line, and a freight from Manchester, running quarter of an hour early, ran on to the branch and into *Eagle*.

While its first class main line was still under construction the G.J.R. obtained an Act (5 Wm. 4, cap. 8) of June 12, 1835, to enable it to purchase the W. & N., and this Act sanctioned the first railway 'take-over', as distinct from legal amalgamation; and the W. & N. tracks actually formed the first part of the G.J.R. to be operated. This purchase was not achieved without some resistance from W. & N. shareholders in order to get good terms. In September 1833, four months after the G.J.R. Act of Incorporation, Moss was authorised by his co-directors to approach the W. & N. regarding tolls and the improvement of its line. Before the end of that year the W. & N. has suggested the G.J.R. could have its railway on payment of £125 for each £100 of stock and the settlement of debts around £20,000. The G.J.R. board declined without thanks. Later the W. & N. came down to £114 16s. a share; but at the G.J.R. general meeting in August 1834 the chairman stated the bigger company had broken off negotiations, and that as the proposed terms could not be adjusted the G.J.R. would have to build its own line to the L. & M.

That was an effective suggestion; and after it had helped to bring the W. & N. to heel in 1834–35 it was resuscitated in 1837, when Moss stated the project then was due to the Birkenhead & Chester Railway having got its Act, and the G.J.R. regarded that line as a possible competitor. This so-called Fidler's Ferry route from Prescot Brook to Huyton would have been 9 miles long as against the 16 miles via Newton. It would have avoided the 1 in 85 gradient south of Newton and the 1 in 90 of the Whiston and Sutton inclined planes on the L. & M.; but it would also have avoided Warrington, from which much traffic could still be expected, and it would not have helped traffic in the Manchester direction. Estimated cost at first was quarter of a million; but other estimates were £300,000 to £400,000; the idea was not pursued, for it was not a good one except as a threat.

Terms for the acquisition of the W. & N. were finally arranged in February 1835. The G.J.R. bought the 518 shares of £100 at par, undertook to pay W. & N. outstanding debts of £15,503, and had to pay the W. & N. shareholders 4 per cent until the G.J.R. main line was open throughout. The purchase price was around £67,000, but for a few years any surplus from the line was shown as reducing the price, which appears variously between £64,853 and £65,476 in the G.J.R. accounts over the years from 1837 to 1842. The G.J.R. had a term in its own Act of Incorporation that it could charge a six-mile toll on anything going a shorter distance, but this was not allowed to be extended to the W. & N. section. The purchase was specifically to make the G.J.R. and W. & N. "one continuous railway under one common control and system of management"; and it rendered through working easier when the G.J.R. main line was opened on July 4, 1837. Thereafter G.J.R. trains and locomotives ran through from the south to Liverpool and to Manchester, the company paying toll charges over the L. & M.

At the 11th half-yearly meeting of the L. & M. the chairman said he looked forward to a considerable accession of revenue from the G.J.R. running over the L. & M. According to *Drake's Road Book of the G.J.R. and L. & B. Railways* (1839) the sum paid was £20,000 a year as rent for the line, but 'tolls' might have been a better word. In any case the arrangement was more complicated, in that as soon as the tolls reached £20,000 in any year the charges per ton and per passenger were to be reduced substantially for the remainder of that year. Accounts for locomotive assistance by the L. & M., probably for banking engines up Whiston and Sutton, were kept separately, and averaged £70 to £80 a month.

The three connections where the G.J.R. joined the L. & M. were known collectively as Newton Junction (Fig. 4), though in timetables the location was often named Warrington Junction. The eastern curve here, leading in the Manchester direction, was opened only on July 4, 1837, along with the G.J.R. main line. The two Newton curves, especially the east one of 660 ft. radius, leading on to the L. & M. main line, straightway assisted in the breakage of many crank axles on G.J.R. locomotives, those accidents in turn leading to the evolution of the famous Trevithick-Allan-Crewe-type outside-cylinder engines. The gradients up the approaching straight averaged 1 in 85 and totalled about a mile in length, but as the uphill section ended at the south junction the normal high piston thrust forces uphill had been reduced before the beginning of the lateral bending stresses to which the axles were subject by the curves. The working here was referred to by Robert Stephenson in 1835 when he said in evidence before a House of Lords Committee: "The Warrington & Newton is another line on which full power is used" (on inclined planes).

Within one week of the opening of the Newton east curve Locke was writing to the G.J.R. board his apprehensions of the effect that curve might have on the six-wheel engines; and he was then instructed to "order the three engines lately used by Mr. Stubs to be repaired in a sufficient measure to be employed in the Manchester carrying." These were the 2–2–0 Planet-type machines which had been used on the W. & N. Possibly the reason why this sharp curve was put in was that no Act was required. The W. & N. Act of May 14, 1829, simply said: "commencing on the south side of the L. & M. at or near Wargrave Lane." Any further construction powers under it had lapsed in 1835; however, only a little land was needed and was bought without trouble from Squire Legh and the Misses Houghton. But Locke had had 18 months to consider all these problems since the board first asked him to report on the connection; and in that time he had rejected as too expensive a Winwick-Golborne cut-off, for which powers were in existence from the second W. & N. Act of May 29, 1830. It is intriguing to reflect that if instead of the Newton east curve, this cut-off had been built within the powers held over the years 1830-36, the Trevithick-Allan-Crewe-type locomotive might never have been evolved.

The G.J.R. had a good deal of trouble with its locomotives in its first few years; and as early as August 1838, at the half-yearly meeting, a statement was made that nearly every one of the locomotive axles (presumably driving axles) had failed or broken in the year since the G.J.R. had been opened. These troubles did even more than increase expenditure and upset line operation; they led to an open quarrel between John Moss, the chairman, and Hardman Earle, one of the directors, which was fought out bitterly at the half-yearly meetings.

The Osbornes, in their *Guide to the Grand Junction Railway* (1838) give a happy account of train working at the Newton triangle in those days:

> "This station (Newton Junction) is situated at the middle of the Liverpool & Manchester Railway, in an angle formed by that line and the curved branches from it which meet the Grand Junction line. The trains for Liverpool and Manchester here pass to the left and right to their respective lines; and the trains from these towns arrive at this station usually at the same minute, and proceed along their curves on to the line of the Grand Junction, the Liverpool train taking the precedence. The sight of both trains connected together, passing along the Grand Junction line, and then separating right and left, and speeding away from each other at the rate of thirty miles an hour is very beautiful; but to see the trains coming from the Liverpool and Manchester line, and watch them running down the curved branches on to the Grand Junction line, is majestic. The precision of time, the order of movement, the noble engines in front with their magnificent trains after them, and the curvilinear course which they take, are all so many particulars which heighten the interest of the sight. There is something of the charm of the wonderful and the sublime in it, and we gaze with admiration and astonishment upon it, as much the fiftieth as the first time.
>
> "The trains of the Grand Junction Railway do not take up passengers on the Liverpool & Manchester line, but they put them down at any station for which they are booked."

Osbornes 'on Newton' may be supplemented by Roscoe 'on Warrington' in 1839, thus:

> "The carriages for Liverpool and Manchester which have come from Birmingham in one train, are here separated; and while the *Firefly* continues to rush forward with those destined for Liverpool, the *Comet* or some other locomotive of equally ominous name, flies off with the Manchester carriages in quick succession. Nothing can exceed the ingenuity of the plan, or the mechanical power, order and exactness with which it is executed. The plan is this: the *separate* trains from Liverpool and Manchester arrive at Warrington a few minutes before the train from Birmingham; the locomotive which has come from Liverpool takes the *united* trains forward to Birmingham, while the engine which has brought its train from Manchester returns back again with the carriages which have arrived from Birmingham."

The engine from Birmingham went on to Liverpool with the carriages for that place. With a marshalling tradition inculcated thus early, it is no wonder that on the northern extensions those marvellous procedures at Wigan and Preston came into being in later years. Certainly nothing *could* exceed the ingenuity at *those* places; but it is to be doubted whether exactness and order were attributes. At Warrington, to effect all these reversals and shunting movements in the early days, there were, according to the Osbornes: ". . . a considerable number of rails . . . for the engines to back and advance and turn round upon, and yet not interfere with the course of the line. This is effected by several short branch lines, which run off from the general line diagonally, and by moveable parts of the rail, which, by being altered in their position, change the direction of vehicles moving over them." Nothing quite so complicated appears on the still existing track plan of the G.J.R. dated 1839/40. In fact, no cross-over is shown between up and down tracks. Also, the only means of turning engines was on two tiny turntables which would necessitate uncoupling the tender and turning it separately. The layout at Bank Quay in 1839–40 is shown in Fig. 3, which shows also the more comprehensive arrangement at Dallum Lane, used for the Warrington goods and local passenger traffic.

Around the opening date of the W. & N. a beginning had been made with the erection on the east side of the line of the first shops of the Vulcan Foundry, then known as Chas. Tayleur & Co.; and the section of line from Winwick up to Newton was after about 1835 often known as the Vulcan incline, as well as by its earlier names of the Newton, Warrington, or Bradley incline. Tayleur himself was a director of the G.J.R. until November 4, 1835, when he resigned because he wanted to quote for some of the locomotives about to be ordered; he did not get any of them, but was successful later.

There is just a bare possibility that the second and third locomotives of the W. & N., named *Newton* and *Vulcan* (renamed *Achilles* at some time prior to September 1834) were assembled at the Vulcan Foundry under sub-contract from Robt. Stephenson & Co. from parts built at Newcastle. They were delivered to the W. & N. on September 1 and December 9, 1831, respectively. Agreement between Robert Stephenson and his partners at Newcastle relative to his collaboration with Tayleur was not reached until June 27, 1831, and it is not likely that drawings or sub-contracts were sent to Tayleur before that date. Even for the second locomotive there would scarcely be time to send parts, re-erect them at a works hardly begun, and deliver by September 1.

The first locomotive, *Warrington*, was built at Stephenson's own works at Newcastle. Dendy Marshall quotes the order book of that firm as showing the engine sent away on April 16, 1831, and delivered complete to Liverpool for £800. Dendy Marshall then says the engine was built at Vulcan, but in relation to the context this was just a slip; and if it had been built at Vulcan it would have been delivered on the spot. Nicholas Wood (1838) shows all three engines built at Stephenson's. Vulcan's own centenary book claims all three W. & N. locomotives as 'Foundry' productions, but that book is notoriously vague and inaccurate on the very early locomotives. From a more accurate but still extremely brief account of the early days of Vulcan in *The Locomotive* for January 1905 it would not have been possible for the Foundry to have participated in deliveries in 1831. None of these three engines appears in the list of G.J.R. engines given by Whishaw in 1840. The boilers, at least, of the three engines were slightly different, and Nicholas Wood gives the barrel diameters respectively as 2 ft. 11 in., 3 ft. and 3 ft., the number of 1⅝ in. tubes as 90, 102 and 88, and the tube heating surfaces (gas side) as 258, 293, and 252 sq. ft. Cylinders in all were 11 in. by 16 in., and driving wheels 5 ft.; grate area was 6.3 sq. ft. and firebox heating surface 35 sq. ft.

In one of its periods of more than usually acute financial shortage, the W. & N., in March 1833, offered to sell one of its engines to the L. & M., but that company was not needing a locomotive at the time. John Dixon, then civil engineer of the L. & M., made a valuation of all three in September 1834 for the ostensible purpose of them being taken over, along with some spare parts, by Messrs. Tayleur and Stephenson. Dixon valued no. 1 at only £250 exclusive of tender, and the other two at £450 apiece. The three tenders were put at £180 the lot. Possibly *Warrington* had been in an accident; otherwise it could hardly have achieved nearly 70 per cent depreciation in 3¼ years while the others had gone down only 35 per cent in 2½/3 years. Maybe *Warrington* was the W. & N. engine which, towards the end of 1833, while running over the Wigan Branch had damaged the *Rocket* of the L. & M., which was one unit of the motive power being supplied at the time by the L. & M. to work the W.B. *Newton* also ran off the line on a straight road about 1½ miles north of Warrington and killed the driver.

Altogether the W. & N. was in trouble with its locomotive stock during its short independent existence. On November 17, 1833, the first class train of the L. & M. from Manchester to Liverpool had to stop at the junction at Newton because the cylinder covers on the engine were loose, and it stopped by the west points. While the driver was tightening up, the W. & N. engine came round the west curve, propelling its carriages and having no one on the lookout, and the carriages crashed into the Mail coach of the Liverpool train, damaging it considerably and injuring a few passengers. This was unlucky for the L. & M., for the day was Sunday, when it ran practically no trains; nor did the Warrington have more than a couple of trains on Sundays by that time.

All three W. & N. locomotives were of the 2–2–0 Planet type, and locomotive advance had been so rapid between 1831 and 1834/35 that they would hardly be considered more than ballast engines by the time the G.J.R. was opened, which indicates the pickle brought by the Newton east curve when these three locomotives had to be put on to run to Manchester. Despite Dixon's avowed purpose in the valuation, there is doubt as to whether the engines were sold to Tayleur. The valuation may have been a preliminary move when the W. & N. asked the L. & M. to provide all the power and work the line; but that company declined the invitation in October 1834. Having acquired the W. & N. early in

1835 the G.J.R. wanted to get rid of it—for a time. The W. & N. continued to work as usual, but under the G.J.R. stores committee, while approaches were again made, this time by the second owner, to the L. & M. to lease it for a while, and this time £3,000 a year was suggested; but terms could not be arranged with an unwilling L. & M. In July 1835 the line was leased to George Stubs, who had been treasurer and general agent of the W. & N. According to a statement made at the third annual general meeting of the G.J.R. on August 26, 1835, the board hoped to get about £3,100 a year from Stubs, which it was calculated would leave a surplus of around £1,000 after the W. & N. 4 per cent dividend was paid.

Stubs seems to have had three locomotives, which probably were the three W. & N. originals, and these were the ones Locke had to put in order for the Manchester trains. According to researches made by Mr. E. Craven, one of the three Kirtley brothers stated some years later that he and his brothers had had a contract for locomotives with the W. & N., but possibly this was just to drive and maintain them, as the Kirtleys had a small shop at Warrington. The G.J.R. board thought enough of Stubs to act as guarantor for him to the L. & M. when a question of some payments came up; but it would not let him borrow any of the new G.J.R. carriages to handle his Haydock Park race traffic, though at the time (June 1837) they were standing idle on the line waiting for opening day. After handing back the line to the G.J.R. Stubs remained for some time with the company as its agent at Warrington.

A final point about the G.J.R. in this area is the construction of the locomotive depot and the principal locomotive repair shops of the company at Edge Hill, on the outskirts of Liverpool, and adjacent to the L. & M. shops. This is perhaps the sole instance of a large railway erecting its principal repair establishment well away from its own line, and reached only by toll charges or running powers. But relations between the G.J.R. and L. & M. were quite close, and several directors were members of both boards, and much of the capital for the formation of the G.J.R. had been subscribed by L. & M. shareholders.

Fig. 4 shows the junctions round Newton and Parkside as they grew from 1831 onwards. Working round the former place was complicated still further by a colliery line from Haydock which crossed the L. & M. on the level and joined the W. & N. at the bottom of the original West curve; and by the extraordinary lead-in of the industrial line from the Muspratt chemical works near the Sankey Canal. The Haydock line was an integral part of the whole scheme, for one of the principal objects in the formation of the W. & N. had been the quick conveyance of coal from the pits near Newton to Warrington. But it may have been this crossing that led to the strictures about crossing the L. & M. on the level which appeared in the second Act of the W. & N. and in the Act of Incorporation of the W.B.

Nevertheless, the Haydock line was not untoward for those days, as can be seen from the map of the layout in 1831. This line and the pits which it served were owned by the Legh family, of which Lord Newton is now the leading representative. The Legh of the 1830s was a brisk and active man in developing his properties. From 1831 he had a locomotive, and then more, of his own; and his engines sometimes conveyed his coal trains as far afield as Manchester, travelling over the L. & M. under tolls.

Before the opening of the G.J.R. the L. & M. was insisting that two policemen or pointsmen would be needed at Newton, one at the East junction and one at the West; but that these men would not be required to stay after the existing hours as the approach tracks from the south towards both Manchester and Liverpool (being the tracks to be traversed by the late trains) had no points requiring attention, being always right for trains going in the normal direction, i.e. they were trailing.

In the years from 1837, when the Newton double junction was in full use, signalling and train movements were still on a rough time basis and not on a distance basis. At Newton special arrangements were in force, and a reference to the map of the layout as it was in 1839-40 shows they would definitely be necessary. In the years immediately following the opening of the G.J.R., trains passing between that system and the L. & M. had to slacken speed to 5 m.p.h., and this was retained by the L.N.W.R. in its early rule books.

In the late 1830s if any second class L. & M. train had arrived at Newton Junction station and a G.J.R. train was seen coming up the Vulcan incline, the engine-man had to stop and allow the G.J.R. train to precede him, either to Liverpool or to Manchester. Also, if a G.J.R. coach train overtook an L. & M. second class train more than three miles distant from Liverpool or Manchester, the second class train had to shunt, if there was opportunity, to allow the Birmingham train to pass. Engines of the G.J.R. had to carry two white bulls-eyes or reflector lamps on their front buffer planks while on the L. & M. Though this was to help identification there was some ambiguity, as the L. & M. engines had to carry "at least one."

By night, a green light at Newton, visible from either of the L. & M. directions, denoted that the points were open for a train going towards Warrington; by day a gilt arrow pointing towards Warrington was the signal. Signal posts chequered red and white were placed at the points leading off the L. & M. line on to the G.J.R. When the chequered side of a board was presented to face a train coming in any of the three directions it denoted that a passenger train was immediately in front, and the engine-man of the second train had to proceed with additional caution. These boards were visible by night and by day.

The G.J.R. had a post at Newton provided with a red lamp, which was hoisted at night whenever any G.J.R. train was near the top of the Vulcan incline, to give notice to engine-men on the L. & M. line, so that, if necessary, they could stop before coming to the crossing. The light was on the south side of the L. & M., and could be seen both from the Sankey viaduct and from Newton bridge.

In the early rule books (1847–49) of the L.N.W.R. these regulations were perpetuated in the main, but enlarged; and the regulations applying to Newton junctions, and the operation of what were still called the Grand Junction trains on the L. & M. section, were seven in number, as follows:

(15). In order to distinguish the Trains while running on the Liverpool and Manchester Branch, the Grand Junction Passenger Trains will carry *two* White Lights, and the Merchandise Trains *two* Green Lights, between Liverpool and Warrington, and the North Union Passenger Trains will carry a *Blue* instead of a White Light on the Buffer Plank of Passenger Trains, and a *Blue* in addition to the Green Light on the Merchandise and Coal Trains.

Special Signals, Newton Junction

(20). By Night, a Green Light, visible from either of the Liverpool and Manchester Main Lines, denotes that the points are open for Trains going towards Warrington.

(21). When a Grand Junction Train from Liverpool is approaching the Junction Points at Newton Junction, at the same time that a Train from Manchester or Liverpool is also approaching, Signals must be given to *both Trains to stop*; and if there is any doubt that there will be danger of collision in the Grand Junction train crossing the Liverpool South Line, the Pointsman must *not* turn the points for the Line to Warrington, but must let the Grand Junction Train run past the points towards Manchester.

(22). Whenever the line at Newton Junction is obstructed, or an Engine or Waggon is being shunted, the attention of the Pointsman on the Liverpool and Manchester Line must be called to the circumstances by *ringing the Bells* at the top of the Incline. *Two Bells* are fixed for the Pointsman at the Junction, whereby Signals may be exchanged between them and the Grand Junction pointsman.

(23). Whenever a Train is ascending the Warrington Incline, whether for Liverpool or Manchester, at the same time that a Train from either of those Stations for Warrington is approaching Newton Junction, the Pointsman will stop the *latter* until the former Train has passed the curve; he will also take care that an interval of not less than *five minutes* is allowed between the passing of any two Trains to Warrington.

(24). If, when any Liverpool and Manchester Second Class Train has arrived at the Warrington Junction, a Birmingham Train is seen coming up the Warrington Inclined Plane, the Engineman must stop, and allow the Birmingham Train to *pass before him* to Liverpool.

(25). If the Birmingham Coach Train overtake a Liverpool and Manchester Second Class Train more than 3 miles distance from Liverpool, the Second Class Train *must shunt*, if there be an opportunity, to allow the Birmingham train to pass. The same rule applies equally to Third Class Trains.

In such fashion were important main-line junctions operated by the Premier Line before the coming of telegraphs, interlocked signals, and continuous brakes! Despite the precautions, there were several incidents at Newton during the first ten years or so. L. & M. locomotive *Star* ran into a laden train of Haydock coal wagons at the crossing; subsequently, the same railway's *Mars* ran through an empty Haydock train; and the

Plate 1a Tait's engraving of Crewe station, 1848, looking north and showing the original works and clock-tower in the distance [*Clapham Museum of Transport*

Plate 1b Tait's engraving of Crewe station looking south from the same point as the view above; the Crewe Arms is behind the station building on the up (left-hand) platform [*Clapham Museum of Transport*

Plate IIa Newton Junction looking east in 1848; Warrington tracks going off to the right; part of the station building in the neck of the V still exists (see Plate III)
[*Clapham Museum of Transport*

Plate IIb Tait's 1848 engraving of Parkside looking west; Wigan branch junction to right; Huskisson's tablet is on the left of the line, close to the overbridge (now carrying the A573 road)
[*Clapham Museum of Transport*

Plate IIIa The remains of the original (1831) Dallam Lane terminal of the Warrington & Newton Railway as they are today

Plate IIIb Parkside East Junction looking west today; rubble on the left marks site of the second station

Plate IIIc Earlestown station (Newton Junction) looking from Warrington lines towards Liverpool; remains of original station building in centre

Plate IIId The Haydock crossing, Newton Junction, looking north, as it is today; eastbound BR dmu below the starting signal

Plate IVa Vale Royal viaduct over the Weaver in the early days of the Grand Junction Railway

Plate IVb Warrington bridge, GJR, over the River Mersey and the Mersey & Irwell canal as it was before the industrialisation of the area; the bridge is still in use today

well-known *Patentee* is recorded to have run at 30 m.p.h. through wrongly-set points at the junction, but did not derail until it "came to a part of the road where the platelayers had the rails out."

Half a century later there was a fatal accident on the incline. Just before midnight on June 20, 1890, a returning banking engine (No. 1870) ran down the incline on the wrong road and collided with a freight (headed by no. 1937) coming uphill, and the driver of the banker died of injuries though neither engine was greatly damaged. There were three men on the banker, one of whom was the Earlestown stationmaster who was going down to Winwick to make sure the signalman there was clear as to instructions that he must accept no trains from Earlestown after 2.15 until the Queen's southbound train had passed. The Queen had left Ballater at 14.50 in the afternoon.

Use of the Newton curves for main-line trains to and from the south remained, for Manchester trains, until the opening throughout on August 10, 1842, of the Manchester (London Road) to Crewe section, built by the Manchester & Birmingham Railway; and, for Liverpool trains, until the opening in April 1869 of the Runcorn bridge and Runcorn-Weaver Junction line. That junction was the first flying junction on an English main line; but it was hardly the first envisaged, because the wording of the W.B. Act and of the second Act of the W. & N. 39 years before left those companies the alternatives only of a flying junction or a burrowing junction where they joined the L. & M. if that company objected to any of its tracks being crossed on the level.

Today, local trains in the form of d.m.u.s still use the curves on services between Warrington and Liverpool and Manchester. The Haydock mineral track no longer exists outside 'the triangle'; within the triangle remain a few lengths of detached track, and also the connection at the south end, which literally comes off the uphill track of the east curve within one yard of the crossing. The station building at the west 'point' is the original.

The well-known main-line cut-off from Winwick junction to Golborne junction (Fig. 4), over which the M.6 motorway now runs, though first projected in 1830, and sanctioned again later for the G.J.R., was not opened until August 1, 1864, under powers granted a third time, by 24 & 25 Vict., cap. 128, of July 11, 1861. Neele records that its first mention in L.N.W.R. passenger timetables was not until February 1872. Some years elapsed after its opening before the Post Office authorities would allow the night mail trains to use it, as Newton was an easy exchange point for mail bags from east and west to go north and south. Eventually Wigan and Warrington were approved as the mail-exchange stations.

The passage of time is such that it is now over a century since Newton and Parkside lost their original importance as junctions and stations. Parkside for many years has been a junction only, with Huskisson's tablet remaining about halfway between the east and west junctions, but with none of the busy scenes depicted in Tait's stone engraving shown in Plate IIb, which is the only known illustration of the old Parkside junction of the W.B. Newton Bridge station is now Newton-le-Willows; and the Vulcan Halt still remains on the 'inclined plane' right opposite the Vulcan Foundry.

Newton Junction remains a station, though renamed Earlestown over a century ago. In 1853 the L.N.W.R. began erection of its new wagon works between the junction and the Sankey canal, leasing some of the ground of the Jones & Potts Viaduct Foundry. The works and surrounding houses were named Earlestown in honour of Hardman Earle, for many years a director of the L.N.W.R., L. & M., G.J.R. and North Union, and also one of the proprietors of the Mersey & Irwell Navigation Co. Selection of this site may have been influenced by an approach of Jones & Potts to the L.N.W.R. board in July 1851 offering the whole of the locomotive-building Viaduct Foundry including shops, cottages, gas works, stationary engines, etc., for the not exorbitant sum of £14,450. The L.N.W.R. declined "not being in want of such a place", but the thought of it must have remained.

III

The Wigan Branch

ON THE same day, May 29, 1830, that the W. & N. got its second Act, to use steam locomotives and to make a branch towards Parkside, the Wigan Branch Railway received its Act of Incorporation (11 Geo. 4, cap. 56). Despite its name, this line was independent of the L. & M.; its 19 sponsors were mainly Wigan-area coal merchants and colliery proprietors seeking a cheaper transport outlet than the canals for their coal going to Liverpool and Manchester, but the preamble to the Act also mentioned passengers. Some of the 'Liverpool party' were shareholders, and by the second annual meeting they were in control on the board. Authorised capital was £70,000 in £100 shares, plus £17,500 borrowing powers; but all capital had to be subscribed before construction began.

First activity was the erection of a grandstand near Parkside, which on September 15, 1830 "they and their friends occupied and from which they loudly cheered the procession." (i.e. the L. & M. opening procession). Almost immediately the cheers must have changed to consternation, for it was just here that Huskisson was run over.

The line began to the east of Wallgate in Wigan, and terminated by an east-facing curve, leading in the Manchester direction, on to the L. & M. at Parkside (Fig. 4). The Act contained provision also for a west-facing curve leading to the Liverpool direction and joining the other curve near Old Town of Lowton; and for a 2.6 mile branch from Inial Hey, a mile-and-a-half south of Wigan, running in a north-easterly direction to the New Springs Bridge over the Leeds & Liverpool Canal. Neither of these branches was built by the W.B., and eventually both were taken in hand by its successors. The original proposal for an either-way lead-in to the Springs branch was never effected, only the south-facing curve being built; but many years later, when the Hindley junction–Haigh junction cut-off was constructed, a north-facing curve was put in at Kirkless to join it.

Springs branch is commemorated to this day on the London Midland Region main line by the signalbox and steam locomotive depot of that name, though the signalbox will disappear with the forthcoming re-signalling between Crewe and Glasgow, and steam locomotives will have gone from the depot by the summer of 1968. Even the depot itself may pass with the changing pattern of traffic and with the probable eventual electrification from Crewe northward; but in its last days, through the winter of 1967/68, it showed another memento of practice long gone by in the shape of two L.Y.R. eight-wheel rigid-frame tenders previously used as sludge tanks from a water-softener.

Why the Parkside West curve (Fig. 4) was not built first remains a mystery. Construction of the W.B. reduced the canal distance from Wigan to Manchester by one mile; but from Wigan to Liverpool the railway journey was 13 miles shorter than by canal, so that all the incentive was to cater for traffic in that direction, particularly as Warrington, too, had been mentioned in the preamble. This omission to connect westward became still more inconvenient when the G.J.R. was opened, for through journeys from the south to Wigan and beyond could only be effected by reversal at Parkside, which became notorious for delays until 1847, when the L.N.W.R., the W.B. successor once removed, put in the half-mile curve, under powers granted to the L. & M. under Act 8 & 9 Vict., cap. 123, of July 21, 1845, just three weeks after the L. & M. itself had been absorbed into the G.J.R.!

A possible reason for the W.B. itself not putting in the west curve in the beginning may have been the proposed W. & N. branch mentioned in the previous chapter, and which in its first state was to have a connection on to the L. & M. just west of Parkside. The W.B. may have thought its own curve could wait until the W. & N. branch was made. After the early months, as already recorded, neither the W. & N. nor the W.B. had enough money to make these short lines; though it is to be noted that during its independent existence the W.B. did not make use of its borrowing powers.

The main line of the W.B. extended for 6.9 miles from Parkside to a station in Wigan almost on the same site, but at a rather lower elevation, as the present Wigan (L.N.W.R.). It was laid at first with a single track, though the formation was made wide enough for two. While single it had to have, according to the Act, at least three passing loops a mile. It was laid with 45 lb. T-form rails 15 ft. long, and seems to have been primitively and poorly constructed. Yet the rail section was not chosen without thought. Apart from the professional advice of Vignoles, the engineer, the directors consulted also Nicholas Wood at Killingworth, the St. Helen's Railway, and Hartley, the well-known Liverpool docks engineer, as to the section. The contractors, Pritchard & Hoof, were not a success; and though they were given also a maintenance contract for two years after the line was opened, this was done no better than the construction, and was taken away from them before the term expired. Legal actions for payment of this and outstanding construction costs went on until the end of 1839, when Pritchard & Hoof were awarded £5,543 plus £645 costs against the North Union Railway, the successor of the W.B. Vignoles stated in 1835 that the W.B. had cost £12,000 a mile.

C. B. Vignoles laid out the line and was engineer of the company. Stretton says he was appointed on the recommendation of George Stephenson, who had to decline the proffered appointment in 1829 as the L. & M. needed all his services. This is unlikely; at that time there was still a certain coolness between Old George and Vignoles, and according to Vignoles' son the *rapprochement* did not take place until 1830, when Vignoles was busy on the St. Helen's Railway. Vignoles was formally appointed engineer of the W.B. at a salary of £500 a year in June 1830, but he had done the preliminary surveys in 1829, and had done them in a great hurry to have them ready in time for the Parliamentary session—

in so much of a hurry that "for three nights none of us went to bed, and when all was finished everyone was completely knocked up." The salary of £500 was to continue until the work was finished, and out of it Vignoles had to pay all his assistants. Within a month he had been asked specifically to report on the best method of making a junction with the W. & N., and in October 1830 there were talks to see what could be done.

Early in 1831 Vignoles told the board he had been invited to assist Alexander Nimmo in surveying the projected Leeds & Liverpool Railway; but as the W.B. was opposing the Bill it gave a decided 'no' to the idea of Vignoles being connected with it. It was Nimmo who had supported George Stephenson years before in the examination of the L. & M. Bill; and on being asked, re Chat Moss, if he would undertake to float a railway over a morass, replied: "Yes; and I would be prepared to float one over the sea if you will provide the money for it."

Over two years from Vignoles' appointment were needed before the main line was complete. It was opened on September 3, 1832; and the only ceremony was that the directors travelled in a separate carriage attached to the first train in each direction and then dined at Wigan. There is no evidence that through carriages were at once run between Wigan and Liverpool or Manchester; nor, when the G.J.R. was opened in 1837, do through coaches between Wigan and the south appear to have been put on; perhaps a wise omission, as even when new the W.B. track seems to have been hardly near G.J.R. standards. In 1837/38, before the N.U. line from Wigan to Preston was opened, the connections to Wigan were off the 9.00 first class train from Liverpool, and off the second class trains leaving at 10.00, 12.00 and 17.30. On Sundays there were connections off the second class trains only, leaving Liverpool at 7.00 and 17.30.

There was from the beginning of the L. & M. in 1830 a stopping place at Parkside, reputed to be the only point between Liverpool and Manchester at which coke and water were available for locomotives. Ackermann's various prints of Parkside show slight additions over the first year or two, but give the general appearance as it would be when the Wigan line was opened. This station was west of the W.B. junction, and the Wigan trains had to reverse at the points, if they came to the station at all, The original proposals were to have also a short stub at Parkside between the two curves, abutting on the L. & M. fencing. The original plan of Vignoles shows the two curves and this centre stub, and gives sections for all three; and this arrangement is shown also on one or two other old small-scale maps, including Booth's. However, this was never built, and by what means passengers changed railways prior to 1839 is conjectural. The shadow of Huskisson lay over the place from the day of the accident. His tablet was on the wall within a year or two; and by 1837, when five tracks were there, Drake was warning passengers: "the difficulty of escaping from a coming train is no small one for a stranger, who, standing upon or among them, would find himself greatly bewildered in any emergency."

In 1839 a new station a little further east, at the point of junction, was built jointly by the L. & M., G.J.R. and N.U. This station was closed in 1878, but the station buildings were occupied as cottages well into the present century. The only remnant at the moment is a pile of brick rubble by Parkside no. 1 box. When this second station was built the extra tracks and buildings at the original L. & M. station were used for years as a goods station. The original Parkside station was just where Huskisson's tablet is located, and was approached from the road down a flight of steps which still exists. The clear-back of the cutting here shows where the building and one of the water cranes of Ackermann's pictures were located. There are still four tracks at Parkside, though the two northernmost are stub-end sidings.

On the original W.B. there was no gradient steeper than 1 in 330. Only when the N.U. line from Preston to Wigan was built did the gradient of 1 in 100 appear, to get the W.B. up to the level of the N.U., which line had to cross Wallgate over a bridge. With the passage of time and various works that gradient, which was 250 yd. long, has flattened out to 1 in 150. Wishaw states that by 1840 there was an intermediate station at "Colborn", but this does not seem to have been there in 1832.

The first chairman of the W.B. was Ralph Thicknesse, a coal owner and private banker in the Wigan area. The only 'Liverpool party' shareholder in the beginning was Edward Cropper; but by the annual general meeting after the first year the redoubtable Theodore Woolman Rathbone was a shareholder and a director, and by the next general meeting he was chairman. Very quickly he made his presence felt on the board; the directors, who were being paid a sovereign a meeting, thereafter were subject to the rule: "Directors to be paid their one sovereign for attendance at each meeting only if they are present within two minutes of the time appointed." This tended to put things on a more business-like footing; unfortunately there was not commensurate business. Like the W. & N. the line was short, particularly as the Springs branch was not built, and it was from this that a big increase in coal traffic could be expected.

In February 1831 Vignoles was instructed to put this branch in hand over the Hindley turnpike and beyond; but the next month his orders were countermanded on the strong objection of one of the directors who said there was not enough money available for this without any guarantees as to traffic. Towards the end of that same year the fluid cash situation was such that not only had a connection with the W. & N. and the Parkside west curve to be deferred, and all preparations for a second track put aside, but the treasurer, James Chapman, had to be directed to sell at not less than cost price 3,000 rails bought earlier and for which there would be no use for some months or more. James Chapman was an original shareholder both of the L. & M. and the W.B.; and in June 1830 he had been appointed treasurer, secretary, and general superintendent of the railway. He remained prominent in the railway scene between Parkside and Preston until the end of 1855, and was connected with all three railways concerned with the main line.

Under such penurious circumstances, it was small wonder that before the line was open for very long the directors began to consider the whole future; and so, when approached officially by the almost moribund Preston & Wigan Railway in August 1833 with the suggestion of an amalgamation they responded with alacrity, an alacrity understandable when it is realised that not only was the Preston & Wigan dominated by the 'Liverpool party' but that two or three of the directors were members of both boards, and James Chapman the secretary for both. Details of this side of the W.B. history are given in the chapter on the North Union Railway.

As the time for opening the line approached, the W.B. had placed no orders for motive power or rolling stock, and asked the L. & M. if it would be prepared to work the trains and provide the stock. This was agreed, but at first only for a term of three months; thereafter it was on three months notice, after the W.B. had been able to get slightly more favourable terms for passengers and goods than the original agreement. The terms of that agreement, which did not leave much for the W.B., were:

> "The L. & M. to find an engine and carriages to work backwards and forwards between Parkside and Wigan and porters to turn the carriages at Parkside. The Wigan Co. to provide the whole establishment of clerks and porters at the Wigan end and a guard for the coach train on their line to clean and grease the carriages. To book the passengers and parcels from Wigan and collect the money for the parcels received at Wigan. To load and unload the merchandise at that end, deliver what may be to be delivered and collect the freights on the same. The fare from Liverpool or Manchester to be 5s. on first-class passengers and 3s. 6d. on second-class passengers.
>
> "The whole of the receipts on passengers and parcels at Liverpool and Manchester or on the L. & M. to be retained by the L. & M. Co., and one half of the gross receipts at Wigan and on the W.B. to be paid monthly by the Wigan Co. to the L. & M. Co. By this arrangement the L. & M. will receive on first-class passengers:
>
> To Wigan — 5s. 0d.
> From Wigan — 2s. 6d.
>
> or on an average, both ways 3s. 9d. per passenger. The L. & M. Co. now receives 3s. on Wigan passengers to and from Newton, the additional 9d. being in consideration of the cost of the locomotive engine and coaches, etc., between Parkside and Wigan.
>
> On second class passengers the L. & M. Co. will receive:
>
> To Wigan — 3s. 6d.
> From Wigan — 1s. 9d.
>
> or averaging 2s. $7\frac{1}{2}$d. per passenger.
>
> The L. & M. now receive 2s. 6d. per passenger to and from Newton for second-class Wigan passengers. Three-halfpence per passenger therefore was all that was left towards providing the engine and carriages on the Wigan line.
>
> With respect to merchandise, the L. & M. Co. provide wagons and engine power, do the business at Liverpool and Manchester and convey the goods between these towns and Wigan for 5s. per ton,

The Wigan Co. to receive the goods and do the business at the Wigan end, for 5s. per ton on all goods moved in either direction. The L. & M. giving credit towards this amount for any monies receivable in Liverpool or Manchester.

These general arrangements lasted the independent life of the W.B.; but in September 1834, when the W.B. had become part of the North Union, that company offered a lease of the whole W.B. main line to John Hargreaves at £3,500 a year, the N.U. undertaking to maintain the track. Within a week Hargreaves had declined, but he sent representatives to offer to carry on the goods trade on the line and pay a sum equal to the gross goods receipts for the previous 12 months, and give accommodation for the coal traffic. Passenger traffic would continue to be worked by the L. & M. This was agreed, but on the understanding that the N.U. advertised the tolls to let, that Hargreaves should send in a formal offer in response, and that this would be accepted. It was through this method that Rathbone and Earle were able to tell a Government commission in 1839: "The N.U. is open to every carrier; there is but one in fact." The contract was signed by John Hargreaves and John Hargreaves Jr., but in July 1835 the latter became the sole lessee.

Hargreaves came to an arrangement with the L. & M. for that company's engine working on the W.B. to assist in the haulage of his goods trains as far as it could do the work while not on the passenger services. The charge for this was to be included in the £100 a month which Hargreaves agreed to pay the L. & M. in return for being handed the goods traffic off that line instead of it being given first to the W.B. and then handed on. As a *quid pro quo* the L. & M. agreed to Hargreaves bringing all the Bolton-area to Liverpool traffic along the Leeds & Liverpool Canal to Wigan and thence via the W.B., instead of over the Bolton & Leigh Railway direct to Kenyon junction. The interests of the Hargreaves family were so widespread that some of their transactions appear tortuous if one does not know the whole story; and the whole Hargreaves story is probably now impossible to obtain.

Long before these commercial happenings the W.B. had taken advantage of L. & M. experience, in fact within a month of the formal opening of that line, for on October 13, 1830, the board decided that the distance between the two tracks should not be less than 6 ft. Vignoles later recommended 6 ft. 6 in., but in April 1831 the board re-confirmed 6 ft. *The Railway Gazette* (September 16, 1938) has suggested that to this decision is usually traced the origin of the term 'six-foot way'. On the L. & M. the inner rails of the two tracks originally were only 4 ft. apart. G. P. Neele's story that L. & M. tracks at first were 4 ft. 8 in. apart: "the idea having been, so says tradition, that at night any wide load of goods could pass along the middle space" must be discounted. In Neele's early days it is quite possible that the tracks at some places *were* 4 ft. 8 in. apart, for the widening was done very gradually and slowly, extending even into the early 1880s, the final works following an accident to two passing trains near Huyton in 1874, when it was shown that the tracks at that place were only 4 ft. 4½ in. apart. *Rocket* and its sister engines projected only 6 in. beyond the rails on each side; the Duke's special carriage on the opening day projected 2 ft. over each side, and its door was wider still, so even if the door had not been open at the crucial moment Huskisson would still have had only 18 in. space as he chose to keep to that side.

Though the W.B. possessed no locomotives of its own, the company's seal depicted Braithwaite & Ericsson's *William IV* (without tender) which in 1830, just after the W.B. was incorporated, was the latest engine for the L. & M., being delivered on September 22, and, according to Ericsson in later life, had been "built to astonish the world" but "proved an utter failure." The decision to depict this engine may have been influenced by Vignoles, who was a friend of Ericsson and had a joint patent with him for improvements in steam locomotives. But the reason for the same engine being included in the seal of the G.J.R., incorporated three years later, is more mysterious, except that as Charles Tayleur was deputed with Richard Harrison to evolve that company's seal, some locomotive in part of the seal was natural.

Dendy Marshall records in *A History of Railway Locomotives Down to 1831* that a locomotive was supposed to be built by Mather, Dixon & Co. for the W.B. in 1832. There is no record of this in W.B. minutes; it may have been built to the order of Hargreaves and used *later* on the W.B. Similarly, Vulcan Foundry's claim that two of its very early locomotives were for Hargreaves for use on the N.U. may be in the same category, for the Vulcan centenary book is too vague for any year to be assigned to the construction of these units. According to *The Engineer*, January 23, 1920, the first two locomotives built by Vulcan were for Hargreaves, and were completed in 1833.

The W.B. had an independent life of only four years, but it managed to leave several legacies that caused trouble abounding and one of which was settled only in the law courts. These needed much attention on the part of the successor of the W.B., the North Union, during the time that line was under construction, and are dealt with more fully in the next chapter. Despite its artless state and practices the W.B., after its absorption into the N.U., and while it was still the only part of that system open, did attain to the dignity of carrying H.M. Mails to Wigan. The mails were brought to Parkside by the evening L. & M. trains from Liverpool and Manchester, and there taken in charge privately by the L. & M. station attendant and handed to the guard of the Wigan train. At Wigan station a messenger met the train and took the bags up-town to the main post office. For these services the G.P.O. paid the L. & M. man at Parkside £5 a year as a personal fee, £5 to the messenger at Wigan, and £20 a year to the N.U.; but the L. & M. was adamant that it would not be responsible for the mails while they were at Parkside.

The Parkside west curve was not opened until 1847. Edward Woods, late of the L. & M., was instructed by the L.N.W.R. in September 1846 to put the branch in hand and complete it as soon as possible after the opening of the Lancaster & Carlisle Railway. The L.N.W.R. at once began to use it for the more convenient running of trains to and from the south and Liverpool, and Parkside station lost much of its importance.

A peculiar service was put on by the L.N.W.R. in 1847 that used both Parkside east and Parkside west curves (Fig. 4). At that time there were 17 trains a day in each direction between Liverpool and Manchester; but five in each direction and two on Sundays were noted in Bradshaw: "By the trains marked NU, being especially North Union trains, the passengers for Manchester or Liverpool will be detained unavoidably at Preston Junction till the arrival of the trains from Preston." These trains comprised through carriages from both Manchester and Liverpool and others from and to Preston; they stopped at most stations on the L. & M. and at all on the N.U. How three trains and three locomotives were handled simultaneously at the simple double-track junction is not known. Possibly the trains from Liverpool and Manchester ran past the Parkside facing points and backed up the further curve to Preston Junction, and so were ready to start off when the Preston passengers and coaches had been interchanged.

Preston Junction was the station, later renamed Lowton, at the neck of the Y formed by the two Parkside curves with the W.B. main line, and is not to be confused with the later Preston Junction a mile or two to the south-east of the town of that name. Lowton lasted until B.R. days, when it was served by locals from Warrington to Wigan and beyond, which stopped at Earlestown, Newton-le-Willows, Lowton, Golborne and Bamfurlong. Today some four northbound diesel multiple-units still use the Newton east and Parkside west curves, including the 17.10 ex-Warrington to Windermere (1967–68 timetables), but there is now no station open on this route between Newton-le-Willows and Wigan.

IV

The North Union

EVEN BEFORE the Wigan Branch Act had been obtained, interests in the Preston area desired to have rail communication with Liverpool and Manchester; and the easiest way to get this would be to prolong the W.B. tracks northward. The first move was a suggestion, in November 1829, that, on the assumption the connection would be made between Wigan and the L. & M., a railway should be built from Fish-house hillock on the south bank of the Ribble and run via Rufford to Wigan, a track which would have been well west of the present main line. Early in July 1830 a promotion meeting was held, followed in the August by a meeting of subscribers, and then by the issue of a prospectus.

On April 22, 1831, an Act (1 Wm. 4, cap. 56) was obtained for the Preston & Wigan Railway, 15½ miles long plus one or two branches, the most important of which was to run from near the present Farington station to Chorley and Walton. Neither this company nor its successor was able to construct the branch, for there was a nasty clause in the Act concerning that fomenter of railway troubles, the Lancaster Canal Co., which appears thus early on the railway scene and continued in it in the same role for many years until its remnants were bought up by the L.N.W.R.

Authorised capital of the Preston & Wigan was £250,000 in £100 shares, plus borrowing powers of £83,000. Subscriptions did not flow in like the Severn Bore. The directors, who had shown much energy in getting the Bill to Parliament and having it passed in less than ten months from the first meeting, had a difficult job in getting money despite the estimates that passenger traffic alone should yield a return of 7½ per cent on a capital of £280,000; and construction could not commence until the full quarter-million had been promised.

Eventually in 1833, after considering whether the whole project should be abandoned, the board on August 8, 1833, resolved that it was "expedient and advantageous to all parties that the Preston & Wigan and Wigan Branch Railways should be consolidated; and if the Wigan Branch agree, then the two parties should jointly apply for an Act, and the united companies shall bear the title of the North Union."

Probably each of the two companies felt it could not do without the other, and three or four months before the W.B. directors had also been considering the future of their railway. At all events the W.B. shareholders, after receipt of the above minute of the Preston & Wigan, were called to a special general meeting three weeks later, on August 28, 1833, at which they showed little hesitation in passing a curiously punctuated, or unpunctuated, resolution: "That it is the opinion of this meeting that the interests of the present Wigan Branch Railway are essentially connected with its extension and continuance to Preston, and that they will be best consulted by agreeing to the consolidation with the proposed Preston & Wigan Railway required by that company as a preliminary." The meeting may have been influenced in this direction by the almost disastrous working agreement come to in August 1832 with the L. & M., which left the W.B. with little revenue, and by the chronic shortage of money. The fusion of the two companies was no difficult matter for leading directors of the two companies were the same. In the talks that preceded the amalgamation, Rathbone, perhaps the most energetic of the Preston & Wigan Directors, appeared for the W.B. and the Preston & Wigan was represented by Hardman Earle and J. Hornby, two more of the 'Liverpool party'. It was no more than a question of Tweedle-Dum and Tweedle-Dee.

Nine months after the W.B. resolution, on May 22, 1834, the Royal Assent was given to an Act (4 & 5 Wm. 4, cap. 25) to unite the W.B. and the Preston & Wigan by the incorporation of the North Union Railway. This was the first railway merger or amalgamation sanctioned by Parliament; and it was the precursor of a number of extremely complicated, inconvenient and ill-tempered manoeuvres, agreements and actions indulged in over the next dozen years or so by the railways from Parkside to Lancaster and beyond, and some effects of which in due time came on to the Lancaster & Carlisle Railway and the L.N.W.R.

Authorised capital of the N.U. by the Act was not to exceed the £320,000 given by the W.B. and Preston & Wigan Acts, which sum was to be consolidated into 3,200 shares; but as no money had been raised on loan by either of the constituent companies, the borrowing powers were raised above the normal to £160,000, and with a proviso that the N.U. could create shares to that amount in lieu of borrowing. By the end of 1839 this sum had been raised by £460,000 in shares and only £20,000 by loans. Another Act (3 & 4 Vict., cap. 5) of March 23, 1840, gave power to raise a further £250,000. The first chairman of the N.U. was Sir Thos. Dalrymple Hesketh, Bart., who had also been chairman of the Preston & Wigan; but the 'Liverpool party' was ever strong on the N.U., and the most active and powerful members of the board were T.W. Rathbone, Edward Cropper, J. Hornby and Hardman Earle.

One condition in the N.U. Act was that until the whole Preston to Wigan line was in public operation the profits from the W.B. line should belong to W.B. shareholders alone, unless two-thirds of them plus two-thirds of the Preston & Wigan shareholders decreed otherwise. This clause, actually suggested first by the Preston & Wigan, proved expedient, for even after the N.U. Act was obtained the subscription list was hard to fill, and no work contracts could be placed until January 1835. Nor was the work then pushed ahead with well-directed energy, and the short main line of 15½ miles (Fig. 5) took over 3½ years to complete.

Few boards of directors can have had more worries and frustrations per mile of construction than that of the N.U.; and few boards can have had such fluctuating and unsatisfactory service from the chief engineer. C. B. Vignoles was more or less inherited from the W.B. and the Preston &

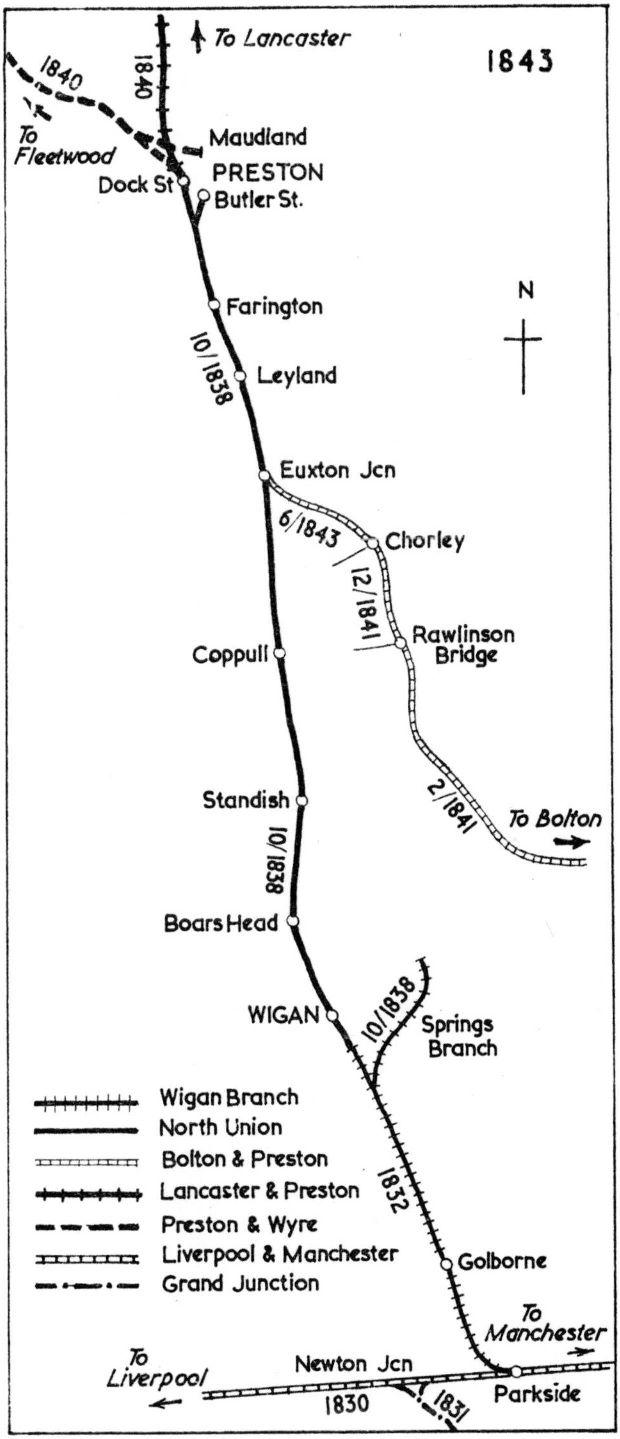

5 Parkside to Preston original owners

Wigan, but without a great reputation on those works. The W.B. construction had not gone as easily and well as the directors thought it should, as it was scarcely seven miles long and had no great works or gradients; and the Preston & Wigan directors, after reading the preliminary report of Vignoles towards the end of 1831, asked him to state what security the proprietors would have against his estimates being exceeded. In a report read at a general meeting of the Preston & Wigan at the end of 1831, Hardman Earle stated: "the directors . . . partake largely in the mistrust so generally and so justly entertained of engineers' estimates, which are proverbially vague, loose and inaccurate".

In June 1834 Vignoles became chief engineer of the N.U. at a fixed salary. The amount was not agreed at that time, probably because there were questions as to bills Vignoles was presenting for the preliminary surveys and plans in relation to the Preston & Wigan Railway; but in January 1835 the salary was settled at £1,200 a year, not a bad figure for a 15-mile line plus supervision of the 7-mile W.B. already built. Work on the Springs branch was not included; when that came it was to be on special terms. Vignoles' trouble was that he was trying to do too much work in other places, including Ireland. After the long delay from the passing of the Preston & Wigan Act the directors were anxious to get on, but Vignoles could never be found. He did not keep appointments he had framed himself, and he did not provide in time the essential information to get on with the staking and to effect the purchases of land.

The general committee of the N.U. directors for several years after the Act met weekly in Liverpool; and there was also a Preston committee which met as needful and was charged with the supervision of the construction and land purchase. Even before the end of July 1834 the general committee was informing Vignoles of the strong remonstrance of the Preston committee at his absence during the whole of the setting out of the line, and that the day when the plans were promised had arrived without any communication at all from the engineer. The general committee had to state that Mr. Vignoles would compel the board to appoint another engineer if it continued to be out of his power to fulfil his engagements. Time after time Vignoles had to be reminded of his absence. The board's irritation increased after construction actually began, because several times Vignoles was not present to give the monthly certificates of the contractors' work so that the board could pay the agreed periodic sums, and this did not improve relations with the contractors.

Vignoles, to quote a happy description of him written in 1842, was: "energetic and fiery, looking the very personification of some new and wild theory, to be put into immediate practice by his instrumentality." But he led the N.U. directors a rare dance with his absences, and by his habit of putting up to them, when he was there, technical and semi-technical questions the decision on which was really his. This led them, or at least the hard-headed Liverpool men among them, to distrust his constancy and also his judgment, so that they did not always confirm his engineering decisions on such matters as rails and sleeper spacing. These matters came to a head on the question of the bridge over the Ribble at Preston, and after this was settled Vignoles gave a little more attention to the N.U. part of his business, and there were fewer complaints from the directors, though they did not cease by any means.

In January 1835, three contracts were placed which covered the whole main line. The Preston contract covered the building of about 2½ miles of line south from the terminus, including the five-arch stone viaduct designed by Vignoles for the crossing of the Ribble, at that point a tidal river. The price for the whole of this contract was around £80,000, and the contractors were Mullens & MacMahon. Rathbone, Edward Cropper and Hardman Earle were also on the boards of the L. & M. and G.J.R., and in comparing relative costs they began to suspect that *pro rata* the Ribble viaduct was going to cost a good deal more than the Dutton viaduct over the Weaver, then being built under the supervision of Joseph Locke. After a reply from Vignoles in June 1835, the board decided to call in Hartley, of Liverpool (as the G.J.R. board had done at the end of 1833 in regard to Dutton viaduct), and told Vigholes they saw no impropriety in this. Hartley positively declined to examine the plans of Vignoles or comment on them in any way, and rather reluctantly agreed to supply a skeleton design of the bridge *he* would have adopted for the crossing of the Ribble.

When his plans were given to Vignoles that engineer said they seemed to involve an altogether new and startling experiment in bridge building. When the board asked if he, as chief engineer of the N.U. would take proper responsibility for erecting Hartley's bridge, he said: "Yes, provided Hartley's views are borne out by other scientific men." Olinthus Gregory, James Walker and William Cubitt were selected and approached. Then Vignoles began to hedge, and said the opinions could not be obtained in a short time; then he had conversations with the contractors and reported that they would not undertake to build Hartley's bridge at the same price and guarantees. The board therefore had to agree to Vignoles' bridge, but it minuted that "the company has no alternative but to adopt in all respects the present plans for the bridge, although unanimously of the opinion that considerable extra expense is thereby incurred." The board then went on to ask why some of the main culverts had been led at an angle involving extra expense; and Vignoles blotted his copy book again immediately afterwards by not being available to sign the monthly contractors' certificates.

Vignoles was very proud of his Ribble bridge and presented a model of it to the Society of Civil Engineers in Ireland. Herapath said (September 1836) it was "exactly the Waterloo bridge but with only five arches." But the above records, and the price accepted by the contractors, must dispose of the story of Vignoles' son that MacMahon made up his price for the bridge on the basis of one of the arches and that his clerk forgot to multiply this figure by five, so that MacMahon had to stand a heavy loss as the mistake was not discovered until everything was signed and sealed. This masonry bridge had five arches of 120 ft. span and the rails were 44 ft. above the river. It was completed in May 1838, but for a short period in 1837 work on it was delayed by a shortage of timber to frame the arches. Because of the estimated cost of its construction, the Preston & Wigan Railway had been given authority to charge pontage and this right was continued in the North Union Act. In his plans of 1831 Vignoles had proposed a 12-arch bridge with necessary piers and iron arches.

There was also a good deal of trouble with the other two contracts, but much of it was due to Vignoles' frequent absences and his inability to keep his finger on the pulse; and Collister, the resident engineer, had to report frequently to the board, for the directors were full of energy and attention. Through the summer of 1836 there were repeated complaints from the board to all three contractors at the slow progress; and eventually in the winter of 1836/37 Hughes, the contractor for the southernmost, or Douglas, contract, had to be relieved of the work. Four days before Christmas 1836 the N.U. board at Liverpool had straightway to draw a cheque for £1,300 and get the money to Wigan that day to pay Hughes's men in the evening, as he had no money. Wm. Mackenzie, who had the centre contract at an ultimate cost of £51,589 for 3½ miles including a two-year maintenance period, was in big trouble in November 1837 when a large culvert taking the River Yarrow through a big embankment burst in a flood. The whole line at this place had to be remodelled by cutting the embankment short at each end and putting over the valley a wooden bridge 400 ft. long and 73 ft. maximum height. At first the board blamed Mackenzie, but after it had apportioned his blame in a half-yearly report he made a spirited yet dignified and objective reply in the press, and reasonable relations seem to have been re-established. Another £2,000 was given to Mackenzie towards the cost of the bridge over the Yarrow.

Largely because of the earthworks such as the big embankments at Wigan and across the Yarrow vale, the cuttings around Boar's Head and through Penwortham hill to the north of Farington, and the substantial bridge over the Ribble, the N.U. was not a cheap line to make. By 1841, including the W.B. and the Springs branch, £582,000 had been expended on it, equal to £23,000 a mile. Both cuttings and embankments on the Preston–Wigan section went to 60 ft. in depth, and Vignoles stated the excavations amounted to 2 million cub. yd. in the 15½ miles of main line. For soils in the vicinity of coal measures he liked to give cuttings a slope of 2 to 1 if they were more than 20 to 30 ft. deep. The line from Preston had to join the W.B. end on; but to do this it had to cross over Wallgate, and therefore the north end of the W.B. track had to be raised, and it was this necessity that brought the 1 in 100 gradient (now 1 in 150) south of the present Wigan station. The N.U Act of Incorporation laid upon the company the duty of making the Wallgate bridge "in character architectural and handsome."

Ruling gradient was 1 in 100 in two stretches between Preston and Wigan, totalling 2.0 miles northbound and 2.8 miles southbound; but with the passage of time and various alterations these have been flattened, and the steepest part today is the 1¾ miles at 1 in 104 from Wigan up to Boar's Head. Vignoles stated in 1845 that he adopted deliberately this ruling gradient, considered steep in 1834/36, having observed that

Plate Va Model of North Union Railway coach; both the model and the original coach were built in 1842 at the NU shops at the foot of Butler Street, Preston [BR, LMR

Plate Vb Lowton Junction (formerly Preston Junction) looking north today; here the two Parkside curves combine, and Anglo-Scottish trains ran through until 1864. Here also Preston carriages were transferred to Liverpool and Manchester trains in 1847

Plate VIc Vignette of Preston & Wyre viaduct at Preston (1850)

Plate VIb Vignette of the North Union station at Preston (1850)

Plate VIa Newton Bridge station on the Liverpool & Manchester Railway in the 1840s; certain Anglo-Scottish trains stopped here until around 1860 to give connections to and from Liverpool and Manchester
[*Clapham Museum of Transport*

Plate VIIa Cornelius Nicholson (1804-1889), a leading promoter of the Lancaster & Carlisle and Kendal & Windermere Railways, and for some years London director of the Great Indian Peninsula Railway [*Courtesy of D. H. Stuart*

Plate VIIb Edward Williams Hasell (1796-1872), chairman of the Lancaster & Carlisle Railway for 28 years from the formation in 1844 [*Courtesy of E. W. Hasell*

Plate VIIc Samuel Barton Worthington (1820-1915), a pupil of Joseph Locke, engineer of the Lancaster & Carlisle Railway 1846-59, and subsequently Northern Division Engineer of the LNWR at Salford [*Clapham Museum of Transport*

Plate VIId Joseph Locke (1806-60), engineer-in-chief of the GJR, and of the lines from Preston to Edinburgh and Glasgow [*Clapham Museum of Transport*

Plate VIIIa Seal of the Grand Junction Railway, showing locomotive akin to Brathwaite & Ericsson's *William IV* [BR, LMR

Plate VIIIb Sir Hardman Earle (1796-1877) director of the North Union, Grand Junction and London & North Western Railways, after whom Earlestown was named [*British Rail*

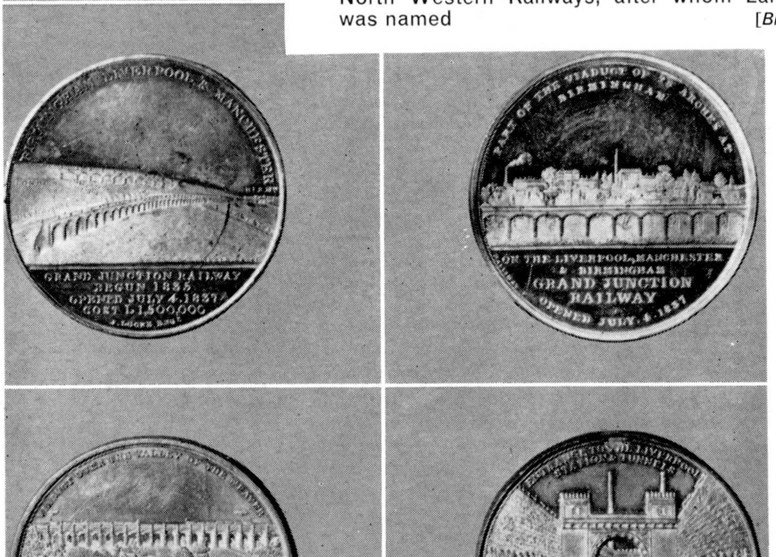

Plate VIIIc A series of medals struck for the opening of the Grand Junction Railway in 1837

locomotives on the L. & M. worked very well on the inclined planes (about 1 in 90 at Sutton and Whiston), and because he expected improvements in locomotives would continue.

The 60 lb. rails were laid on wooden cross sleepers on the embankments and at certain other points, but in cuttings or where the railway was over the surface of the land stone blocks were used. There was considerable discussion among the directors about the rail section and weight; the measurements were changed two or three times, once after a substantial contract had been placed. The board was not disposed to take Vignoles' recommendation without enquiry, and Locke seems to have made suggestions about the rail section when asked informally by those who were members of both G.J.R. and N.U. boards. Nor would the directors allow Vignoles to space out the sleepers and stone blocks to 5 ft,. as he proposed; they said, quite rightly, that this would involve heavier rails, and above 60 lb. a yd. they were not prepared to go. But the first rail contract, placed with Harford of Bristol, did not run well, because of some defective rails and other causes.

At this time Vignoles was pushing flat-footed rails on longitudinal timbers, though he had none on the N.U.; nor would the N.U. directors take them in 1840–41 when Vignoles put them forward for the relaying of the W.B. The advantage he saw at the time was not his flat-footed rail spiked direct to the sleepers, as is now almost universal, but the continuous support given by the longitudinal sleepers, and the possibility thereby of going back to cast iron rails! In view of what he was doing on the N.U. during 1835–38, it is interesting to note that in a report to the Midland Counties Railway at the end of 1836 he stated: "sleepers are laid on embankments with the avowed intention of being replaced after a few years by blocks." This was not very politic on his part when Rathbone and Cropper were members also of the Midland Counties board.

The Preston–Wigan main line was not the only headache of the N.U. directors over the years 1835–38. The W.B. from Wigan to Parkside had been lightly and poorly laid. After its opening the contractors, Pritchard & Hoof, got a two-year maintenance contract, which was carried out to no higher standard than the first construction, and by the time the N.U. got its Act some parts were even dangerous. Less than two months after the formation of the N.U., the secretary, James Chapman, who had been secretary and manager of the W.B., was ordered, "in the absence of the engineer to get John Smith and such other workmen lately employed on the Wigan Branch to get on immediately with the repair and bring it into the state prescribed." In May 1835 a maintenance contract for a year at £400 was given to Smith & Eckersley to cover the Parkside–Wigan section, and this seems to have been satisfactory, for it was renewed for another two years at £500 a year until such time as the whole N.U. was open and the company took over the maintenance.

In its independent days the W.B. had never had enough money to build the Springs branch (Fig. 5), though there was considerable potential coal traffic. The company tried to get various coal owners to guarantee certain yearly traffics, but did not meet with a response sufficient to invest the money. When the N.U. was formed it was charged by the Act to complete the Springs branch and to have it open to public working before or at the same time at the Preston–Wigan main line. From time to time construction was deferred; then in the first half of 1836 Vignoles staked out a line and gave estimates for the construction of the branch at: £19,324 for double track, £13,270 for single track, and £14,105 for single track but with bridges and land for double track. Thereafter the branch was put in hand, but only at a gradual pace, and it was not opened throughout until the same time as the main line in October 1838. The contractor's price for the earthwork, bridges and laying one set of rails was £6,990.

A trouble on the Springs branch was a 1 in 30 gradient near mid-length, and how to work it caused the N.U. directors much thought. Horses, locomotives, an engine-worked incline, and a self-acting incline were all considered. There was some horse working on the incline, and also over the rest of the branch by those leading their own coals, but as a whole the traffic was operated by a steam locomotive. Only empty wagons were hauled against the 1 in 30 gradient. Braking regulations for loaded trains downhill have not survived, but after one accident a strict rule was issued not to exceed 8 m.p.h. on the incline.

By 1846 the N.U., then comprising almost 40 miles of route, was carrying 1,000 to 1,200 tons of coal a day, and the Springs branch contributed a considerable quota, for the number of working collieries along it had grown. Traffic grew further, and G. P. Neele records that by 1867 this branch "was worked on a system existing solely in the intelligence of the local superintendent, Mr. Hill, under whose control all the coal traffic and all the breaksmen working the coal trains to the south were placed." In the early 1840s many northbound trains from Wigan along the main line were banked up to Boar's Head by a locomotive stationed at Wigan for the purpose. This engine was not worked so lightly as most bankers, for it had to bring empty coke wagons back from Coppull, and there was a time when it had additionally to lead coal trains from Springs branch junction to Parkside when not otherwise engaged.

Intermediate stations between Wigan and Preston were at Standish, Coppull, Euxton, Golden Hill and Farrington (then spelled with the double 'r'). Euxton station disappeared last century, though replaced to some extent by Balshaw Lane & Euxton; Golden Hill was renamed Leyland within the first year. Though Preston station soon came to be considered a miserable affair, and drew remarks alike from the Railway Commissioners and the public, it gained a few encomiums when it was erected by having a double way with a roof 120 ft. long by 40 ft. wide. According to Vignoles' son, it was not nearly so grandiose as that engineer wanted to make it. For many years the platforms remained only a few inches above rail level, and it was long years before the L.N.W.R. actually bettered the accommodation and layout, though there were one or two spasmodic tries. Even in 1848 the Government inspector said the accommodation at the N.U. station was "utterly insufficient for the traffic passing through it."

From June 1840 the main double line passing outside the station (Fig. 5) was used to give connection with the newly-opened Lancaster & Preston Junction Railway. It passed through a 77-yd. tunnel under Fishergate to join the L. & P. at Dock Street. Public entrance to Preston station was from Butler Street, and was to the north end of what later came to be the East Lancashire (Lancashire & Yorkshire) part of the station. Butler Street was on a down-slope from Fishergate; at the other end of the line Wigan station was approached up a ramp from Wallgate. More about Preston station in its later days is given in Chapter XVI, and a map of the peculiar arrangement of lines just north of the N.U. tracks is given in the map forming Fig. 6 (Chapter VI). Around 1850 the station was enlarged and rebuilt, though still inadequately; at this time the entrance was changed from Butler Street to what is now the ramp down into the present station, but that ramp in 1850 led down along the west face of the station, and not into the centre as it does now.

The projected branch from somewhere near the present Farington station towards Chorley and Walton, authorised first in the Preston & Wigan Act of 1831, was never built, because of an unusual qualifying clause. This branch was to run east to make connection with the existing tram-road of the Lancaster Canal Co.; but the Act contained a provision that work on it was not to begin "without first having obtained from the company of proprietors of the Lancaster Canal Co. an undertaking that within six calendar months from the completion of such branch they will take up their present railway or tramway in Walton-le-Dale"—surely one of the most peculiar conditions put in any Act, particularly when related to a body such as the L.C.C.

At length the whole N.U. work was finished and the directors had an opening trip of their own on October 21, 1838. Their train seems to have been only one open carriage; though the contemporary accounts say it was 'propelled' by the locomotive, that word in those days was used almost indiscriminately for pushed or pulled, though in this case it would certainly be better for the directors to have the locomotive behind. The train seems to have gone through from Parkside to Preston, 22½ miles, in 45 min. without any ceremonial stop at Wigan, probably because October 21 was a Sunday. No. 2 engine pulled the coach, and its 30 m.p.h. average would be sufficient for a Bury-type 2–2–0 on unconsolidated track. Engine no. 5, of the same type, acted as pilot in advance. Rathbone, Hardman Earle, J. Hornby, and the chairman of the Preston committee, W. Taylor, were the leading board members present. Public opening was on October 31, 1838, and the transport of mails began a week or two later. At this time the second station at Parkside was brought into use, a little to the east of the old L. & M. station and against the junction.

Five weeks before the N.U. opening to Preston the London & Birmingham Railway had been opened throughout, and from the end of October 1838 a continuous journey of 218 miles 51 chains from Euston to Preston became possible, though it involved two reversals, at Birmingham and Parkside, and there were no through carriages at first. The exact distance is that given by the Government commissioners reporting in 1840 on the routes to Scotland. Not until August 19, 1839, do through coaches between London and Preston appear to have begun, and on that day, too, through fares and bookings were initiated, though for first class passengers only. This latter facility had been delayed somewhat because the G.J.R. had not adopted Edmondson's card ticket machines, and only a strong remonstrance from the two more northerly companies led it to do so.

Train services and fares in October 1839 are given respectively in Tables II and III. Through Preston–London carriages ran on the 9.45 and 18.27 departures from Preston, and on the 9.30 and 20.30 ex Euston. Other services, with a change en route were given off the 2.57 from Preston, and off the 8.45 and 11.00 out of Euston. Through Preston–London fares first class were 54s. 6d. by the day train and 57s. by the night mail.

While the northern railhead remained at Preston there were seven trains going south over the N.U. and six coming north, all with connections at Parkside, or through coaches to or from Liverpool and Manchester There were three trains a day in each direction on Sundays. Most trains stopped at all stations, and the overall time for the 22½ miles between Preston and Parkside was around 60 min. for first class trains and 75 min. for local trains. The average length of station stops according to Whishaw writing in 1840, was 1.8 min. Intermediate fares over the N.U. line were as given in Table III.

When the service began in 1838 a few trains headed by N.U. locomotives throughout seem to have run from Preston to Liverpool and Manchester, but toll charges and fares on the L. & M. were high, and over the first six to nine months payments to the L. & M. amounted to nearly half the N.U. operating expenses, though of course these payments were largely the L. & M. portion of the normal through fares. From October 31, 1838, to June 30, 1839, total operating expenses were £15,015, so that the L. & M. share must have been £7,000 or more. On the other hand, there had been a clear operating profit of £16,013 in the same period, and most of this came within the last six months, as traffic built up slowly to the end of 1838. By the summer of 1839 there was little through locomotive working, coaches of the two companies simply being exchanged at Parkside. Despite these altered arrangements the N.U. was as big a help to the L. & M. as the G.J.R. had been two years earlier because of the number of passengers brought on to the pioneer line; and at the end of 1839 *The Railway Times* estimated the L. & M. was getting £20,000 a year in fares from N.U. passengers and other N.U. tolls.

In the first six months of N.U. operation 68,500 passengers were carried, and the receipts for these and for parcels amounted to £12,646; and in the ensuing eight months to the end of 1839 the number of passengers carried was 135,482 and the receipts £22,796. Coaching revenue increased to £28,861 for the first six months in 1840 and to £26,247 in the second six months. Not all this traffic was carried in the N.U.'s own coaches, for L. & M. vehicles ran through to Preston. At the end of 1840 the N.U. owned 20 first class, 15 second class, 12 carriage trucks and 6 horseboxes. Even if L. & M. through coaches housed 40 per cent of the passenger

Table II—Train Service between Preston and Merseyside, and Preston and London, October 1839

Departures from Preston to Liverpool and Manchester	Departures from Liverpool for Preston (3)
2.47 mail	7.15 mixed
7.00 mixed	8.45 1st class
8.20 1st class	11.00 1st class
9.45 1st class (1)	14.30 2nd class
14.20 2nd class	16.45 mixed
16.20 mixed	19.15 1st class(2)
18.27 1st class mail (1)	

(1) Including through carriage to London

(2) Passengers for Preston have to await at Parkside the arrival of the G.J.R. train leaving Birmingham at 17.00.

(3) From Euston, through carriages for Preston were included in the 9.30 and 20.30 departures from August 1839.

Table III—Fares from Preston (North Union Railway), 1839

From Preston to	Single Fares	
	1st class	2nd class
Farrington Lodge	1s. 6d.	1s. 0d.
Leyland	1s. 6d.	1s. 0d.
Euxton Lodge	2s. 0d.	1s. 6d.
Coppul	2s. 6d.	2s. 0d.
Standish Lane	3s. 0d.	2s. 6d.
Wigan	4s. 0d.	3s. 0d.
Golbourne Gate	5s. 0d.	4s. 0d.
Liverpool or Manchester	7s. 6d.	5s. 0d.
London (through day coach)	54s. 6d.	—

traffic, when around 300,000 passengers a year were being carried (317,500 in the year 1843/44, bringing in £36,767) this meant a pretty good user for the tiny N.U. two-axle carriages, an illustration of one of which, from a model built for a Preston Guild week, is given in Plate Va.

Soon the layout of Preston station proved insufficient to cope with the growing traffic, for from the summer of 1840 the P. & W. and L. & P. systems were bringing in and taking out more and more passengers; but only trifling enlargements and improvements were made to the Butler Street premises. By the first half of 1844 the remarshalling of the mail train for the south had to be transferred to Parkside "to obviate the great delay which took place in Preston, where there were 5 or 6 trains with 500 passengers at once to attend to." This move simply transferred the mail-train delay to Parkside, which, despite its five tracks, was no more suited to remarshalling operations than Preston.

Moreover, drivers were not inclined to treat timetables seriously, and as the general operation was still a little naïve, the railway system scarcely having attained puberty, trains were not connecting at Parkside as they should, which led to cumulative delays north and south. In the end, after discussions with the L. & M., Chapman drew up an 'official' scale of tolerances for up trains at Parkside, as given in Table IV. In the reverse direction, as delays were not unknown on the G.J.R. and L. & M. systems, a locomotive of the N.U. was sent specially to Parkside each day by 14.30 for the particular purpose of bringing on any passengers arriving with the 11.15 ex Birmingham, apparently a notorious late-comer, who missed the scheduled connection for the north; and this special train would stop at any station on the main line to Preston to set down.

Station working at Parkside was not helped by 'local times' then in force all over the country, for trains from four directions converged there, and on occasion exact instructions had to be given to the stationmaster to consider local time as something different. Only from 1846, largely due to the efforts of Henry Booth, did standard time come into force; and by then, through the formation of the L.N.W.R., its adoption in south Lancashire became easier, for there was only one operator covering London–Birmingham–Parkside–Preston, Liverpool–Manchester, Manchester–Crewe–Chester, and other lines.

At Preston were the principal carriage sheds of the N.U., to the west of the station and alongside the through tracks entering Fishergate tunnel; and near the passenger station in Butler Street were the locomotive repair shops, an engine shed and a goods depot. The shops could take five engines and tenders, and the establishment had a smithy and a fitting-and-machine shop with four lathes and a planer driven by an 8 h.p. stationary engine. The first locomotive to be owned by the N.U. was bought at the end of 1836 for £900. It seems to have been lying at Wigan without tender, and belonged to the Haigh Foundry; a contract was placed with that builder for a tender at about £60, but the vehicle had to have its springs suited for earthwork. The locomotive was lent to Hughes, the contractor; but from January 1837 Hargreaves was allowed to have the use of it at two guineas a day as long as the company was not actually in need of it. Presumably Hargreaves used it on the Wigan Branch. No information about its type or dimension now seems to exist.

By the end of 1840 there were 13 locomotives in the stock of the N.U., of which the above was not one. Eleven were of 2–2–0 Bury type built by the Haigh Foundry, Jones, Turner & Evans, and Benjamin Hick; and all of these had been built to specifications drawn up by Edward Bury for the N.U. Bury's firm did not get any of the orders, but Bury himself was paid £424 4s. 2d. for the specifications and for the supervision of the construction of the first six of the engines and tenders. All engines except nos. 1 and 12 had 12 in. by 18 in. cylinders; and all except nos. 1 and 13 had 5 ft. 6 in. wheels and were 9 tons in weight. No. 12 was a 2–2–2, also of 9 tons' weight, but with 13 in. by 18 in. cylinders; and no. 13 was a 2–2–2 with 12 in. by 18 in. cylinders and 5 ft. wheels supplied by Bourne & Bartley, who were probably just suppliers, and it has been suggested that this particular locomotive had been built by the Haigh Foundry. In the last two engines advantage was taken of the trailing wheels to get a larger firebox, and the firebox heating surface was 70 sq. ft. compared with

39 to 44 sq. ft. in the four-wheelers. In experiments made in 1840 by Whishaw with nos. 3, 4 and 5 engines, the highest speed attained was 42.8 m.p.h.; train weights were from 20 to 24 tons including the engine, and on the odd occasions when steam pressure was recorded it was 50/52 lb. per sq. in.

According to the Gauge Commissioners' report of 1846 the N.U. then had 17 engines of its own, of which four had been obtained from Jones & Potts in 1844, and some of the earlier ones had been withdrawn. Presumably no locomotives came over with the absorption of the Bolton & Preston Railway, as Hargreaves had the power contract for that line. On the lease of the N.U. to the L.N.W.R./Manchester & Leeds (L. & Y.) combination at the beginning of 1846, the former took over eight engines and the L.Y.R. five; the other four presumably were sold. For a time these engines continued to work the N.U. section; but in July 1847 the Crewe Committee of the L.N.W.R. recorded: "That the present N.U. engine stock, which was very defective from the first, be considered as four good new engines and tenders, and that whatever is needful beyond that must be supplied and charged to capital." The four N.U. engines thus taken into stock were numbers 177–180 and named *Chimera*, *Friar*, *Nun*, and *Monk*, but none had a long life on the L.N.W.R. According to *Tuck's Railway Shareholders Manual*, the N.U. had (presumably at the time of the take-over) 16 engines and 59 carriages; and there were at work on the line 13 engines and 1,071 goods and coal wagons belonging to colliers.

Passenger train weights as recorded by Whishaw were light even for those days, and the tiny engines had no difficulty in coping with them. On a day in April 1840 the driver of the early morning up mail from Preston, on receiving the right-away signal, started off in the dark without noticing that the train was not coupled on. Another locomotive was procured quickly and set off with the mail. After six miles or so the light-engine driver realised he *was* light, and stopped; but the train was close behind and a collision ensued, the mail engine was derailed and a number of passengers injured. On another occasion, in 1841, a coal train ran down the Chorley–Southport stage coach at the Euxton level crossing, the crossing-keeper having forgotten to close the gates to the road when he went for his midday meal.

In October 1841 James Chapman was telling the House of Commons Select Committee on the Bill for railway regulation that he did not think that on the N.U. there was any danger of collision through fast trains being sent off at too short an interval after slow trains; yet only a month before an alarming accident had happened at Farington station when the down mail from London ran into a preceding local standing in the station. The driver of the latter, seeing the danger approaching, started his engine and then jumped off. The suddenness of the start broke the coupling and left the train standing; the engine ran on at some speed, passed by Preston station on the lines through the Fishergate tunnel, and was finally stopped somewhere up by Maudland on the L. & P. as it slowed down.

The N.U. locomotives already described worked the passenger traffic;

the goods traffic was let to John Hargreaves Jr., who worked the trains with his own engines and rented the goods depot at Preston which had been built by the N.U. When the N.U. was approaching completion various toll charges were agreed with the L. & M. for traffic between Parkside and Liverpool to the west and Manchester to the east. These were: each passenger to either of the two termini 1s. 0d.; each ton of goods 2s. 0d.; and varying mileage charges for shorter distances, goods generally being about 2d. per ton/mile, but minerals, salt and lime being 1d. per ton/mile. Some short time after the opening Hargreaves Jr. was granted the operation of all N.U. freight traffic, including that on the W.B. section which he was already working, at a yearly rental resolved as from July 1, 1839, at £5,000, he paying the L. & M. its 2s. 0d. a ton for goods going to Liverpool or Manchester. The Railway Returns of 1841 showed that this must have been equivalent to Hargreaves paying the N.U. at an approximate rate of 1½d. per ton/mile whereas his average charge for goods was 4d. a ton/mile. Hargreaves could also carry parcels up to 56 lb. weight as long as he did not charge less than 1s. 0d. for any parcel between Merseyside and Preston and paid half the sum to the N.U. Through the winter of 1839/40 Hargreaves also was allowed the use of the spare engine kept in steam at Wigan to bank his freight trains up to Boar's Head if it was not on N.U. trains, and for this he paid 2s. 0d. a mile both ways.

A critical account published in November 1839, getting at the N.U. rather than Hargreaves, said: "The North Union professes to follow the example of the London & Birmingham (in allowing all carriers, under certain conditions, to convey goods over the line), but as yet only one carrier has established himself upon the line, and as he is the lessee of the Bolton & Leigh Railway, it is conjectured that his wealth and influence may virtually enable him to retain the entire carriage of goods upon those two lines." This was simply a paraphrase of what Rathbone and Hardman Earle had said before the Government railway committee.

As from January 1, 1844, the N.U. absorbed the Bolton & Preston Railway after the vicissitudes to be described in the next chapter. From that date the N.U. had a 'productive mileage' of 39.75. They were important miles—all of them, for the Springs branch was then surrounded by collieries which put much traffic on the line, and the remainder could all be classed as main line. The N.U. made only one further addition to its mileage, in the form of the ¾-mile branch at Preston to the Ribble docks, which was joint with Preston Corporation down to Strand Road and belonged to the Corporation in the dock area. The Act, 8 and 9 Vict., cap. 116, of July 21, 1845, authorised a capital of £20,000 and loans, for one-third that sum. In making out its case for absorption by the G.J.R. and M. & L., the N.U. calculated the Ribble Docks branch would lead to an increase of 12,000 tons of coal a year carried 12 miles for shipment, and that this would bring in £2,000 a year at 1d./ton-mile. The docks branch, much of it through tunnel and at gradients of 1 in 29–33–37 for half-a-mile, was opened in October 1846 under L.N.W.R. auspices, as by that time the N.U. had been taken over. Despite the sharp curves, of 530 ft. radius over much of the length down to Strand Road, L.N.W.R. 0–8–0 coal engines worked the line regularly in later days.

In 1846 the N.U., important because of its traffic and its place as a link in the Anglo-Scottish chain, and profitable despite its comparatively short length, came to an end as an independent operator, though not as a legal entity. The acquisition of the Bolton & Preston by the N.U. in 1844 had solved the N.U.'s own problem in regard to the Manchester traffic, and from October 1, 1849, passengers from the N.U. to Manchester were no longer booked via Parkside except by the mail trains. However, the fusion of the B. & P. did not solve the L. & M.'s problem of losing traffic between Manchester and the north; but that railway itself, with the associated Bolton & Leigh and Kenyon & Leigh Junction Railways, had been absorbed into the G.J.R. on July 1, 1845, by 8 and 9 Vict., cap. 198. In August and September of that year the N.U. invited the G.J.R. and Manchester & Leeds to take over or lease jointly its railway and property. Within a fortnight the N.U. offer was accepted, on terms extremely advantageous to the N.U. but causing a loss of £20,000 a year to the two lessees for some years and even £8,000 after seven years. The lease took effect from January 1, 1846, though the vesting and lease were not authorised by Parliament until July 27, 1846, under 9 & 10 Vict., cap. 231. Before this date of Royal Assent, the G.J.R. itself had been absorbed into the L.N.W.R., the Act of Incorporation of which was 9 & 10 Vict., cap. 204, dated July 16, 1846, a happening provided for in clause 50 of the Act of July 27. Thus the G.J.R. was an active lessee of the N.U. only for six and a half months, and was never a legal lessee at all.

The other joint lessee of the N.U., the Manchester & Leeds Railway, had already amalgamated with the neighbouring Manchester, Bolton & Bury Railway & Canal Co. as from July 1, 1845, though retaining its existing title, under 9 & 10 Vict., cap. 378; and of course it was the M.B.B. line which fed the direct Manchester traffic into the N.U. The Manchester & Leeds, as such, remained joint lessee with the L.N.W.R. until July 9, 1847, when, under Act 10 & 11 Vict., cap. 163, its name was changed to the Lancashire & Yorkshire Railway, which included also the six other railways in the two counties that the Manchester & Leeds had acquired or was in process of acquiring.

From 1846 the N.U. line thus was vested jointly in the L.N.W.R. and the L.Y.R., and was run by a joint committee of management. From this time the Parkside–Euxton Junction section was worked on L.N.W.R. account, the Bolton to Euxton Junction section to L.Y.R. account, and the Euxton Junction to Preston section on joint account. This last section remained joint until January 1, 1922, when the L.Y.R. was merged in the L.N.W.R. one year before Grouping. Thus until 1922 the West Coast Route between Crewe and Carlisle was never under single ownership, though it had been operated as a single unit since 1859, and had been considered as such for Anglo-Scottish traffic by the various owners since 1846.

The N.U. remained as a legal entity for 42 years after its lease to the L.N.W.R./L.Y.R. combination. The terms of the leasing Act of July 27,

1846, provided for a fixed annuity of £66,063 18s. to the N.U. as from January 1, 1846. This sum was to be payable after heavy useless rents of £8,000 and £825 18s. 9d. due to the Lancaster Canal Co. as a result of a Bolton & Preston Railway arrangement of 1837, in two half-yearly instalments; and had to be divided £47,732 13s. 4½d. among the holders of the £477,326 of A stock (i.e. original N.U. stock) and £18,331 4s. 7½d. among the holders of the £261,874 of B stock (i.e. the original B. & P. stock). These amounts gave returns of 10 and 7 per cent respectively, a remarkable return which resulted in the L.N.W.R. and L.Y.R. losing money for years, the loss in 1852 to the L.N.W.R. being calculated at £5,076. The L.N.W.R. was responsible for 60-94ths of the payment and the L.Y.R. for 34-94ths. On the 1846 lease coming into effect, the L.N.W.R. came into possession of the 1,000 shares in the Lancaster & Carlisle Railway held by the N.U., on payment of 34-94ths of their market value to the L.Y.R.

In 1888 the N.U. company was dissolved as from July 1, under the provisions of Act 51 and 52 Vict., cap. 176, of August 7. Its stocks were converted into 4 per cent debentures of the L.N.W.R. and L.Y.R. in the proportions for which those two companies were liable for the N.U. dividend. The holders of A stock received £250 of debentures for each £100 of their holding, made up, after adjustment of fractions, of £160 L.N.W.R. and £90 L.Y.R. Each £100 of B stock received £112 of L.N.W.R. debentures and £63 of L.Y.R. debentures.

Table IV—Arrival tolerance at Parkside for up N.U. trains from September 1844

Trains leaving Preston at	Due to arrive at Parkside	
	not before	not after
3.27	4.17	4.25
8.25	9.30	9.35
10.50	11.45	11.50
14.20	15.30	15.35
16.25	17.25	17.30
19.53	20.40	20.43

V

Bolton & Preston Railway

SOON AFTER the N.U. got itself to Preston in 1838 a long series of troubles began among the railways focusing on that town, and in which the Lancaster Canal Co. was often found as a catalyst, in the true meaning of that word as 'increasing the speed of reaction without being itself permanently changed.' On July 15, 1837, the independent Bolton & Preston Railway was incorporated by 7 Wm. 4 & 1 Vict., cap. 121. This was one of the most complicated and lengthy railway Acts framed up to that time, and had 263 clauses for the 20-mile line. It contained provisions which nullified each other yet left heavy financial commitments and sources of friction in the process; and it provided both the seeds of discord and the ground in which they could sprout and flourish. The original capital sanctioned by this Act was £380,000 plus borrowing powers of £126,500. Both the John Hargreaves—senior and junior—were among the original shareholders.

The B. & P. line was surveyed by John Urpeth Rastrick, but the engineer of the railway was Alex. J. Adie. Originally the approach to Preston was to be along the tram line belonging to the Lancaster Canal Co. that crossed over the River Ribble to the end basin of the canal on the north side of Fishergate. The purpose for which this tramroad had been built in 1802–05 was to connect the Preston end of the Lancaster canal with a branch of the Leeds & Liverpool canal some five or six miles s.s.e. of Preston. The Act for its construction (32 Geo. III, cap. 10) was dated 1792. The B. & P. could have possession of the tramroad and adapt it for steam locomotives if it saw fit. It did not actually exercise this power, and horse-drawn trains of the lessees continued to use the tramway until 1862 as far as through traffic was concerned. The L.N.W.R./L.Y.R. combination, as successor to the N.U., was permitted to close the Bamber Bridge–River Ribble section in 1864; but not until powers were granted under a general-purpose Act of July 21, 1879, could the remainder be closed legally.

Perhaps the 1 in 6 gradient and succeeding tunnel north of the Ribble bridge led to the abandonment of the tramway approach, and the immediate promotion of an amending Bill to divert the B. & P. route westward from Chorley to near the N.U. by Euxton, and then run parallel to that railway as far as Preston, but with a separate station in the town. So close were the tracks of the N.U. & B. & P. to be from Euxton to Preston that Herapath wrote in 1837: "We cannot understand on what principle the Bolton & Preston can apply to Parliament to grant a new line to run for several miles together parallel to, and almost osculating, the North Union." It is difficult now to understand why the B. & P. applied for this amending Act. Its Act of Incorporation stated that it would be advantageous if the N.U. could be made available for purposes of traffic between Chorley and Preston; and because of this the B. & P. was forbidden to buy any land or begin to construct any separate line from Harpers Lane at Chorley to Preston for three years after the passing of the Act.

A petition presented by the N.U. against the amending Bill charged the B. & P. with having a capital £88,000 too small on £349,000; and of having presented to the House a deed with one-half of the subscriptions executed, there being at the same time a private deed releasing the parties from the payment in part of the deposits. However, a month or two later arrangements were made for the B. & P. to have running powers over the N.U. from Euxton Junction into Preston "on payment of a toll hereafter to be fixed." Nothing was said about the separate station. In due time the toll was fixed at 1s. 0d. per passenger. The amending Act sanctioning the abandonment of the original approach to Preston and the construction of the diversion from Chorley to Euxton was passed on July 4, 1838 (1 & 2 Vict., cap. 56). Though nothing was said in the running powers arrangement about a separate station, the B. & P. Act of Incorporation had provided that the L.C.C. should set out 2,000 sq. yd. of its land to the north of Fishergate to be converted by the B. & P. into stations and warehouses. These establishments could have been only infinitesimal in size, and the area of land was changed by the amending Act to a strip 10 yd. wide from Fishergate to the dock, on which to lay a double track, plus another 2,000 sq. yd. alongside.

However, it was a long time before the running powers over the N.U. were exercised. The B. & P. opened the first section of its line, from Bolton to Rawlinson Bridge (or Nightingale Bridge), two miles south of Chorley, on February 4, 1841, as a single line; the short section on to Chorley was opened on December 22/23 of the same year (Fig. 5). Sir Frederic Smith, the Government Inspector, tried to get the B. & P. to lay the double track for which the formation was made; but P. Sinclair, the company's secretary, wrote that they were not doing that under any circumstances until the Chorley–Euxton section was almost complete, and that might be one-and-a-half to two years away. Sinclair did say the B. & P. proposed to have only one engine in steam, which was fortunate, for Smith recorded he saw neither signal nor lamp posts at any of the stations.

From the opening to Rawlinson Bridge a coach service ran between that point and Preston at an inclusive rail-road fare. There were three trains a day in each direction. Those northbound left Manchester at 8.00, 14.30 and 18.00, and Bolton at 8.30, 15.00 and 18.30, and the connecting coaches left Rawlinson Bridge at 9.00, 15.30 and 19.00. In the reverse direction the timings were so arranged that the coaches had only a short lie-over time at Rawlinson Bridge. Coaches left the Bull and Red Lion inns at Preston at 7.30, 14.00 and 17.30, connecting with southbound trains leaving Rawlinson Bridge at 9.00, 15.30 and 19.00. There was no service on Sundays .These timings just permitted the one engine in steam, with a very quick turn-round at Rawlinson Bridge.

Passengers travelling by the first northbound train arrived in sufficient time to get the train to Lancaster leaving Preston at 10.45, or the canal packet for Lancaster and Kendal at 11.00, or the train to Fleetwood at 11.15. Passengers by the second train had a connection for the packet boat to Lancaster at 17.00 and for the Fleetwood train at 17.15. In the reverse direction, passengers by the afternoon train from Fleetwood arrived at Preston in time to catch the B. & P. coach at 17.30. Through rail-road fares were as given in Table V.

Due to heavy and difficult works in the Chorley area, the remaining 3½-mile section from Chorley to Euxton Junction was not opened until June 22, 1843. The same year work was begun on doubling the Bolton–Chorley line. The difficulties around Chorley were in cutting through Hartwood Green hill, composed of alternate layers of sand and clay, out of which the contractor had to pump water continuously by seven steam engines totalling 60 h.p. Originally a 350-yd. tunnel of 20 ft. by 22 ft. 6 in. section had been proposed, and work on it was begun in February 1841; but after 18 months of trouble a decision was made to turn it into an open cutting. This involved removing 650,000 cub. yd. of earth, and throwing a bridge over the deep cutting to take the turnpike road. The cutting had to be provided throughout with retaining walls, and these were strutted with 16 flying masonry arches with a span of 26 ft. 9 in., the tops of which were covered by stone slabs to protect the masonry and mortaring from weathering. A photograph of these arches and the road bridge after nearly a century of service was published in *The Railway Magazine* for November 1938.

This opening-up did not end the troubles on the Chorley–Euxton section, for a short tunnel remained, and also another short cutting up to 70 ft. in depth that had a small retaining wall. A slip on this occurred on the evening of November 8, 1890, and a 'Lanky' Manchester to Blackpool train headed by locomotive no. 870 ran into the debris in the dark, without fatalities. This train had been held 11 min. at Bolton awaiting a connection from York, a reminder of cross-country services as they were in better days.

At its northern end the B. & P. was to have its own terminus at Preston; and in the promotion the company had been drawn into the tentacles of the L.C.C. For what seems the enormous annual sum of £8,000 a year plus 2s. a sq. yd. rent, the L.C.C. agreed to lease the tramway, and facilities north of Fishergate, for the use of the B. & P., though with a certain amount of joint use by the L.C.C. Altered arrangements made

Table V—Rail-Road Fares 1841

	From Manchester		From Bolton	
To:	Inside	Outside	Inside	Outside
Horwich and Blackrod	4/–	2/6	1/6	1/–
Rawlinson Bridge	5/–	3/–	2/6	1/6
Clayton Green	6/6	4/–	4/6	2/6
Bamber Bridge	7/–	4/6	5/–	3/–
Preston	7/6	5/–	5/6	3/6

in 1838–40, involving different land and property, led to the rent becoming £825 18s. 9d. a year additional to the basic £8,000. This site later became known as the Maxwell House station (Fig. 6, Chap. VI), though as a station it was never used by the B. & P. itself. When the running powers from Euxton to Butler Street station were obtained from the N.U. the ground north of Fishergate, and the tramway, became useless to the B. & P., but it could not get out of the £8,825 18s. 9d. annual payment, most of which had been ratified by Parliament, and this had to be taken over by the N.U. after the absorption of the B. & P. On the other hand the L.C.C. allowed the B. & P., and later that company's successors, £600 and then £1,000 a year to maintain the tramroad, which made the net money payment around £7,825 a year.

At its southern end the 14.5-mile B. & P. made end-on connection with the Manchester, Bolton & Bury Railway at Bolton, and so gave a more direct and convenient route from Manchester to Preston and beyond than the existing route via the L. & M., Parkside, and the N.U. At Bolton there was also to be a quarter-mile branch to the Bolton & Leigh Railway, of which the Hargreaves had a lease. As the B. & P. neared completion there was jealousy on the part of the L. & M. and the N.U., particularly as at that time (1843) the N.U. was at loggerheads with the Lancaster & Preston Junction Railway, with whom the partly-completed B. & P. had been developing closer relations in regard to using jointly a second station at Preston independent of the N.U. At this time, too, the Hargreaves of Bolton were providing under contract the motive power for the B. & P. and the L. & P., and were also operating freight trains under toll on the N.U. Further, the Hargreaves had the motive power contract for the Manchester, Bolton & Bury Railway. The branch to the B. & L. was never built.

The first thing to come was the first rate war. The B. & P. through fares initially were the same as those of the L. & M./N.U. route, viz. 7s. 6d. first class and 5s. 0d. second class, or 'inside' and 'outside' as the classes were termed here. These fares were the same as the B. & P. had been charging for the rail-road journey. The distance was 30 miles as against 36 miles via Parkside, and the B. & P. proposed to trust to this shorter distance and time to get them the traffic. But in less than a fortnight the N.U. reduced its fares to 5s. 0d. first and 3s. 6d. second; the B. & P. followed suit at once. After another two weeks the N.U. came down to 3s. 0d. and 2s. 0d. respectively, and again the B. & P. followed. The N.U. was charged with deliberately delaying the B. & P. trains between Euxton and Preston to get that company a bad reputation for punctuality, and the Bolton company retaliated by running coaches along the road between Euxton and Preston, and by threatening to resuscitate the powers to use the Canal Co.'s tramroad (often known as the Walton or Summit tramroad) as proposed in 1837.

All this was simply losing money for the two companies and distorting morale, and negotiations soon began. The Bolton was the more conciliatory of the two; probably this was due to the powerful 'Liverpool party' on the N.U. board, who had money at their disposal, and also knew that in any case it would not be too long before the N.U. itself would be taken over by their own master company, the G.J.R., as the north-spreading railway system became a trunk route. The Bolton first offered two-fifths of the passenger traffic and half the goods traffic between competitive points if the N.U. would grant running powers between Euxton and Preston, with accommodation at those places and the intermediate stations at Leyland and Farington, for an overall sum of £100 a year. This suggestion was refused, whereupon the Bolton suggested three-quarters of the total traffic for itself while continuing to pay existing tolls. Again the N.U. refused, and the Bolton came down to three-fifths; but the N.U. stuck out for fifty-fifty and the existing tolls.

In the autumn of 1843 a fusion of the two companies was agreed as from the beginning of 1844. The fares at once went back to what they had been until the June, after four months at the lower rates—the kind of instantaneous measure that helped public and Parliament to frown upon railway monopolies. The ratifying Act came later, and was 7 & 8 Vict., cap. 2, dated May 10, 1844; its purpose was "to effectuate" the sale of the B. & P. to the N.U. At the time, the amount of paid-up capital of the N.U. was £477,326 and of the B. & P. £262,000. By this Act the N.U. had to take over the yearly payment of £8,825 18s. 9d. to the L.C.C. to which the B. & P. was committed.

Though Vignoles had nothing to do with the construction of the B. & P. the engineering side of it came under his view when the N.U. and B. & P. were amalgamated, for after the completion of the N.U. he became consulting engineer to the company at a retainer of 50 guineas a year. Much of the B. & P. track was on longitudinal sleepers, and it was here that Vignoles began to have doubts about that form of construction, which formerly he had pushed vigorously. In his evidence to the Gauge Commissioners in 1846 he said: "On the Bolton & Preston, now part of the North Union, the line is laid on longitudinal sleepers. On the North Union part they are cross sleepers chiefly; in some parts blocks are laid on the old system . . . On a foggy morning when an engine comes to the longitudinal sleepers she invariably slips, and that slipping does not take place on the cross sleepers. Now that is a practical disadvantage which has affected my opinion on longitudinal sleepers." "Can you account for it?" he was asked. "Not at all. I would not believe it at first. The resident engineer, Mr. Coulthard, reported that to me two years ago. 1 in 200 is the gradient on the Bolton & Preston . . . The slipping occurred so repeatedly that I rode on the engine once or twice to satisfy myself." Vignoles then said there was more moisture around the rail with longitudinal timbers, and that the ballast was mainly sand.

The unyielding nature of the longitudinal-sleeper road may also have contributed to the trouble. Though Vignoles did not specifically tell the Gauge Commissioners, some at least of the B. & P. had been laid on continuous stone blocks instead of timbers; the blocks were 5 ft. long by 2 ft. wide, and were "embedded in brick sleepers"—perhaps the most unyielding track ever laid in England.

VI

Preston & Wyre Railway

WITH EACH northward projection of the railway system through Lancashire the town next ahead took up the question of a railway seriously; and with the Preston & Wigan works little more than started two further railways out of Preston were projected: first, the Preston & Wyre, leading to Fleetwood, and, secondly, one running almost due north to Lancaster.

The Preston & Wyre Railway & Harbour Company (the P. & W.) was incorporated on July 3, 1835, under 5 & 6 Wm. 4, cap. 58, with a capital of £130,000 in shares plus £40,000 in loans, to make a line between Preston and Fleetwood. Preston Corporation was one of the shareholders, but did not have a large block. On the other hand, John Abel Smith, the London banker, subscribed 27 per cent of the original capital; and then he went on to buy Roa island, near Barrow, to try and develop Piel as a harbour for passengers and for ore shipments from the developing Furness haematite beds, probably hoping that a Fleetwood–Piel steamer service might form part of a Lancashire–Scotland through route. The prospectus was unusual in bearing no date whatever; but it stressed that by shortening the sea passage, packet boats from Glasgow, Greenock and other Scottish ports would "be enabled to lower their fairs" (*sic*). More, it claimed: "so soon as the railway shall extend, as it is proposed, from the Irish Channel to the German Ocean, even the town of Kingston-upon-Hull will traffic to the Wyre through Preston, as the most convenient and most economical channel leading to all the western parts of the world".

The whole length of 19¾ miles, mainly single track, was opened on July 16, 1840, to a Preston station (Maudland) east of the Lancaster line, which was crossed on the level by a double track. The proposed level of the Lancaster line had been 5 ft. above that of the P. & W., and that railway agreed to raise its permanent way to cross on the level; but the Lancaster & Preston Junction Railway (L. & P.) had to make a connection so that P. & W. trains could run on to the main line and so through on to the N.U. system.

On July 21, 1845, another Act (8 & 9 Vict., cap. 125) was obtained for the construction of three branches: one from Poulton to Blackpool (Talbot Road), 3¼ miles; another from Kirkham to Lytham, 4¾ miles; and the third a three-quarter mile branch to Lytham dock. All of these were opened in 1846, the first-named on April 29 and the Lytham lines on February 16; the length of the P. & W. then totalled 28¾ miles, including a slight diversion of the main line at Poulton to give a better connection to the Blackpool branch, and a spur that was put in to give the possibility of a direct run between Blackpool and Fleetwood.

Building of the Fleetwood line was retarded because of monetary

Plate IXa Crewe-Allan 2-4-0 with original four-wheel tender replaced by a six-wheeler. These engines were used on the Crewe-Carlisle line until replaced by Ramsbottom engines in the 1860s

Plate IXb Crewe-Allan 2-2-2 of the type supplied by LNWR for working Lancaster & Carlisle passenger trains, 1846-57

Plate IXc One of the numerous Northern Division rebuilds into 2-4-0T of a Crewe-Allan 2-4-0 tender engine

Plate Xa Original laminated timber arched bridge over the River Lune at Lancaster
[*Courtesy C. L. Parkinson, AMInstCE*

Plate Xb Ticket for the official opening of the Kendal to Windermere section of the K&W Railway; the short section from Oxenholme to Kendal had been opened in September 1846
[*BR, LMR*

KENDAL & WINDERMERE RAILWAY.

Opening through to Windermere,

On TUESDAY, 20th April, 1847.

SECOND CLASS

LEAVING KENDAL AT 12 O'CLOCK, NOON,

TO RETURN AT 6 P.M.

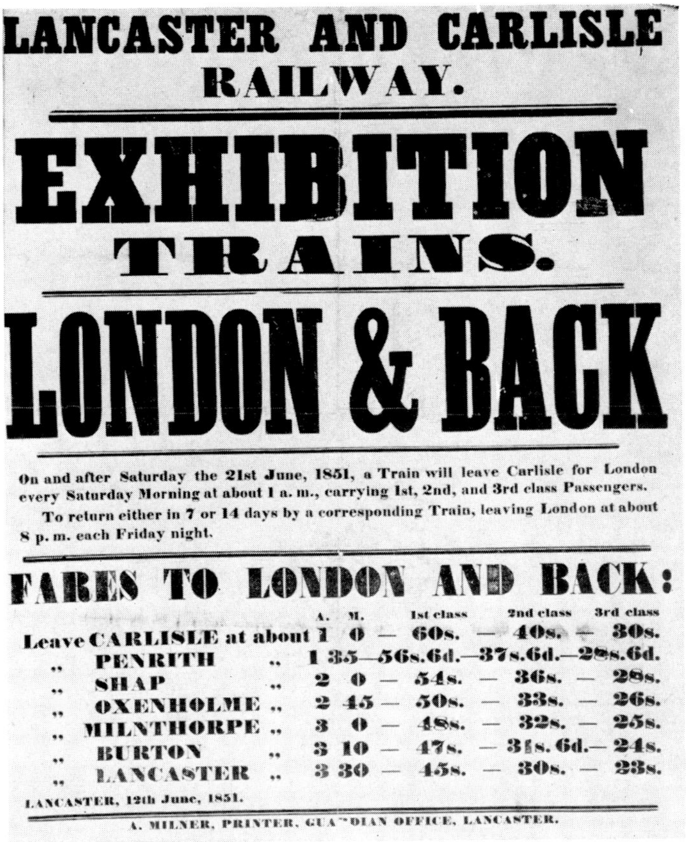

Plate XIa Lancaster & Carlisle Railway poster for excursion trains to the Great Exhibition of 1851 in Hyde Park

[*Clapham Museum of Transport*

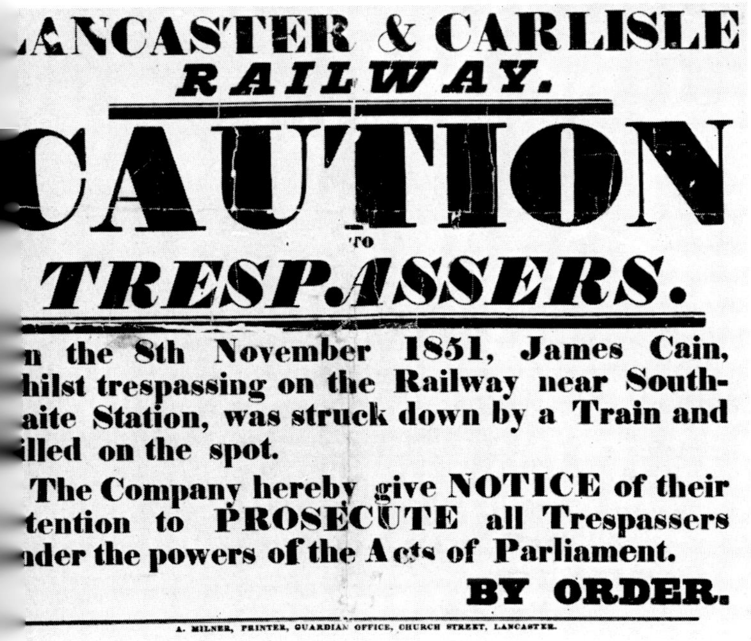

Plate XIb A curious trespass notice of the L&C Railway

[*Clapham Museum of Transport*

Plate XIIa The Carret Marshall tank engine built in 1851 for the Kendal & Windermere Railway, taken over in 1858 by the Lancaster & Carlisle, and passed into the London & North Western Railway's stock in 1859 [*BR, LMR*

Plate XIIb Lancaster & Carlisle 2-4-0 locomotive built by Fairbairn in 1859 after incorporation into the LNWR stock, fitted with a Crewe chimney and renumbered in the duplicate list

difficulties, for the original cost calculations were most optimistic and were only around half the final cost. At its northern end the line ran down the west side of the Wyre harbour, part of which was crossed by a big embankment between high and low water levels, which enclosed a considerable amount of land from the sea. In 1850 a westward diversion had to be made over the last 2½ miles into Fleetwood, as the sea had burst in, and this diverted line was opened on January 13, 1851. The original line and the diversion were to the first Fleetwood station; the later station, a little further on, was opened on July 15, 1883. Gradients on the P. & W. scarcely exceeded 1 in 300. At first the line had only a single track, but the land was wide enough for a double way. About a mile and a half of the line was laid on longitudinal sleepers.

Local trains to and from Fleetwood used the P. & W.'s own Preston terminus at Maudland; but some through trains or carriages to the south went over the connecting loop to the L. & P. and through Dock Street to the N.U. line and station. Maudland (P. & W.) was closed to regular passenger traffic (though not to goods) in February 1844, and thenceforth all regular passenger trains used the N.U. station in Butler Street on the south side of Fishergate. Before that there had been for some time an omnibus service between Maudland and Butler Street in connection with the three local trains a day each way, the charge for which was 6d.; and the N.U. booked passengers from its station through to Fleetwood at a charge of 3d. a time initially. Fares between Preston and Fleetwood were 4s. first class, 3s. second class and 2s. third class.

Passenger traffic was slow in growing. Over the year ending June 30, 1844, the line carried 21,782 first class, 27,202½ second class and 66,680½ third class passengers, and the receipts totalled £10,640. Fleetwood in those years had not grown to a fish, cargo and cattle port; and over the period just quoted the P. & W. revenue from goods and cattle was only £147.

The level crossing at Maudland was always a trouble and quickly led to an accident which reflected the way many small railways were worked at the time, a decade after the opening of the pioneer L. & M. On December 18, 1840, the extreme south end of the L. & P. was being ballasted from a train of wagons drawn by a horse, train and ballasting operations being in the sole hands of Henry Taylor, employee of a contractor. Despite being told by the policeman on duty at the crossing that a P. & W. train was due, he made a further trip, and at 16.50, in the dark, the P. & W. train duly ran into the wagons at the crossing and killed the ballast man. The inquiry revealed that the L. & P. policeman could not show a red light in any direction as he had sent his lamp to Lancaster for repairs; the P. & W. train had no lights at all. The policeman said he had instructed the ballast driver to cross over from the up line to the down, but the deceased had not obeyed and the policeman had no power to force him. The Government inspector then showed that a down train to Lancaster was due on the spot at 16.53, so it seems that the time of Henry Taylor had come in any case. Other matters made clear at the inquiry were that the P. & W. did not have any printed regulations at all; and that five months after the opening the Fleetwood traffic was so sparse that there were no passengers on this evening train.

Maudland (P. & W.), though closed to regular passenger trains from February 1844, continued to handle some excursions. On Sunday, September 18, 1845, at eight in the morning, an excursion for Fleetwood comprising nearly 30 goods trucks crammed with passengers started slowly out of Maudland, and while going over the crossing was cut in two by an up train from Lancaster, running late and travelling at something like 30 m.p.h. instead of the 7 or 8 m.p.h. it should have been doing at the approach to the Maudland area. Yet no one was killed, though many in the trucks were injured. The L. & P. engine was said to be a light four-wheel type (it would be one of the Bury-type 2–2–0), and the two trucks that took the main force of the collision "hung across it like a pair of panniers."

From 1850 the Maudland crossings became still more complicated because a third track owned by yet another company was put across the L. & P. line a few yards to the north. The Preston & Longridge Railway, incorporated on July 14, 1836, by Act 6 & 7 Wm. 4, cap. 122, was opened on May 1, 1840, and worked by horses until June 12, 1848, when locomotives were substituted; it ran only to Deepdale, a mile or so to the east of the north-south main line. Up to 1850 its only relation to the west coast route was in the amount of stone brought down from the Longridge quarries for constructional work on the railways, though the substantial amount used in the building of the N.U. had been brought by carts as the Longridge railway was not then open.

In 1849 this railway was leased at £3,000 a year to the Fleetwood, Preston & West Riding Junction Railway, sponsored by the P. & W., and incorporated by 9 & 10 Vict., cap. 246, of July 27, 1846. In its history this new company laid only one mile of line, and that a very awkward one, for it went west from Deepdale through a separate F.P. & W.R. station at Maudland, crossed the L. & P. main line on the level, and then connected with the P. & W.'s Fleetwood line. The one mile to Maudland and beyond was opened on January 14, 1850, to goods trains. At the end of 1851 the line was taken over again, and closed, by the P. & L. because the F.P. & W.R. could no longer pay the rent. Stranger still, the F.P. & W.R. re-incorporated in 1856 by 19 & 20 Vict., cap. 44, of June 23, purchased the P. & L. outright under an agreement dated March 14, 1856, and resumed the service, extending the passenger trains from Deepdale to Maudland as from November 1, 1856. The purchase price of £48,000 was to be paid in instalments, £6,000 on taking possession on August 31, 1856, and then seven biennial payments of £6,000.

There was never a passenger service off the F.P. & W.R. over the L. & P./L. & C. crossing, but at the crossings there were two keepers on duty for many years, one L. & P./L. & C. looking after the P. & W. crossing and the other a F.P. & W.R. man. Despite the paucity of east-west traffic the old Lancaster & Carlisle Railway would never agree to the withdrawal of the Longridge-line keeper unless the track of that railway was actually taken up. Perhaps the reason was the fear continuously engendered by the celebrated crossing—St. Nicholas at Carlisle —at the other end of the system. For a year or two there seems to have been yet a further level crossing on the main line between Maudland and Fishergate, for city maps of the 1850-52 period show a line from the L.C.C. tramway in the dock area crossing over to a coal depot at the junction of Dock and Pitt Streets.

The reconstituted F.P. & W.R. came into the joint hands of the L.N.W.R. and L.Y.R. by Act 30 Vict. cap. 95, of June 17, 1867, on the terms of an agreement made on May 12, 1866, by which those two companies entered into possession on July 1, 1866. No changes were made until 1885, when Maudland (F.P. & W.R.) station was closed and a south loop to the main line opened, after which Longridge-line passenger trains used Preston main station until June 2, 1930, when the passenger service was withdrawn. The L. & C. crossing was removed in 1885, but the F.P. & W.R. tracks remained as far as the east side, and one siding still extends close up to the west-coast main line opposite Pugin's beautiful spire. The P. & W. Maudland crossing also remained until 1885/86, when the Maudland goods station was abolished, and the whole Maudland-area railway system was simplified from that shown in Fig. 6 to that shown on the right-hand side of Fig. 18 (Chap. XVI).

As far as the railways in the Maudland area were concerned, the P. & W. was the first to get its Act. This gave it a legal priority that led eventually to a curious situation. When the L. & P. got its Act two years later, powers were given to the P. & W. to have full authority over the L. & P. traffic at the crossing for the purpose of securing a free and undisturbed use by the P. & W., but so that "as little interruption and interference as possible" should be made "to the free and commodious passage" of L. & P. trains. This was the clause that led some 20 and more years later to Blackmore, the L.Y.R. superintendent, always insisting to G. P. Neele, the L.N.W.R. superintendent of the line, that his goods trains and light-engine movements from Maudland (P. & W.) to the Blackpool line took precedence over the Anglo-Scottish expresses. Another humorous feature of this crossing and its regulations was that though the P. & W. had a lead of two years in gaining its Act, and so had legal priority, the L. & P. line was opened three weeks before that of the P. & W., and so had physical priority.

At first the P. & W. owned no locomotives or carriages. In time for the opening, an arrangement was made with the N.U. to supply power and stock at the rate of 2s. 4d./train-mile if one engine was used or 2s. 6d. with double heading. Coaches were supplied at 1d. a mile first class and ½d. a mile second class. Power for goods trains was not furnished in the beginning as the N.U. had insufficient engines; but P. & W. freight traffic was trifling in the first few years, and wagons were tacked on to passenger trains. Locomotive power was supplied under varying terms until the end of June 1842, when the P. & W. could no longer afford to pay the N.U. charges, even though that company offered a rate of 1s. 8d. a train-mile in the end. Distinct from the L. & P., the relations between the N.U. and P. & W. remained amicable; the N.U. well recognised that its small neighbour was poverty-stricken, and also that a good deal of first class traffic came on to the N.U. by reason of the boat services out of Fleetwood. The N.U. did what it could to help, and at Preston reduced its booking fee from 3d. to 1d. for Fleetwood passengers.

After this the P. & W. managed to acquire some locomotives of its own, and according to a return completed in 1845 had 6 engines, 23 carriages and 86 wagons having a total value of £17,550. By the time it was leased to the L.Y.R./L.N.W.R. combination two years later it must have acquired more locomotives, for five of its engines were taken into L.N.W.R. stock and seven or eight went to the L.Y.R. Only two goods engines were put into the L.N.W.R. capital list; the three other engines went straight into the duplicate stock "being of very inferior description." The L.N.W.R. numbers and names given to the two goods engines were 258 *Ribble* and 259 *Windermere.*

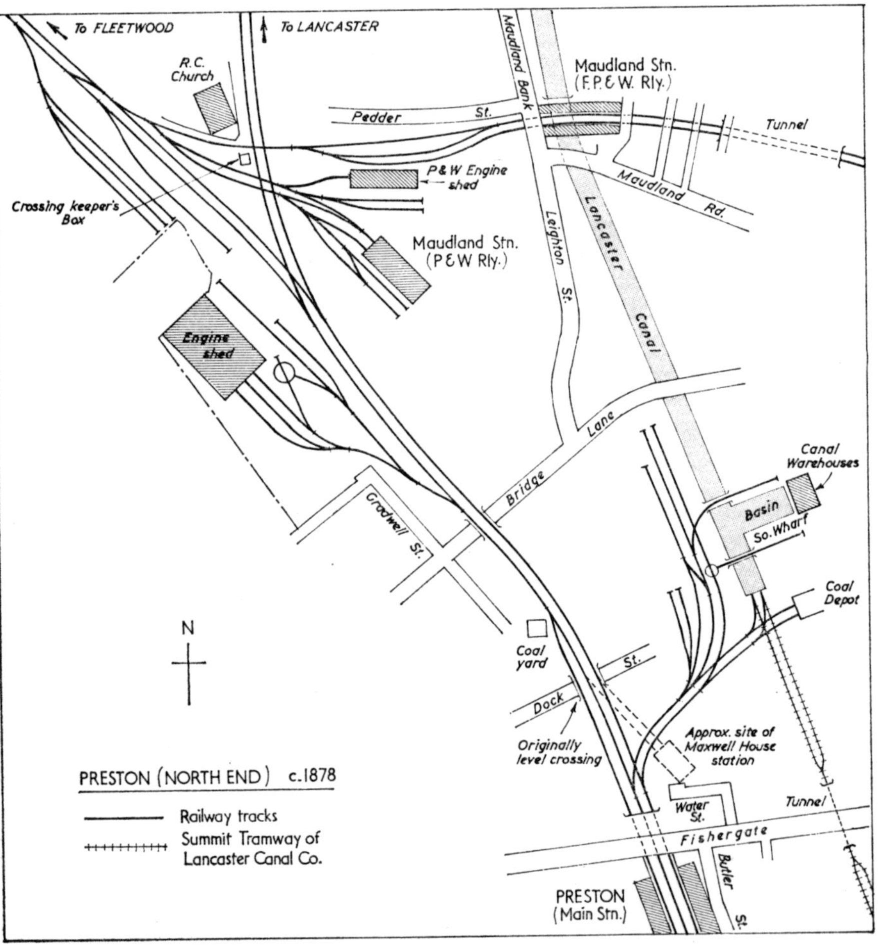

6 Layout at Preston North End about 1878

The P. & W. never came into the financial orbit of either the N.U. or the L. & P. After tentative approaches by the East Lancashire Railway, it was leased to the L.Y.R. by 9 & 10 Vict., cap. 306, of March 1, 1847, after power had actually been given in the M. & L. Act of March 3, 1846, for it to be amalgamated with the Manchester & Leeds Railway. The L.N.W.R. was to participate in this lease to the extent of one-third the profit or loss, but its interest in the contract, agreed with the L.Y.R in 1847, was not legalised until two years afterwards, by 12 & 13 Vict., cap. 74, of July 28, 1849. The actual date of the deed of agreement for the amalgamation was May 15, 1847, and the agreement was with the M. & L., being seven weeks before the M. & L. changed its name to the L.Y.R.

Financial arrangements were complicated. Originally the P. & W. was to be paid a gross rental of £38,000 the first year, beginning March 1, 1847; £41,000 for the second year; £44,000 the third year; £47,000 the fourth year; £50,000 the fifth year; and £54,000 a year for all subsequent years. For the better interests of P. & W. shareholders if they wished to sell, these annual rentals were converted into guaranteed rates of £7 1s. 6d. per cent p.a. for the first eight years from 1847, and from then on £7 17s. 2d. per cent in perpetuity. At the same time the loan debt was capitalised and the whole P. & W. capital then stood at £666,000 for 28¾ route miles, a contrast with the £130,000 plus £40,000 for 19½ route miles ten years earlier.

By an Act (28 Vict., cap. 22) of May 26, 1865, the L.Y.R. was authorised to raise another £16,000 capital and the L.N.W.R. £8,000 to finance the widening of, and other improvements to, the Blackpool branch of the P. & W. system; and by an Act (34 & 35 Vict., cap. 64) of June 29, 1871, the Blackpool & Lytham Railway (incorporated May 17, 1861, by 24 Vict., cap. 9), was amalgamated with the P. & W. company, and a half-mile junction railway between the two was authorised in July 1873. In 1888, under Act 51 & 52 Vict., cap. 176, which covered also the dissolution of the N.U., the Preston & Wyre company was dissolved as a legal entity as from July 1 of that year. Every holder of P. & W. stock received L.N.W.R. 4 per cent debentures equivalent to one-third of his holding plus L.Y.R. 4 per cent debentures equal to two-thirds of his holding. This meant that the holder of a P. & W. £25 share who had been receiving guaranteed interest at £7 17s. 2d. per cent received £33 of L.Y.R. stock plus £16 of L.N.W.R. stock. From 1847 onwards P. & W. shareholders got a far higher return than they could have anticipated if the line had remained independent.

As one investment book of 1853 put it: "This railway is one of the curiosities of railway history. As an independent line its career was anything but fortunate; then by one of those kaleidoscopic changes sometimes observable in railway affairs, this concern, which had been insolvent from the beginning, and had never declared a dividend, became suddenly a 7 per cent guaranteed line . . . the lessees took possession in March 1847 . . . last year (1852) the loss to the L.N.W.R. was £8,250." So the loss to the L.Y.R. that year must have been approximately £16,000, and losses approaching this order were sustained for nearly ten years.

These various details of the P. & W. are given here because, strange as it may seem today, the Preston–Fleetwood line for some years formed part of a West Coast route to Glasgow. The P. & W. had powers for improving Fleetwood harbour. The Preston & Wyre Dock Co. was formed in 1837, but in 1839 was absorbed by the P. & W. Sir Peter Hesketh Fleetwood, the local Lord of the Manor, from whom the town took its name, was the originator and moving spirit in the railway and all the harbour improvements, and in the formation of the town. A census taken in the summer of 1841 showed Fleetwood to have 1,500 inhabitants; and the enumerators remarked "five years ago there was not a soul abiding in the district, it being a rabbit warren."

Even in 1839, before the line was actually opened, P. & W. statements were that the railway could and should form part of the route to Scotland, though at that time the route envisaged was by boat over Morecambe Bay to somewhere in Furness, then by rail to Whitehaven, Maryport and Carlisle, proposals probably supported strongly by John Abel Smith. The idea of sailings to Scotland may have been due to George Stephenson. The first engineer of the P. & W. had been Landmann, of London & Greenwich Railway fame, who laid out the line; but well before the opening he had been succeeded by George and Robert Stephenson. In a report dated June 5, 1839, to the directors of the P. & W., George said: "a railway being in a rapid progress from Glasgow to Ayr which will have the effect of materially shortening the voyage from Glasgow to Lancashire, your harbour will evidently offer much superior advantage to steam vessels from Ayr than the port of Liverpool." Early in 1840 Sir Peter Hesketh Fleetwood moved in the House of Commons that the terms of the Commissioners appointed to report on the various Anglo-Scottish schemes should be widened to include the P. & W. and Fleetwood harbour; but owing to the thinness of the House he withdrew his motion.

From Fleetwood harbour a packet boat, the *Express*, plied daily from 1840 to Bardsea, a trip of one to one and a half hours, to give a connection from south Lancashire to the Furness and Lake Districts. From May 1841 a boat connecting with the principal trains from the south sailed three evenings a week to Ardrossan, from which Scottish port there had been a rail connection to Glasgow from August 12, 1840; and on the first southbound trip there were 40 cabin passengers. This service replaced a thrice-weekly (twice weekly in winter) sailing between Liverpool and Ardrossan instituted in August 1840, and which, in its turn, had given a quicker journey than, though not superseding, the Liverpool–Greenock boats.

It was of this extraordinary Fleetwood–Ardrossan route that *The Railway Times* made its statement about the convenience, so often half-quoted without any particulars of issue that the relevant parts may well be repeated here. In the issue of May 22, 1841, an editorial said of the Fleetwood route: ". . . which in respect of celerity and, we believe, of cheapness also, really leaves but little to be desired. A person may now leave London at daybreak, and proceeding by railway to the new port of Fleetwood, embark there in a noble steamer, in time for breakfast next morning at Edinburgh or Glasgow! How much *more* can any reasonable man want?" It is only fair to the long-deceased editor of that journal to record that these words seemed merely a sop to Sir Peter Hesketh Fleetwood, and that within a month the paper was supporting the Lancaster and Carlisle direct route, to the proposals for which it had already given attention. As part of the amenities of Fleetwood there was erected at the time "M. Vantini's magnificent new hotel", the North Euston; but the station to which passengers were brought was primitive in the extreme.

A passenger leaving Euston with the early morning train had an all-night crossing to Ardrossan, and arrived in Glasgow 25 to 26 hours after leaving London, and did so at a fare of £4 2s. first class rail and "leading cabin on boat." This was 5s. cheaper than the all-rail fares for a 13-hour journey a dozen years later. The rail-sea-rail service was not without competition, because from the opening of the railway to Lancaster in 1840 there was a connecting coach service between that town and Glasgow via Penrith and Carlisle. This was more or less as quick as the boat service, the throughout journey from London to Glasgow in 1845/46 taking 26 hours by the morning departure from Euston and 28 hours by the 20.45 night mail. Such journeys were not without incident. Even before the beginning of the Lancaster & Carlisle Railway the Fleetwood route was perturbing the coach proprietors, and from Lancaster northward the mail and stage coaches began to race to see which could get to the termini first. There was a fatal accident from this cause four miles north of Kendal in 1841, and it was the second on the Shap road.

These rail-road and rail-sea arrangements lasted until long after the opening throughout of the L. & C. The coach departure point was altered to Kendal in September 1846, when the railway was opened as far as that town; and then to Carlisle from the end of December the same year. On September 10, 1847, the Caledonian Railway was opened from Carlisle to Beattock, and the coaches moved on; but not until February 15, 1848, was the Caley line from Beattock northward opened, so permitting through rail journeys between London and Glasgow, and London and Edinburgh, by the West Coast Route.

The Fleetwood–Ardrossan service was begun by the *Fire King*, but then for some nine years was operated by the steamers *Her Majesty* and *Royal Consort*, each of 700 tons and 350 h.p. Sailings from Fleetwood generally were on Monday, Wednesday and Friday evenings after the arrival of the trains from the south. Departure times from the south to catch the boat in 1846 were: London 8.30 and 10.00; Birmingham 13.45; Liverpool 15.35; Manchester 17.15; Bolton 17.35; and Preston 18.20. A special boat train awaited the arrival of the steam packet at Ardrossan to take passengers to Glasgow.

Sailings in the reverse direction were also on Monday, Wednesday and Friday. A boat train left Glasgow at 15.30, and the ship sailed from Ardrossan at 17.00; it was due in at Fleetwood in time to connect with the early trains to the south. Scheduled arrivals were 9.30 at both Manchester and Liverpool; 18.00 and 20.45 at London; "and other places with equal expedition." Fares from Fleetwood to Glasgow, including steward's fees, were: cabin and first class railway 20s.; cabin and second class railway 18s. 6d.; deck and third class railway 5s. In 1847 these services came under the L.Y.R.; they were continued, and presumably continued to draw a certain amount of traffic away from the all-rail route to Glasgow, for as late as the summer of 1849 the L. & C. was reminding Capt. Laws of the L.Y.R. that he had not yet honoured his promise of taking the Fleetwood boats off the Scottish service.

Two minor but interesting events are connected with the South–Fleetwood–Scottish rail-sea route. In 1846 Mr. Thos. Cook conducted his first excursion to Scotland, and took his passengers by rail to Fleetwood and thence by boat to Ardrossan. In 1847 Queen Victoria, along with Prince Albert and their two eldest children, after a cruise round the west of Scotland and into the Irish Sea, put into Fleetwood and journeyed on to London by train.

VII

Lancaster & Preston Junction Railway

DESPITE EARLY pecuniary difficulties in the shape of insufficient capital, the P. & W. and its directors seem to have been a gentle and peaceable combination. No so, however, with the other railway building concurrently north of Preston. Its relations with its transport neighbours were complex, elusive and cantankerous; though the evidence shows that at least one of those neighbours, the Lancaster Canal Co., was equally unaccommodating. and another of them, the N.U., scarcely more efficient, and perhaps just as slim, though with a much harder-headed directorate.

Advantages of a railway between Lancaster and Preston had been outlined first in the *Lancaster Gazette* as early as September 1832; but it was largely the 'prospect' made by Joseph Locke for a line from Preston to Glasgow at the end of 1835 that led to a public meeting being convened in the Town Hall at Lancaster on April 12, 1836, when the formation of a railway from Lancaster to Preston was agreed, and a provisional committee appointed to direct the necessary surveys and plans. The resolution was carried through with energy. Locke was engaged to make the survey, the project was quickly put before Parliament, and an Act (7 Wm. 4, cap. 22) was obtained on May 5, 1837, for the incorporation of the Lancaster & Preston Junction Railway (the L. & P.), with an authorised capital of £250,000 plus borrowing powers of £83,000. A second Act (3 & 4 Vict., cap. 4), obtained in March 1840, authorised another £125,000 by loan.

Probably the L. & P. was the most peculiar railway with which Locke was ever associated professionally—and the peculiarity began with himself. At the time, he was engaged by the G.J.R. as it chief engineer on the understanding that he would give all his time to that company unless he had the specific permission of the directors to do otherwise. In fact, his salary was raised from £1,200 to £2,000 a year in March 1836 on that express condition. Two months later he wrote to the G.J.R. board that he had been offered the appointment of engineer to a line from Preston to Lancaster, and asked what were the board's views. The directors replied that they had no reason to object to Locke becoming consulting engineer to that railway—a simple but tremendous difference of which Locke took no cognisance, and acted as engineer, laying out the line and supervising the contracts, but having A. S. Gee as his assistant spending much time on the line.

Locke estimated the cost of construction at £250,000; and a report of the committee, signed by George Burrow (Mayor of Lancaster in 1836) as chairman, in 1837, says: "From the accuracy of his (Locke's) calculations, as proved in the completion of the Grand Junction Railway, the Provisional Committee place full reliance upon his estimates, and consequently expect that the L. & P. will be completed at less expense per mile, and that being nearly level it will be worked at a less cost, than almost any other line hitherto made in this country."

Locke's estimates for the L. & P., however, were well exceeded. This was partly because new Standing Orders required the height and width of bridging to be increased; and because the company had to pay £90,000 for land instead of the £25,000 estimated. These of themselves were not enough to raise the cost from the quarter-million estimated to the final almost £400,000; and Edmund Sharpe, one of the contractors, inferred that Locke might have been tempted to design the structures of lighter material and workmanship than was consistent with safety and durability, and he instanced the failure of the Galgate skew bridge against which he said he had protested before he built it. There must have been other factors; indeed, there was always something unaccountable about this survey and construction and Locke's later activities where they touched upon the L. & P., particularly at its northern end, as is mentioned in a subsequent chapter.

The line was laid with 65 lb. rails on cross sleepers on embankments and with stone blocks in cuttings. It had no great works upon it, and the steepest gradient was 1 in 500; the work proceeded steadily and the 20¼ mile line was opened formally throughout on June 25, 1840, public traffic beginning the next day. The Lancaster terminus was 'up Town', about a mile south-east of the present Castle station, and was a handsome station; at Preston the line ended at Dock Street without any accommodation at all. So far, so good, or reasonably so; except for the estimated returns of 10 per cent, later increased to 18 per cent, on the original capital, and, three or four months before the opening, the first rumblings of trouble with the N.U., trouble which persisted for a long time, and the thick end of which was passed on to travellers at Preston.

From the public opening there were five through trains a day in each direction, of which two, the 8.45 and 17.30 from Lancaster, had through coaches for Euston, with corresponding London arrival times around 21.00 and 8.15. Two other trains a day, the 7.15 and 13.00, had connections to Liverpool and Manchester. The original service was: Lancaster dep. 2.00 (mail), 7.15 (mixed), 8.45 (first class), 13.00 (second class), and 17.30 (mail). Preston departures for Lancaster were at: 6.45 (mail), 10.35 (mixed), 12.30 (first class), 16.40 (second class), and 19.15 (mail); but Preston departures were soon altered to 7.05, 10.45, 12.40, 16.40 and 19.15, and the mid-day second-class out of Lancaster to 13.30. On Sundays there were only the two mails in each direction, but by 1841 these had been supplemented by a mixed train at 8.00 from Lancaster and a return from Preston at 17.30.

Time between Lancaster and London by the day train was just over 12 hr., so that in the beginning there was no acceleration on the southern part of the journey, for the time between Preston and London had been about 11 hr.; four years earlier, when a coach all the way was the only method, the London–Lancaster time had been 26 hr. Fares between Lancaster and Preston were 5s. first and 3s. second; third class varied from 1s. 6d. to 2s. over the first year or two. Only one train a day in each direction had third class carriages; this was the 'mixed' train, and by it the first class fare was reduced to 4s. and the second class to 2s. 6d. First class fare between Lancaster and London in 1840 was £2 19s. 6d. by day train and £3 2s. by the night mail.

Complete almost to the last detail, the long vicissitudes of the L. & P. have been happily written by M. D. Greville and G. O. Holt in a small book published in 1960. Only those events and activities relating to the west coast trunk line and the L. & P. neighbours at each end need chronicling here; in all conscience they are complicated enough.

First of the difficulties was to do with Preston station and the connection with the North Union. As early as October 1836, exactly two years before its own line to Preston was opened, the N.U. offered to buy land for a railway to Dock Street and extend its line to that point, and vest the whole of the railway and land north of Fishergate in the Lancaster company as soon as that railway should have formed its line, on the condition that the L. & P. paid the purchase money and cost of making the railway within a month after the money had been laid out; the two companies were to be permitted to use each others' lines within the borough of Preston on payment of a one-mile toll. The provisional committee of the L. & P. declined all this without giving any particular reason; that is understandable, for the committee at that time was still six months off getting the Act. Not to be deterred, the N.U. countered with further proposals no more onerous. After discussing these and the possibility of a joint station near Dock Street, the L. & P. committee was still not willing to come to any specific arrangement, whereupon the N.U. decided to extend its line from alongside the Butler Street terminus to Dock Street as long as the works were not begun before it appeared definite that the L. & P. would get its Act. In March 1837, when the Act seemed certain, the L. & P. convenanted to pay the N.U. £1,500 when that company completed the extension northward to Dock Street, near the end of the Lancaster canal, and tunnelling under Fishergate to get there.

At first sight the various offers of the N.U. seem generous and the attitude forthcoming, for at the time these proposals were being made the N.U. had purchased the land and garden of Dr. St. Clare and other property in Butler Street for its terminus and depots. On the other hand, the N.U. Act itself stated that the line was to go as far north as Dock Street, that is, on the north side of Fishergate, so the N.U. had been committed to make the extension, though at one time it proposed to abandon construction. Yet that company succeeded in making the L. & P. pay £1,500 towards the cost without any compensating privileges.

By the time the L. & P. was opened, Butler Street station had been in operation for nearly two years, and the double-track connection to Dock Street had been completed for six months. This extension at first by-passed the platforms at Butler Street in a manner similar to the archaic layout perpetuated for so many years by the L.S.W.R., Southern Railway and Southern Region of British Railways at Dorchester, though at Preston there was no equivalent to the Dorchester down platform except the separately-owned Dock Street 'site' a full quarter of a mile away.

After the L. & P. opening the N.U. asserted that the single payment of £1,500 did not include free use of the short connecting strip and the N.U. station; the L. & P. said it did, but there is difficulty in reconciling this view with an offer the L. & P. had made in October 1839 to pay £300 a year for the use of the N.U. station in Preston. Possibly the trouble arose because the L. & P. began to realise the N.U. might have pulled a fast one over them. Certainly the N.U. pushed on the Dock Street extension quicker than necessary, and was claiming payment of the £1,500 in December 1839. For seven months this completed extension lay useless for anything except N.U. carriage storage.

The N.U. in the meantime had agreed to supply motive power to the L. & P. This had not been arranged without some hesitation and prevarication on the part of the L. & P.; and only when the opening of the line was six weeks away did the L. & P. finally agree to the arrangement suggested by the N.U. The main term was the pooling of the locomotive stocks of the two companies and the establishment of a uniform system of locomotive management under the supervision of the N.U.; but the L. & P. had to supply sufficient locomotives to the pool to cope with train mileage equivalent to that scheduled for the L. & P. train service. Also, if the N.U. furnished locomotive power to any third railway from out of the pool, that was to be considered as N.U. business. This last term was included because, during the procrastination of the L. & P., the N.U. had agreed to supply some of the locomotive power needed by the P. & W. from the opening of that line to Fleetwood.

Terms for locomotive power ultimately agreed were the same as those charged to the P. & W. by the N.U., that is 2s. 4d./train-mile with one engine and 2s. 6d. for double-heading. Almost immediately the N.U. began to complain that the state of the L. & P. track was injurious to the locomotives, and within a month of taking up the working was writing that it could no longer undertake to provide locomotives in the present state of the track unless the time from Lancaster to Preston was increased to 80 min. Nor did the N.U. approve of the L. & P. practice of stopping passenger trains between stations in order to do a little ballasting from a truck at the tail end. As its share of power, the L. & P. bought six Bury-type four-wheel locomotives similar to those in use on the N.U., but all were not delivered in time for the opening.

Henry Booth of the L. & M. was called in to arbitrate on the station and locomotive differences between the two companies, and some kind of agreement seems to have been patched up for a year. In June 1841 the N.U. gave notice to terminate the locomotive working arrangement at the end of that year, the excuse being that it was not worthwhile. Rathbone had stated it was no more profitable than obtaining an odd shilling or two; and James Chapman told a Commons committee in October 1841 that the arrangement was very good for the L. & P. but very indifferent for the N.U. Probably the daily troubles weighed more with the N.U. than the actual financial result.

The L. & P. considered the notice received from the N.U. as applying to both the station arrangements and the locomotive working, though the N.U. note was clear enough, and in first acknowledging receipt the L. & P. did not raise any other questions. The L. & P. thereupon initiated collaboration with the B. & P., whose line was then open as far as Chorley. This railway more than a year earlier had proposed to the L. & P. that they should share a joint station at Preston. In 1841 the B. & P. not only agreed to build its proposed station on land rented by it from the L.C.C., although it was nowhere near getting there itself, but helped to arrange for locomotive working over the L. & P. This latter business was not hard to fix, because John Hargreaves Jr. was already supplying under contract the locomotive power for the one engine in steam between Bolton and Rawlinson Bridge for the B. & P., and also for the Manchester, Bolton & Bury Railway at the other end of the B. & P. He seems to have taken over the six L. & P. locomotives and arranged the operation, and agreed to hand the engines back at a valuation whenever the arrangement terminated. This did not ease the friction with the N.U., over which Hargreaves was still working all the freight traffic under toll, because the B. & P. already was anathema to the N.U. To complete the catalogue of the relations, Hargreaves was also working the L. & P. freight traffic under toll, and continued to do so until the end of 1845.

The L. & P.'s southern terminus was a 'site' (it could hardly be called more) at Dock Street, reached by a flight of steps and a path from Fishergate. Some L. & P. trains terminated there; others did go on to the N.U. station, though with a change of engine. Passengers going through had to pay an N.U. toll of 6d. after the agreement between the two companies ceased at the end of 1841; and it has been said that many of those with light luggage, or with none at all, preferred to get out, climb the stairs, cross Fishergate, go down the Butler Street ramp to the N.U. station, and rebook, well knowing that they would be in ample time to rejoin the train they had left. All this did not enhance the reputation of either railway with the public or the town council.

Early in 1842 the promised B. & P. station at Preston materialised, and the L. & P. built a very short connecting line (see Fig. 6); but it remained a dead-end station, and the Lancaster company's trains could not run through it and, as B. & P. trains, reappear on the N.U. tracks south of Butler Street under running powers. Nevertheless, the possibility of this, added to the rate war in 1843, led the N.U. to desire the amalgamation with the B. & P. as already recorded, though strictly on its own terms.

By the middle of 1842 the constant friction and the disappointing receipts from the passenger traffic led the L. & P. into the hands of the Lancaster Canal Co., after overtures for purchase had been made to the B. & P. and then to the N.U. The leasing terms seemed good at first, but in later years the association with the L.C.C. led to immense trouble and mortification for the L. & P., and then not with its old antagonist the N.U., but with its new end-on neighbour, the Lancaster & Carlisle Railway, with whom it should also have been on good terms.

On July 14, 1842, an agreement was made to lease the L. & P. as from

September 1 of that year for a period of 21 years to the L.C.C. at a rental of £13,000 p.a. Only after this was application made to Parliament to authorise the lease, and the Act (6 & 7 Vict., cap. 4) was given Royal Assent on April 3, 1843. It did not state clearly the terms on which the lease was to be effected, and this omission led to further trouble later. Under these arrangements the L. & P. local traffic continued to use the so-called Maxwell House station at Preston built by the B. & P.; but when that railway was merged in the N.U. at the beginning of 1844 the use of the station was withdrawn, and the Canal company had to reach an agreement with the N.U. for the use of Butler Street station at a rental as from February 13, 1844.

Up to the time of the lease the L.C.C. was a strong competitor of the L. & P. Probably that was not a hard job, for the canal boats were comfortable and warmed in winter, whereas the L. & P. trains continued to be the acme of discomfort and the working primitive. The boats were 70 ft. long and 6 ft. wide; they were of light construction to carry up to 70 passengers and could "be drawn by two horses at a canter." There were no locks between Lancaster and Preston. Up to the beginning of the lease the boats had reasonable connections at Preston with southbound trains; and an omnibus service, free for through passengers, ran between the canal basin and the N.U. station. Boat fares between Lancaster and Preston were 1s. 6d. cabin and 1s. second cabin, considerably cheaper than the railway fares. Between Lancaster and Kendal, where there was no competition, the fares were 3s. cabin and 2s. second cabin. The Lancaster–Kendal boats ceased in September 1846 when the railway was opened. The canal timetable over the years 1842–45 when the L.C.C. was running both trains and boats is given in Table VI. Passenger traffic on the L. & P. grew slowly during the L.C.C. lease. For the year ending June 30, 1844, a total of 124,093 passengers was carried, of which 32½ per cent was first, 24¾ per cent second, and 42¾ per cent third; they brought in a revenue of £19,041, and for the same period goods receipts were £3,089.

As soon as the whole of the Lancaster & Carlisle Railway was in operation from the end of 1846, there was in theory a 308-mile grand trunk route from London to Carlisle, owned in different parts by four companies and with the traffic operated by four companies not identical with the owning quartette. Nine separate companies had been concerned in the formation and eight in the construction. The odds were thus against smooth and uniform working; but there was one part definitely weaker than the others, and that was the 20-mile section from Preston to Lancaster owned by the L. & P. In the words of the L. & C. board in 1848, the L. & P. line was "still a disconnected link in the otherwise uninterrupted chain of railway communication, in united and friendly hands, from London to Perth." While admitting the general truth of this, one has also to admit that the day-by-day operation of that section of 'the chain' just south of the L. & P., the N.U. was only fractionally more efficient than on the L. & P.

Weakened and debilitated by its incessant differences with the N.U. and the Lancaster Canal Co., and by the legal ineffectiveness of the directors, with money so short as to preclude stock and track being in good order, and with the signalling primitive even by the standards of 1845–46, the L. & P. line could be described only as ramshackle. The direction of the company was in such a peculiar legal tangle that for a time there seems to have been only one director, and he had no power to work without others and no power to appoint others. This tragio-comic situation has been fully explained by Greville & Holt in their little book on the L. & P.; only the direct relations with the L. & C. and the grand trunk route need attention here.

First mention of the L. & P. in the L. & C. records is four months before the L. & C. Act of Incorporation was obtained, when, at the end of January 1844, John Wakefield, George H. Head and Cornelius Nicholson were appointed to form a special committee with two representatives of the L. & P. to make arrangements with the Lancaster Canal Co., at that time the lessee of the L. & P. Thus early was the L. & C. desirous of working in complete harmony with the L. & P., or gaining control of it to make sure a first class main-line railway was available all the way from Preston to the Border as soon as the railway was completed to Carlisle.

The special committee must have done good work, for in March the L. & C. provisional board recorded: "That the arrangement with the Lancaster Canal Co. to take a perpetual lease of the canal for £11,000 a year, the Canal Co. collecting the Toll and keeping the docks in repair the same as at present; and the option of the L. & C. within two years to take an assignment of the lease of the L. & P. upon paying £2,500 a year additional rent in perpetuity be adopted and confirmed." These early intentions came to nothing, probably because of the indefinite terms of the L. & P. lease to the Canal Co.; but the L. & C. board again determined at the end of the same year to try and become possessed of the reversion of the L. & P. from the L.C.C. if it could be obtained on fair terms, and further proposals were exchanged between the three parties.

Matters dragged on until 1846, when agreement seemed to get far enough for a Bill to be promoted; but it was withdrawn when it was seen that the agreement could not become effective, and that it was not even clear with whom agreement had to be reached. The opening of the L. & C. was now in sight; and the board decided that whatever might be the arguments with the Canal Co., or the exact legal position, it was going to ensure as far as it could proper working through between Preston and Carlisle. The beginning was modest enough; it was a simple minute in April that as between July 1 and the opening of the railway to Carlisle the L. & C. would work the L. & P. with what stock that small line had in hand, that being the L. & C. view of a previous agreement which had not been ratified. This could not be done, as the L.C.C. refused to surrender stock or line. But as from September 22, when the public service began between Lancaster and Kendal, the L. & C. simply ran its through trains on from Lancaster over the L. & P. tracks to the N.U. station at Preston. The last-named system was then for all practical purposes the L.N.W.R., which had close ties with the L. & C., and certainly the L. & C. would not have adopted such a measure unless it had the concurrence of the L.N.W.R.

Naturally this extraordinary practice of the L. & C. was fraught with danger—legal and physical. As far as the former was concerned, the L. & C. furnished a record of all trains so run, and put by regularly sums of money to cover any toll charges that might be claimed, for there were no legal running powers. This went on until 1849, and in those days the railway department of the Board of Trade had no authority to stop such practices; it could only admonish and recommend.

As for physical danger, there was plenty of it—every day; but no actual crash for two years. This illegal operation did not go unnoticed, and though the Government itself did nothing the Railway Commissioners were remonstrating with both companies within a month or two. An idea of the looseness of working on the L. & P. section is given by the reaction of the L. & C. directors to the remonstrance; they told their engineer, Worthington, to instruct expressly all concerned to be more careful over the L. & P., and under all circumstances to keep a distance of at least 800 yd. between all moving trains, even though 600 yd. was the distance prescribed by L. & P. regulations. This easy instruction to modify a most primitive 'space' system, which itself must have been grafted on to an equally primitive 'time' system, could not have been so easy to obey implicitly; and there was further complication in that the L.N.W.R. was providing the L. & C. with engine-men, locomotives and carriages, so that it, too, was legally involved.

L. & C. trains ran non-stop between Lancaster (Castle) and Preston (N.U.); the L. & P. trains continued to run from Lancaster (Penny Street), to stop at all stations, to terminate at Dock Street, and—to carry the Lancaster mails. Just what traffic regulation there was outside Lancaster, where the junction between the two companies was out on open line, is now unknown; perhaps it was like that at Kinnaber in the 1895 Race to Aberdeen, but with the security of lock-and-block replaced by the insecurity of a red flag which wound itself round the post in any wind.

Eventually, at the beginning of August 1848 the L. & C. shareholders authorised the board to adopt any measures expedient, and, if needful, to make an independent line of railway between Lancaster and Preston. This was simply a threat; in this case Parliament would *not* have sanctioned a second route; it would have made the L. & P. and L.C.C. put the house in order, as the Railway Commissioners, with no executive power, had asked them to do more than once. However, the whole question was brought conveniently one stage further by the inevitable crash; that this should have been delayed until August 21, 1848, can be regarded only as a miracle. As usual on occasions important for the L. & C., *Dalemain* was the engine, though be it remembered it was an L.N.W.R. engine working for the L. & C. on a line over which neither company had a right to pass. This crash at Bay Horse, and the report on it by Capt. Laffan, are detailed fully by Greville & Holt; suffice it here that Laffan stated categorically the rightful possessor of the line

London and North Western Railway.

OFFICERS' MEETING.

At a MEETING of the HEADS OF DEPARTMENTS and others, held at Birmingham, on Saturday, the 19th December, 1857;

PRESENT:

Captain HUISH, in the Chair.

Mr. BRUYERES.	Mr. MILLS.	Mr. M'CONNELL.
,, NORRIS.	,, STEVENSON.	,, RAMSBOTTOM.
,, BINGER.	,, BROUGHTON.	,, CARTWRIGHT.
,, PARSONS.	,, BRADSHAW.	,, LEYLAND.
,, ROBINSON.	,, CARTER.	,, WINBY.
,, ORMANDY.	,, HUNTLEY.	,, GREW.
	Mr. SWINYARD, *Sec.*	

The Minutes of the last Meeting were read.

692. The arrangements made at a Meeting of Representatives of the Caledonian, Lancaster and Carlisle, and London and North Western Companies for the extension to Preston and Scotland of the 9.0 a.m. Down Train from London to Manchester, and the running of an Up Auxiliary Mail from Scotland and Preston to London, instead of from Crewe only, were submitted, and the following hours of working were recommended: —

9.0 a.m. from London to run to Preston.

Up Auxiliary Mail fr. Crewe to run from Preston.

Down Train.

Euston - - - - -	dep.	9. 0 a.m.
Crewe - - - - - -	arr.	12.55 noon.
Departure for Preston - - -		12.58 p.m.
Departure for Manchr. - - -		1. 0 ,,
Newton Bridge - - -	arr.	1.45 ,,
Departure from L'pool - - -		1.10 ,,
Arrival at Newton Bridge - -		1 40 ,,
Preston - - - - -	arr.	2.25 ,,
Carlisle - - - - -	,,	5. 0 ,,
Do. - - - - -	dep.	5.15 ,,
Edinburgh - - - -	arr.	7.50 ,,
Glasgow - - - - -	,,	8. 5 ,,

Up Train.

Aberdeen - - - - -	dep.	6. 0 a.m.
Glasgow - - - - -	,,	1.15 p.m.
Edinburgh - - - - -	,,	1.30 ,,
Carlisle - - - - -	arr.	5.45 ,,
Do. - - - - -	dep.	6. 0 ,,
Preston - - - - - -	leave	9.45 ,,
Arrive at Newton Bridge - -		10.30 ,,
Arrive at Liverpool - - - -		11.10 ,,
Warrington - - - -	arr.	10.45 ,,
Crewe - - - - - - -	,,	11.30 ,,
Do. - - - - - - -	dep.	12.20 a.m.
Euston - - - - - - -	arr.	5.30 ,,

Plate XIII Minutes of LNWR officers' meeting in 1857 dealing with train services

Plate XIV Group of old Lancaster & Carlisle and LNWR Northern Division drivers at Crewe in 1879 or 1880, with Richard Moon (left hand top), F. W. Webb (right hand top), George Whale (left hand bottom), and A. L. Mumford (right hand bottom). The drivers and the year they began railway service were: (top row, left to right) Thomas M. Hale (1841), William Morris (1841), Thomas Stockton (1838), Ralph Mort (1839), William Manners (1840), John Meers (1837); (bottom row, left to right) John Murphy (1828), Thomas Stronach (1838), Thomas Valentine (1838), James Middleton (1830) [*British Rail*

Plate XVa Ramsbottom's DX goods engine as built at Crewe for the LNWR from 1858 to 1872 in the original form

Plate XVb Webb four-cylinder compound 4-4-0 No. 1907 *Black Watch*, banked in the rear, passing Scout Green on the 1 in 75 with a Preston-Glasgow train

Plate XVIa The last of the Webb Jumbos as LMSR No. 25001, *Snowdon*, at Keswick on a train of ex-Midland stock about 1930 *[B. H. Ellston*

Plate XVIb Webb's rebuild of a 6ft 2-4-0 class with special friction drive-and-braking mechanism; the original wheel centres with crank bosses were retained and the size of the balance weights reduced. The original name *Banshee* was removed when the friction drive was fitted

was uncertain, that the signals were quite insufficient for "a great chain of railway communication with the north." and that the framework of the last L. & P. carriage was "so rotten that I could scrape a hole in it with my fingers". The *Manchester Guardian* of the time reported: "The carriages are completely broken in pieces, excepting the wheels and axles." In the actual crash, and the behaviour of the drivers, this accident bore remarkable resemblance to that on the N.U. at Farington in 1841, described already in Chap. IV,

The Railway Commissioners intervened again, and a solution *had* to be found; but as the L. & P. was involved the situation was naturally dragged out to its uttermost, and Locke was instructed to make a survey for an alternative route west of the L. & P. This went nowhere near anywhere, unless Garstang, Cockerham and Glasson could be called anywhere. At last, on November 13, 1848, agreements were made between the three companies concerned for the L. & C. to take over the management of the L.C.C. including the L. & P., and these were confirmed at shareholders' meetings of the three companies all held on July 2, 1849. Parliamentary sanction was given by Act 12 & 13 Vict., cap. 87, dated August 1, 1849, the purpose of which was to amend the several Acts relating to the L. & P. and transfer the management to the L. & C. Motive power and rolling stock remained L. & P. property, and were subsequently sold by auction; the remainder of the possessions, with odd exceptions, were taken over by the L. & C.

From August 1, 1849 the Canal Co. relinquished its lease of the L. & P., paying its proportion of the stipulated rent up to that date; but as it was giving up some 14 years of its lease, it was to receive from the L. & P. the sum of £4,875 p.a. for those 14 years. Option of purchasing this annuity was reserved to the L. & P., and the proprietors were not long in exercising it, and came to that decision at a company meeting on April 12, 1850. One-twelfth shares were created up to the number of 10,833 to finance this purchase, and they brought in £45,137. The L.C.C. was then paid £48,115 3s. 6d. principal and expenses, less proceeds of certain sales in 1849 totalling £2,976 13s. 5d. But altogether the Canal Co. is said by one account to have made a profit of £67,391 out of its lease of the L. & P. The L.N.W.R. leased the L.C.C. waterways under an indenture dated December 22, 1859 (when the L. & C. lease to the L.N.W.R. was completed), and this was confirmed by an agreement dated February 8, 1864, on a yearly rental of £12,665 17s. 6d. This did not include the southern separate length from Walton summit (the end of the Preston tramroad) to Kirkless, near Wigan, which under agreement dated July 1, 1864, was leased in perpetuity to the Leeds & Liverpool Canal Navigation (whose system it joined) at £7,075 a year. In 1885 the L.N.W.R. bought the L.C.C. property outright at a sum said to be half a million pounds, and the Canal property was formally vested in the L.N.W.R. as from July 1 of that year. The L.C. Company was formally wound up as from January 1, 1886.

Financial terms with the L. & C. were that the L. & P. should receive 7-22nds of the net profits derived from the working of both lines. Out of its proportion the L. & P. had to pay the interest on its existing mortgage debt of £113,000; but it had to receive entire the dividend on the 1,111 shares it held in the L. & C. In the promotion of the L. & C. in 1843 the L. & P. had promised to subscribe £65,000, that is 1,300 shares of £50; but it had difficulty in finding this money, so much so that just before the opening of the line to Carlisle the L. & C. had to give notice to the L. & P. that its shares were forfeit, as no notice had been taken of the several calls, and letters to the secretary had gone unanswered. This seems to have served its purpose, and the call monies were paid on the 1,300 shares. Yet so tight did money remain for the L. & P. that in 1848 it had to sell 189 of these shares to pay the final calls on the remainder. The chairman said they had been sold at a considerable premium, so that not only were the last calls paid but the L. & P. was able to buy 65 quarter shares of its own company which had been over-issued.

By its shareholding and the terms of the share acquisition, the L. & P. had the right of appointing a director to the L. & C. board; but in the years of the L.C.C. lease the legal tangle was such that the L. & C. refused to allow the nominee to attend its board meetings. When in July 1848 Joseph Bushell announced he had been nominated by the L. & P., the L. & C. sent him a copy of the board resolution, that "they greatly regretted being unable (acting on legal advice) to recognise any of the official acts of the gentlemen who at present assume to conduct the affairs of the L. & P., whilst under other circumstances it would have been most agreeable to them to receive Mr. Bushell as one of their colleagues."

The transfer-of-management Act of 1849 gave the L. & P. the right to have a second director on the board of the L. & C., and also the right to appoint some person to examine the L. & C. accounts; but the L. & C. ensured by the terms of this Act that it could choose which member of the L. & P. board should become the second representative. By this time the position was clear; and the L. & P. first nominee, Bushell, and the L. & C. choice for the second, Wm. Jackson, became valued members of the L. & C. board, and Jackson was elected deputy-chairman after the L. & C. became a holding company.

Remaining to be settled to the advantage of the L. & P. were the outstanding toll payments for the L. & C. trains having run over the Lancaster-Preston line from September 22, 1846, to July 31, 1849. Robert Stephenson was appointed arbitrator, and arrived at a total sum of £83,616 19s. 3½d., but of this £55,551 10s. 7½d. had to go to the L.C.C. which had the lease and management of the L. & P. during that period.

A result of all the financial arrangements and the holding of 1,111 L. & C. shares was that L. & P. stock became a good investment. The rate was always above that of the L. & C., as indicated in the graph Fig. 9 in Chap. IX, and rose to 10 per cent in 1858; and so in its very last year as a legal entity the L. & P. earned for the first time the rate predicted at the preliminary meetings 22 years earlier, and on a capital greater than that authorised in 1837. These happy results were not simply because of good management by the L. & C., but rather because the very existence of the L. & C. brought the through main line on which so much depended.

When at last in 1849 the L. & C. had the L. & P. and its line to Preston, an announcement was made in the July that from August 1 all trains between Preston and Lancaster would run to and from Castle station in direct connection with L. & C. trains, but Penny Street terminus seems to have been used for some little time afterwards for local trains. Thereafter it was a goods station for a short time until it was sold with about two acres of land adjoining. Of the four L. & P. stopping trains a day in each direction, two were continued, but using Castle station; the other two were replaced by L. & C. trains which then made stops at the intermediate stations.

In taking leave of the L. & P. one term in the management Act of 1849 may be mentioned, as it aroused opposition from certain L. & P. shareholders led by the father of Sir Edward Watkin. This was to do with the Scottish Central management contract described in Chap. IX. In the arrangements whereby the L. & P. was to receive 7-22nds of the net profit of the combined L. & C./L. & P., it was stated that the profit or loss from the S.C. contract (if the action at law then under way should result in any liabilities) had to be a debit or credit on the balance before any division took place. This meant L. & P. shareholders might have to stand a proportion of any working loss, or of litigation charges, on matters in which they had been in no way connected. This objection, though quite a legitimate one, was outvoted at the L. & P. meeting.

The end of the L. & P. as a legal entity came after a life of 22 years when, under Act 22 & 23 Vict., cap. 124, dated August 13, 1859, the L. & P. was fully amalgamated with the L. & C. The L. & P. shareholders received £101 18s. 1½d. of L. & C. ordinary stock for each £100. Just after this Act received the Royal Assent, the L. & P. at its final meeting on September 10, 1859, also had to approve the leasing of the L. & C. as a whole to the L.N.W.R., details of which are given in Chap. IX.

Table VI—Lancaster Canal Boat Times and Train Connections, 1845

Kendal dep.	Lancaster dep.	Preston arr.	Preston dep. by train	Liverpool or Manchester arr. by train
—	6.00	9.20	9.45	12.00
6.30	9.50	13.20	14.20	16.00
8.30	11.50	15.20	16.20	18.00

Manchester dep. by train	Liverpool dep. by train	Preston dep.	Lancaster arr.	Kendal arr.
9.00	8.45	11.00	14.20	18.20
11.15	11.00	13.30	16.50	20.30
14.45	14.30	16.00	19.20	—

VIII

The Grand Trunk Route

IDEAS OF rail communication between England and Scotland far antedated the slow spread northward from Warrington of the railways just described. They were inherent in Anderson's suggestions of 1801, though the Doctor could have had small inkling of the way steam traction would develop. They were specifically mentioned by Thomas Gray from 1820 onwards, and he refers to 'steam wagons'. They were considered as practical in the *London Magazine* and elsewhere in 1825, when one writer reckoned a London to Edinburgh journey could be done on a railway for two guineas and in a time of 15 to 16 hr.

Definite West Coast proposals seem to have arisen first in the *Carlisle Journal* of August 22, 1835, in an editorial supporting a route through that city in preference to an eastern route. This editorial was written by John Steel, the editor and principal proprietor, who was a firm and discriminating backer of railways, though a rival journal which he had trounced tried to dub him as a supporter of canals. Steel set out in parallel columns the pros and cons, as he saw them, of the two general routes; but his main theme was that already the railway was working or in a forward state of construction over the 219 miles between London and Preston, whereas there was no direct route of any kind between London and York which had even got as far as an Act. Also, he wrote, any line from Newcastle to Edinburgh must cross the Cheviots unless it took to the coast, and in that case it would have to cross the Lammermuir hills, whereas any railway beyond Carlisle could avoid the more mountainous range of south Scotland by making Dumfries, Kilmarnock and Glasgow the object. Alas, in the end, the four miles at 1 in 96 up Co'path in the east are more than balanced by 10 miles up at 1 in 74–88 near Beattock and the four miles at 1 in 75 up Shap; even the G. & S.W. route along the line of Steel's suggestion is not without its gradients.

Stretton states :". . . after examining various routes he (Locke) finally arrived in Carlisle on August 19." three days before Steel's article; but wrote there was no evidence that Steel had an interview with Locke. How Stretton came to make that statement is not clear. A preliminary search showed that Locke's name did not appear among the distinguished guests at the Bush Hotel, Carlisle, during August; but the present writer felt at first that perhaps, with the Grand Junction not yet on everyone's lips, and with Giles still in charge of the London & Southampton, Locke was not considered eminent enough for his name to appear in the same list as that of Baron Rothschild and family.

A further search showed that though the old G.J.R. board minutes never gave the names of officers in attendance, but only the names of the directors present, there was a board meeting at Liverpool on August 19,

1835, of which one of the minutes records: "Mr. Locke having brought up his Report on the construction of the bridges . . . Resolved that six additional bridges be erected." With communications as they were at the time, it would not have been possible for Locke to have attended a board meeting at Liverpool in the morning (11.00 was the normal time of the G.J.R. board meeting) and arrive in Carlisle the same evening. Moreover, seven days later the G.J.R. general meeting would almost certainly necessitate Locke's presence in Liverpool, especially as only on August 12 had he been confirmed as chief engineer at £1,200 a year.

Thus it would seem that Stretton was in error, and that to Steel may go the credit for originating the project for a complete railway system from Preston to Edinburgh and Glasgow. Considering the time of its publication, and the concise and practical information in it, the statement was one of the most powerful 'railway' editorials to appear in the press during 130 years; and it contained also the suggestion that in view of the importance of the subject the Government itself might well facilitate a survey. Certainly this issue of the *Carlisle Journal* would be brought to the attention of the G.J.R. board.

The next mention of such a line from Lancashire to Scotland is in the minutes of the G.J.R. board dated October 21, 1835, when Locke, as chief engineer of the company (his sole appointment at that time), was directed "to make an early opportunity to inspect the country north of Preston to see if there was a practicability of a line to Carlisle", an instruction supplemented at the next board meeting on November 4 by another "to report on the practicability of making a railway communication between Preston and Glasgow." This alone disposes of Stretton's claim that Locke arrived in Carlisle in August in accordance with G.J.R. instructions.

Locke reacted at once to the board's directions, and at the November 18 meeting the board recorded receipt of a letter from him describing the result of his inspection of the country; and on January 27, 1836, he presented his full report. The board was so pleased with it that John Moss, the chairman, sent a copy to James Loch, M.P., and it was he who caused the report to be circulated and so brought the whole question of a west coast route to Scotland into the eyes of public and Government. Loch was agent and auditor for the Marquis of Stafford (first Duke of Sutherland), and it was under his agreement that the Sutherland evictions had been carried out.

Though Locke did not make a survey, but only a rapid inspection in which he took very few levels, his eye for country and the comparatively enormous area he covered by coach, horse and foot in the matter of a fortnight, produced a report which created a firm and practical basis on which the whole question could be examined and built up technically, commercially and economically. The work of the many men of all kinds later associated with the west coast route stems from this concise appreciation; and no better introduction to the rise and progress of the Crewe–Carlisle–Glasgow trunk route can be given than an extensive quote from Locke's report dated January 27, 1836. It gives the outlook of some of the foremost railway minds of the time; Locke, though he walked the country and drew up the report, should not be separated from the G.J.R. directors, who had prescient minds and also provided the right atmosphere for Locke's powers to develop through his vital years in the middle and late 'thirties of last century.

Quoting from Locke's report:

"It is at all times desirable in the selection of lines of this description to embrace as many towns as possible . . . Kendal appeared to claim consideration, and my earliest attention was directed to ascertain how far the levels of the country would permit the line to be carried in that direction. It will suffice to inform you that although there is no difficulty in reaching Kendal there are very great ones in leaving it . . . unless worked by a stationary engine or made through a long tunnel. The only opening which appeared to me worthy of notice was that by Long Sleddale and Hawes Water . . . I also tried the Lake District by Milnthorpe, Windermere Lake, Ambleside, Rydal and Raise Gap . . . but a tunnel two miles long through Raise . . . and private properties induced me to seek other ground . . . I then tried Kirkby Lonsdale and Shap Fell . . . and believing this to be more favourable than any I had yet seen, I caused some levels to be taken . . . and I found that without incurring any greater rise than 1 in 100 the summit at Shap Fell might be passed with a tunnel a little more than 1¼ miles . . . In the very short period which I was enabled personally to devote to this survey . . .

"Beginning at the terminus of the N.U. (in Preston) . . . leaving Garstang one mile and Lancaster about three miles to the west . . . passing into the vale of Lune near Claughton . . . hence keeping by the valley to the east of Kirkby Lonsdale. Lancaster must be approached by a branch, and this arises from the great difficulty in passing through the town. There would be required a tunnel of half-a-mile long or an expensive bridge across the river there, besides increasing the distance by upwards of three miles. I have given this part much consideration, and think it better to recommend a branch, which would not exceed four miles in length.

"The line will continue in the Lune valley all the way from Kirkby Lonsdale to its source near Shap Fells, leaving Sedbergh and Orton about two miles to the east, and after passing under part of Shap Fell by tunnel, will pass into the valley of the Lowther by Bampton and Askham, cross the River Eamont above Eamont bridge, and continuing to the west side of the town of Penrith. Kirkby Lonsdale to Penrith would be above 34 miles at the following inclinations:

2¼	miles	up at	1 in 200
3	,,	,,	1 in 530
5¾	,,	,,	1 in 176
2½	,,	,,	1 in 240
4½	,,	,,	1 in 140
3½	,,	,,	1 in 100

$1\frac{1}{4}$	miles up	1 in 260	summit tunnel here
$7\frac{1}{4}$	,,	down 1 in 165	
$1\frac{3}{4}$	,,	level	
$2\frac{1}{2}$	,,	down 1 in 100	
1	,,	level	

"These gradients are not insurmountable by locomotives; none are as steep as on the Liverpool & Manchester Railway.

"The summit at Shap taken isolatedly may be fairly considered as an impediment . . . but the object to be attained by passing through or over this ridge is not merely local; it is not for a railway from Kirkby Lonsdale to Penrith . . . the line must be viewed as a whole, having 140 miles on one side and 40 miles on the other side of the summit . . . and we may even extend it to a London–Glasgow railway with 140 miles on one side and 250 miles on the other, on which locomotives may travel easily . . . The whole distance London to Glasgow is 417 miles and would be traversed in $21\frac{1}{2}$ hours; the mail now occupies more than double that time and the ordinary stages nearly treble.

"On the cost of the line one cannot speak at the moment with any degree of confidence; but I should say it cannot be executed at less than £14,000 a mile . . . Two great lines from Scotland to England cannot pay, and if only one is to be made there can be no question as to the route it ought to take."

In the opinion of most persons at that time the Lake District terrain would have to be avoided, but at least one detailed survey through it was made. The other possible ways, as clearly shown by Locke's examination, were only those going well east or well west of that area. The former would for much of its length be over wild country with little in the way of inhabitants or industry, and would involve steep gradients and probably tunnels. The second would be a 'Great Way Round', and would involve crossing Morecambe Bay or one of its wide inlets, though it would gain much traffic from the mineral area around Whitehaven; the haematite deposits around Barrow had not then been realised, though some iron ore was being worked near Ireleth, and there had been small shipments from Barrow since the beginning of the 19th Century, with land transport by carts.

The preliminary inspection of 1835 went up to Glasgow; and beyond the Border Locke recommended Steel's route via Dumfries, Nithsdale, Sanquhar and Kilmarnock, because he found 10 miles at 1 in 75, leading to a summit nearly 1,000 ft. above the sea, would be needed north of Beattock, and he did "not wish to recommend a line having such a plane as this." Nothing much more was done in 1836 except at Lancaster in regard to the L. & P.; but in the Spring of 1837 meetings were held in Glasgow to forward "the great national work of a railway from Glasgow through Carlisle to Lancaster, to join the main line southward." From these meetings Locke was asked to conduct another survey over Scottish ground. This he seems to have done roughly; but then the Annandale party, headed by J. J. Hope-Johnstone, came into the picture, and for that group Locke resurveyed the Annandale and Vale of Evan route with the specific object of reaching conveniently both Edinburgh and Glasgow. It was really this widening of the project to get one line which would go a long way north of the Border before the division into two branches serving the two chief cities that led to the Caledonian line being built, despite the difficulties north of Beattock.

In 1837 Locke was by no means happy about it, even though from his resurvey he said he could get up Beattock by ten miles at 1 in 93. His much briefer inspection at the end of 1835 gave a closer approximation to the gradients finally adopted, though at that time he felt he might have to use a stationary-engine plane to get up. He emphasised in 1837 regarding the ten miles at 1 in 93:

> ". . . a plane like this ought not to be adopted without sufficient reason. There are practical disadvantages in such an inclination, which nothing but the necessity or (all things considered) the economy of the case would justify our encountering, and although the important object to be attained will far outweigh any disadvantage it possesses, yet still it would be premature to say that this plane ought now to be adopted . . . I would repeat that although there is no ground for rejecting this line, I would not in the present state of our information on the general question pronounce in its favour."

Another interesting feature of Locke's report of 1837 to the Annandale group was that after a nine-mile fall at 1 in 97 Edinburgh was to be entered via Liberton with a one-mile drop at 1 in 42 to a terminal near Newington; but a resurvey of the last few miles in 1838 got a 10-mile gradient at 1 in 100 and came in via Powburn to Newington without any steeper final drop than this.

At the southern end of the Preston–Glasgow route Locke's report of January 1836 led immediately to the Lancastrians taking action to ensure they got a railway of some pretensions and were not put at the end of a four-mile branch from Galgate. In the getting of it they were astute enough to invite Locke to lay out and build the line. They also knew their line would benefit from any Scottish extension; and this is reflected in the report of the provisional committee of the L. & P. dated June 19, 1837: "The construction of the line to Glasgow may also be regarded as a probable event. Mr. Locke, having examined the line and found it practicable, has already received instructions from a committee in Glasgow to complete the surveys with a view to the construction of a railway." Locke, however, in undertaking the L. & P. construction, seems to have made a mental reservation to himself that when the Anglo-Scottish line was begun he would leave the L. & P. near Galgate and bring Lancaster back to the branch he proposed in 1835.

This 1835 inspection of Locke on behalf of the G.J.R. must have had some part in George Stephenson's advocacy of the Great Way Round. There have been suggestions that Stephenson's friendship with the Earl of Lonsdale, who had great coal interests in West Cumberland, led him to support and survey the West Cumberland route; but this friendship seems to have come a little later, and bore fruit in the Whitehaven &

Furness Junction Railway (8 & 9 Vict., cap. 100, July 21, 1845). The coastal idea did not originate with Old George himself. West Cumberland interests initiated the project, and a committee of the Great Caledonian Junction Railway asked him on September 1, 1836, to report on a line to Scotland. This seems to be the first recorded railway use of the word 'Caledonian'; in succeeding years it was used loosely for all kinds of west coast railway ideas before coming to be associated with one company. Stephenson's commitments at that time did not enable him to do anything, and nine months went by. Then a committee of the Whitehaven, Workington & Maryport Railway on June 6, 1837, invited him to take up the work and make "an ocular survey" of two routes between Lancaster and Carlisle; the first was to go via Ulverston and Whitehaven, the second via Kirkby Lonsdale and Penrith, with a view to completing railway communication between England and Scotland. This was where the Lonsdale influence may have come in, for the Lowther family had extensive interests around Whitehaven and took considerable holdings in the two railways that *were* built in that district; and it also owned much of Shap Fells and the Lowther valley.

Stephenson spent the first fortnight of August 1837 making a circular walking and riding tour; but he did not make a proper survey and took very few levels, and his whole report bears no mark of him being really interested in either scheme. He could hardly recommend the Lune valley, which would be 40 miles away from West Cumberland, and he suggested the coast route on a trace followed more or less by the several railways which later made up the Furness Railway, with the exception that Stephenson proposed to cross Morecambe Bay by a curved embankment from Poulton-le-Sands (Morecambe) to Humphrey Head instead of using the much shorter crossing from Arnside ultimately adopted. At Whitehaven the projected line was to link up with a railway from that town to Maryport, which had just been surveyed by Hall, and for which a Bill was being promoted. At Maryport the line would join the Maryport & Carlisle Railway, surveyed in detail in 1836–37 by Old George himself, and the Act for which (1 Vict., cap. 101) was obtained on July 12, 1837. Years later the Whitehaven–Maryport line came into possession of the L.N.W.R., though cut-off from the parent system by 28 miles.

Reclaimed land was to be a feature of this scheme. Stephenson suggested that if the railway paid half the cost of the embankment and the owners of the reclaimed land the other half, it would be a good investment. He himself put no estimate of costs in his brief report; the figures associated with his name were added by the committee in their comment on the report, and were said to be "estimated on data furnished by Mr. Stephenson." Cost of the 49½ miles from Lancaster to Whitehaven was given as £341,500, and £90,000 from Whitehaven to Maryport. A feature of Stephenson's levels was that once clear of Lancaster his route was nowhere more than 40 ft. above sea level, though he needed a tunnel in Furness to achieve this. Stephenson did not think much of the practicabilities of the eastern route from Penrith to Kirkby Lonsdale; but apart from walking over the fells he made little effort to find a way, and simply

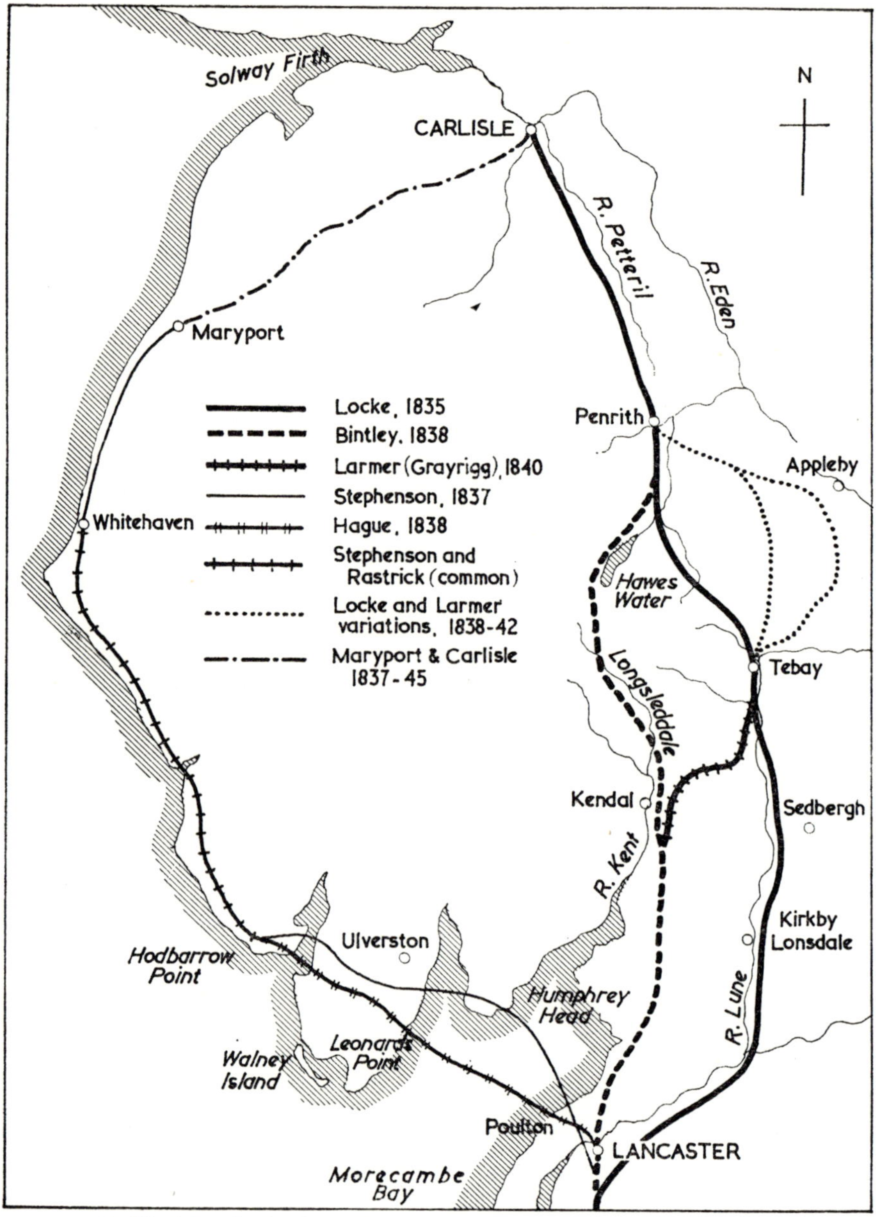

7 West Cumberland and Fell routes, Lancaster to Carlisle, 1835–42

said the possible routes would have objectionable inclinations and a tunnel, the rate and length of which respectively he had not ascertained.

There is a story that Stephenson ridiculed Locke's Shap line by saying the gradients would be so steep that the engines would run away and find themselves in the sea. Perhaps this legend arose from the West

Cumberland committee; its printed comments on Stephenson's report said that the long 1 in 100 to 1 in 200 gradients of Locke's route might give rise to such speed that on the curves "the danger of precipitating the whole train into the glen below would be imminent." Train control at that time was not by continuous brakes; and it may be noted that Locke himself in his 1837 report to the Annandale committee said relative to Beattock, for which he proposed ten miles of 1 in 93: "In the descent, however, there is more danger, and this is a question of importance. Perfect machinery and perfect watchfulness on the part of the attendants would leave no room for apprehension; could these be depended upon, the objections to such planes would be materially lessened."

Though Stephenson's report of 1837 showed little enthusiasm, he returned to the subject in a manuscript report to the P. & W. in June 1839 when he wrote that the cost of the Morecambe Bay embankment would be too great and the scheme too hazardous unless the Government took it up; and he suggested the Cumberland people might be got to make a harbour at Duddon, and that boats should go across from Fleetwood to provide a through rail-sea route to the west of Scotland, as a railway across Shap Fell was out of the question. Old George could never adjust his mind to the practicability of Shap; and a happy later reflection on this is given by Michael Robbins in the *Journal of Transport History*, November 1965, quoting R. B. Dockray's diary entry of his journey over the Shap line on May 17, 1850. Dockray wrote: "The long and steep gradients by which the high ground at Shap is surmounted do not very sensibly check the speed of the trains. I remember when we Stephensonites used to think those gradients of so much importance that they would drive all the Scotch traffic along the railways on the eastern side of England."

After Stephenson's report was delivered the West Cumbrians maintained some interest, but did nothing until 1838, when, led by Sir H. le Fleming Senhouse, they formed another provisional committee, this time for a Caledonian, West Cumberland & Furness Railway, and commissioned two further detailed surveys. They also solicited, and received, small subscriptions from some of the more southerly railways to cover the cost of the surveys, e.g. from the North Union. One of the surveys, by John Hague, was specifically on the practicability of the embankments across Morecambe Bay and the Duddon estuary. The second, by John Rastrick, was for a survey of the whole line from Lancaster to Maryport, but using the line of embankments suggested by Hague.

Hague, who received his instructions in February and March 1838, varied Stephenson's line across the bay, and projected a still longer embankment from Poulton-ring, south of Bare, straight across to Leonard's Point in Furness, just north of the mouth of the Gleason brook, a distance of 10 miles 51 chains. The Duddon was to be crossed from Ronhead Crag to Hodbarrow Point, 1 mile 65 chains. Hague reckoned the Morecambe Bay embankment would require 10,435,785 tons of material, of which 6,149,370 tons would be brought in by the sea through tide and wave action. These old engineers stuck to the exact calculated figure; they did

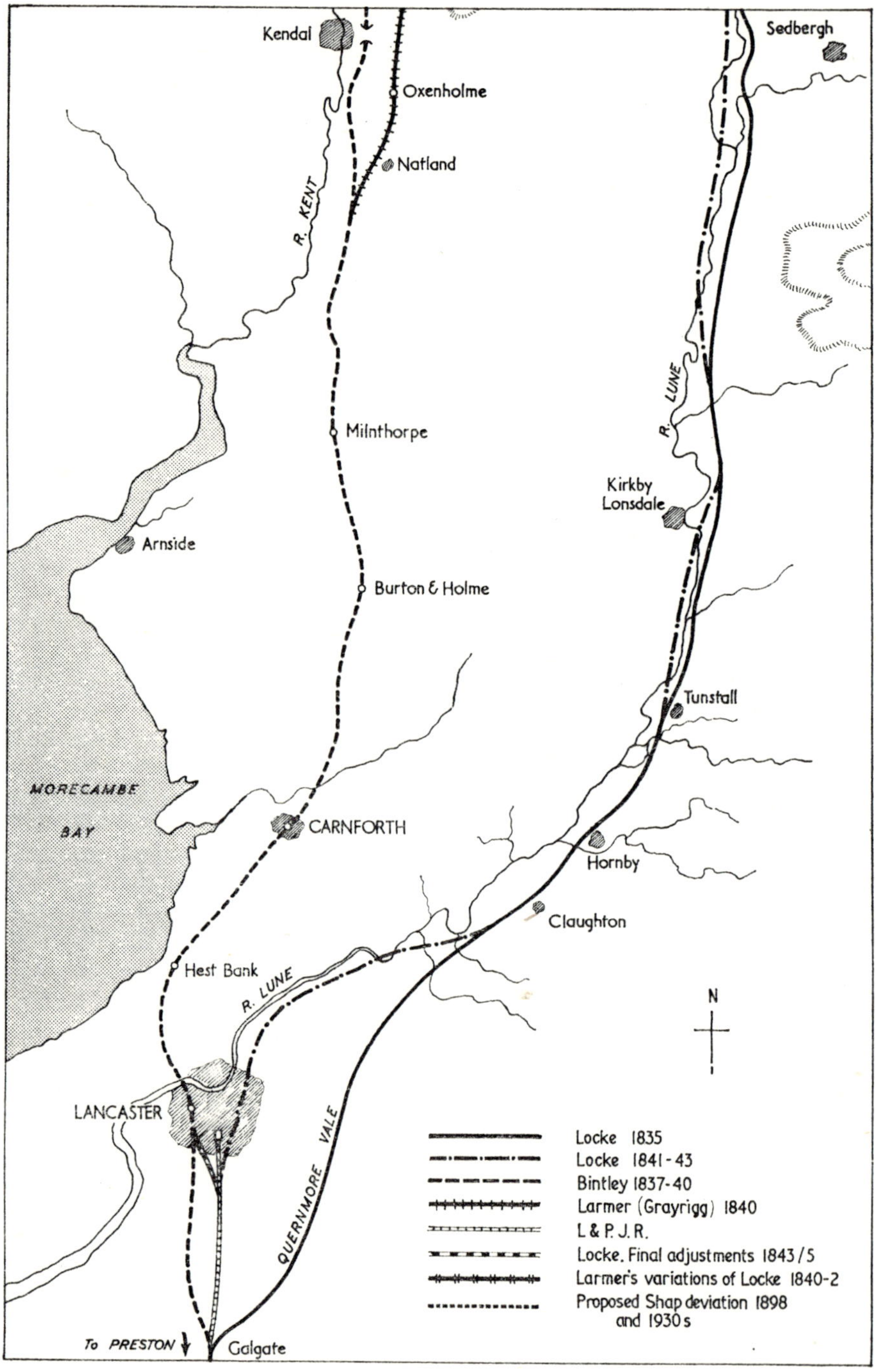

8a Lancaster to Penrith, various proposed routes, 1835–45

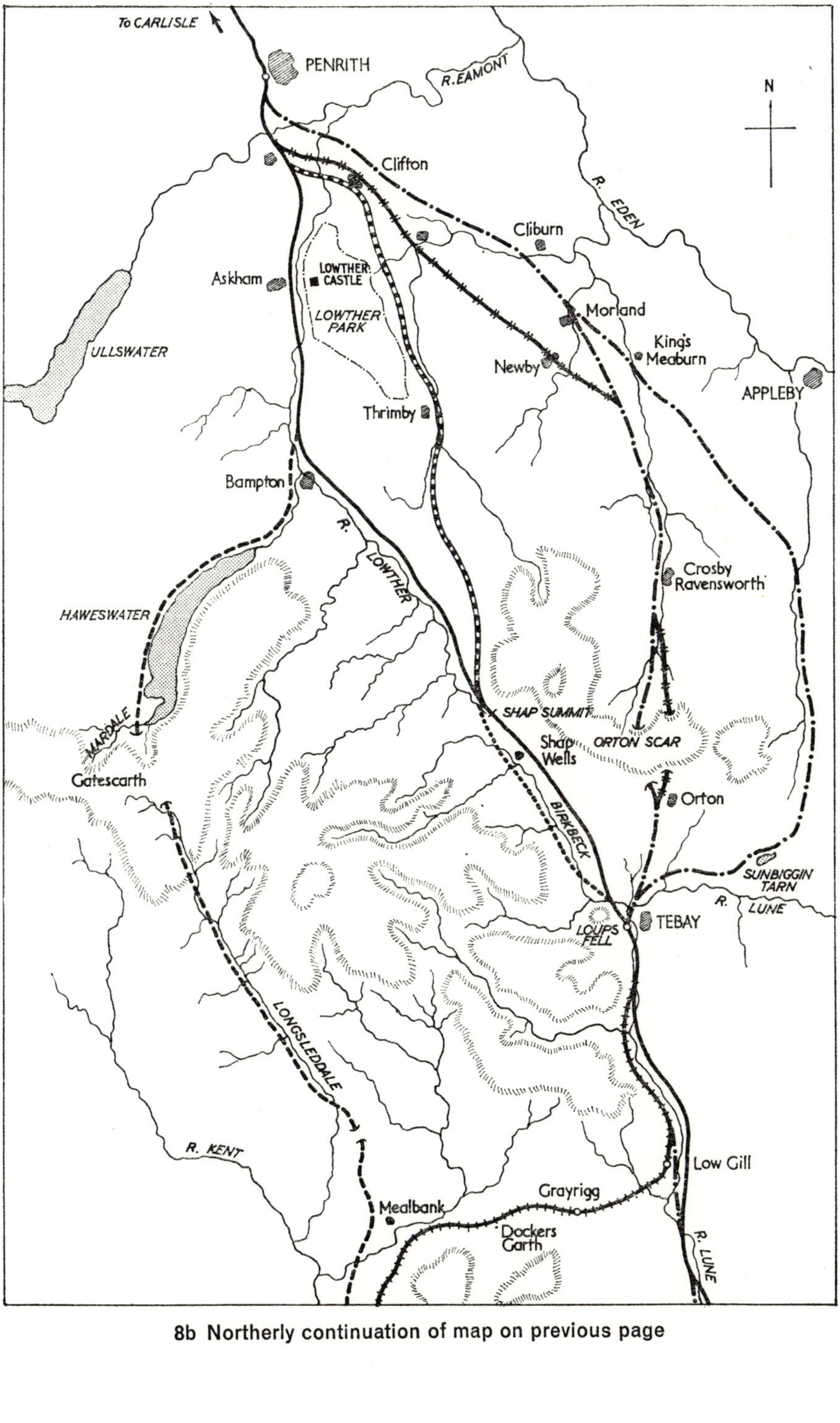

8b Northerly continuation of map on previous page

not round 'em off, perhaps because they feared a charge of making their investigations in a vague and unprofessional manner. Hague similarly estimated the cost of the two embankments at £434,131 9s. 4d.; that is, almost the same figure as the West Cumberland committee reckoned for the whole line to Maryport after considering Stephenson's appreciation of the preceding year.

Reclamation of land was a big possibility from this scheme also. Hague estimated 46,300 acres from Morecambe Bay and 5,700 acres in Duddon Bay, and at £23 an acre this represented £1,196,000. Stephenson's estimate for land reclaimed by his crossing of Morecambe Bay was approximately 20,000 acres, but he said up to 40,000 acres *could* be reclaimed. One supporter of the Shap line reckoned Hague's embankments would reclaim enough land to enable the proprietors to get a return of 1 or 2 per cent; but neither he nor any of the reporters seems to have considered to whom the reclaimed land might belong; nor did the Government commissioners who examined the scheme in 1839–40. But the whole proposition aroused wide general interest; and a letter in the *Lancaster Guardian* in 1839 recorded that the rights of the subject went out to high-water mark of ordinary tides; and that as thence to the low-water mark the shore belonged to the Crown, it was probable that the Crown's rights would extend over half of Morecambe Bay.

Rastrick received his instructions in October 1838, and his report, addressed to the 'West Cumberland, Furness & Morecambe Bay Railway', was dated December 24, 1838. He surveyed a line of 66.9 miles from Maryport to Lancaster without steep gradients. Towards the end of the report, after stressing the absolute necessity of *some* line between Lancaster and Carlisle, he warned the provisional committee: "If you do not bring forward this line of railway (the West Cumberland scheme) and support it with all your might, West Cumberland will for ever remain in the back settlements."

One further extract from Rastrick is of interest: "I have not thought it necessary to survey or level a line up to the important town of Ulverstone, as the railway to that town will be laid on the embankment which Mr. Hague proposes to make for the ship canal . . . vessels on the canal could be towed by locomotive engines expeditiously and at low expense." This refers to Hague's proposal to dredge a canalised channel at right angles to the west end of the main embankment to get ships up to the Ulverstone canal by Bardsea. Yet such an early proposal for towing ships by locomotives was not the first; such schemes had already been suggested in 1825 generally, and again a few years later in regard to Panama.

Rastrick's report to the West Cumberland committee was printed and circulated over the name of 'John M. Rastrick', of 454 Charing Cross East. The Government commissioners, in their second report, June 1840, included this report *in toto*, but over the name of 'John Urpeth Rastrick' at the same address.

Nothing more came at once from these West Cumberland proposals. Lancashire, Westmorland and Cumberland interests kept the matter of a western route to Scotland going through 1837–39, with several preliminary meetings and surveys; and as the original interest of 1836–37 was dying down, a meeting was held in Penrith in November 1837 to forward an independent line from that town to Carlisle, a distance of about 20 miles. This had the support of the Earl of Lonsdale, and also some backing from the inhabitants of neighbouring towns such as Appleby. At a subsequent meeting in Carlisle, George Dixon, then High Sheriff of Cumberland and a director of the Newcastle & Carlisle Railway, promised the support of that line for a Carlisle–Penrith railway.

Several meetings were held over the next two years to form a company with a capital of £170,000, that being Locke's estimate after George Larmer had made a survey and taken levels. Locke wrote: ". . . it will hereafter form a link of the Great North and South Railway . . . it will form the beginning of the northern district of the greater scheme." Progress in getting subscriptions was slow; then, according to an account written some seven years later, after a good deal of money had been promised, "too large a number of railway jobbers, a race even then in being, though not so numerous as it has since become, got mixed up with the project, and it was judiciously resolved by the local committee to abandon it altogther."

Locke's suggested route up the Lune valley did not suit the inhabitants of Kendal at all, particularly as that engineer had begun his very first report by stressing the importance of the town. Of all the fairly scanty populace within miles of any practicable route between Lancaster and Penrith they were by far the keenest to have a railway. Many of the efforts over the years 1837–43 to get and keep things going seem to have derived from Kendal under the spur of Cornelius Nicholson (1805–89); in the Carlisle area Colonel Graham of Mossknowe was the rallying point over those seven years, and at Penrith it was E. W. Hasell.

In 1837 Nicholson wrote what is now a rare pamphlet on 'The London & Glasgow Railway'. He wanted Kendal on the route, and it was mainly with that object in view that the pamphlet was published; but he emphasised: "If we cannot obtain a line through Kendal it is our manifest duty to throw our weight into the scale in favour of one or other of the lines previously proposed . . . The mistake with many persons in the Kendal neighbourhood is that they cannot look further than between Penrith and Lancaster . . . It is not the Penrith and Lancaster railway we advocate but the London and Glasgow, the Lancashire and Lanarkshire—nay, the English and Scottish connecting railway."

As Locke's 1835 inspection had suggested the Lune valley route, and a Lowther valley continuation which did not suit Lord Lonsdale, that engineer was invited by the Kendal and Penrith provisional committees for a Lancaster and Carlisle line to try and find other routes that might obviate their objections. From these instructions he reported in 1838 on two other possibilities: (1) a line up the Lune valley to Tebay as before, but continuing more east of north through Orton, King's Meaburn, Morland, Cliburn and Eamont to Penrith; (2) from Lancaster by Carnforth to Kendal, up Longsleddale, tunnelling through the hills to Mardale, and running alongside Hawes Water to Askham and Penrith, a proposition he had rejected out of hand in 1835. Locke said route (2) would be 12 miles shorter than route (1), but would have steeper gradients than the ruling 1 in 130 of the Orton line. He appreciated Kendal's anxiety to have a railway, but reiterated his preference for his original Lune-Shap survey, and stated the 1¼-mile tunnel envisaged in that route would present fewer difficulties than the works of the Hawes Water line. But his surveys, certainly of the Kendal line, seem to have been cursory, as if he was not really interested in anything but the Lune valley line and was not inclined to treat very seriously these commercial men who would eventually have to see about getting the money.

George Larmer, working independently for the Carlisle and Penrith committees, summarised the various routes which had been surveyed or given brief preliminary inspections by September 1839 as:

Lancaster to Carlisle

Via Kendal and Longsleddale	65*	miles of which		2½	miles in tunnel	
Via Lune Valley and Shap	67	,,	,,	1½	,,	,,
Via Lune Valley and Orton	67	,,	,,	1	,,	,,
Via West Cumberland	96	,,	,,	¾	,,	,,
Via Lune Valley and Appleby	75	,,	,,	none in tunnel		

* Plus 2 miles to join L. & P. south of Lancaster.

At that period Larmer counted on a shorter tunnel through Orton Scar than he suggested later, but his approach from the south was at 1 in 120, and from the north at 1 in 140; with the longer tunnel his southern gradient also became 1 in 140.

As the Shap proposals gradually became more widely known, West Cumberland speeches began to characterise them and the tunnel as the dream of a madman while, to quote an almost contemporary account: "they were lifted into a fourth Heaven when they talked of the magnificent embankment of 10 miles to span Morecambe Bay." Two or three years later George Hudson vituperated that Shap was one half of the year covered in snow, and during the other half was unable to maintain one goose an acre, and he talked wildly that the route would cost £35,000 a mile. George Stephenson himself felt that snow conditions might be experienced for weeks at a stretch; fortunately his prognostications have never been realised, and considering its height and openness 'Shap' has been singularly free from snow interruptions.

In 1837/38 the Kendal provisional committee employed a local surveyor, Job Bintley, first to survey a route from Lancaster to Kendal, and then another from Kendal to Penrith. Something will be said later about the former. For the Kendal–Penrith line Bintley concentrated on the Longsleddale-Askham route, and must have been on the ground almost at the same time as Locke's men, but he surveyed that line in much greater detail. His proposals were to tunnel from Longsleddale under Gatescarth, cross Mardale on a bridge, and run along the west side of Hawes Water to Bampton, Askham, Yanwath and Penrith. His summit tunnel would have been 2¼ miles long, and his estimate of its cost was £80,000 a mile,

Plate XVIIa Crewe shed in the early 1890s, showing (back row, just outside building): 519 *Shooting Star*, 6ft 3cc 2-2-2-0 class; 2464 "Cauliflower" 0-6-0; 1305 *Doric*, 7ft 3cc 2-2-2-0; "Cauliflower" 0-6-0; 1213 *The Queen*, a "Jumbo" 2-4-0; a 0-6-0 goods engine; in the foreground 1311 *Celtic*, 7ft 3cc 2-2-2-0, and behind it No. 1979, a 0-6-0; to right, 395 *Scotia*, a "Jumbo" 2-4-0 [*British Rail*

Plate XVIIb St Nicholas railway level crossing at Carlisle in 1875; to left is the N&C loop; in the centre running south under road bridge is the LNWR main line; and running from left to right is the N&C Canal branch

Plate XVIIIa Crewe station looking south from the north end in the early 1890s, showing on right the beginning of the suspension bridge leading to the works, and along which ran an 18in gauge railway

Plate XVIIIb Looking north from the same point, showing the old works and clock tower, and, on the right, the crossover to the Manchester line. The sheds on the up side were demolished when the fly-unders were built early this century [*LGRP*

Plate XIXa Carnforth station looking north in the late 1890s; main-line platforms to right, and the then single Furness platform to the left

Plate XIXb Glasson terminal station at the turn of the century; open ground lever frame in left foreground, Webb six-coupled tank on right

Plate XXa Grayrigg station looking north in the 1890s; the shelter on the up platform (to the right) was used as the local Sunday school until the 1939-45 war

Plate XXb Docker Garths viaduct today after 122 years of main-line service, latterly with axle loads and lineal loadings three times those of the original engines

or about £184,000 total. Some objection was made later against the great depth of the three working shafts for this tunnel, viz. 824, 762 and 347 ft. respectively; but Bintley rejoined that the tunnel shafts on the Manchester & Sheffield Railway, then under construction by Locke, were 582 and 579 ft. He reckoned that from first to last his main tunnel might take six years to complete.

By 1838 there was wider recognition that the railway which was seen to be inevitable between Carlisle and Lancaster would have much more than local interest. As no signs of any agreement as to route on the western side were seen, and no practical measures for either east coast or west coast lines had been initiated, Hodgson Hinde, M.P. for Newcastle, moved in the House on June 7, 1838, for the appointment of commissioners to report on the best line of communication between London and the manufacturing districts of England, Edinburgh and Glasgow. There was opposition to this, and on a vote of 53 for and 53 against the Speaker gave his casting vote against. The next year, as nothing had been done in the meantime, Hinde, later a director of the Caledonian Railway, returned to the subject. This time his motion was carried, and in November 1839 the Government appointed two commissioners, Sir Frederic Smith and P. W. Barlow, to report on the various proposals for lines from England to Scotland, eastern and western, and to report also on communications between London and Dublin.

As soon as the appointment of the commissioners was announced, the Kendal provisional committee renewed their efforts, and gave instructions for another survey, this time by George Larmer, who, prior to his Carlisle–Penrith surveys, had been responsible as resident engineer for the construction of the western end of the Newcastle & Carlisle Railway, which included the great Cowran cut and the Wetheral viaduct over the Eden. His first survey for the Kendal committee simply began around Low Gill and went northward, departed from Locke's Shap route at Tebay, and going thence north to Orton and taking the general line of Locke's alternative, but with some variations.

The Kendal committee also sent an urgent invitation to the well-known Francis Whishaw to come north and go over Bintley's line, and he spent 10 days on the ground in March and April 1840, covering an amount and nature of ground that in later years would have qualified him for the Fell & Rock Climbing Club. He reckoned he could shorten Bintley's main tunnel by 400 yd., and said that in comparison with the Orton route the approach cuttings to the summit tunnels should also be taken into account, and he gave the comparison included in the accompanying table. The tunnel figures may be compared with Bintley's estimates given previously, but Whishaw proposed four vertical shafts for the Longsleddale summit tunnel, whereas Bintley had suggested three. Influenced, he said, by some members of the committee, Whishaw gave up Bintley's idea of a 'tidal' crossing at Lancaster, and went back to the L. & P. terminus and the Larmer general line of departure to the north, envisaging a bridge 530 ft. long and 60 ft. high. He also stressed that north of Kendal there would be two bridges of 80 to 90 ft. in height and 1,000 and 530 ft. in length over the Rivers Mint and Sprint, structures to which Bintley does not seem to have invited attention.

Whishaw's Estimates of Three Summit Sections, 1840

Orton (Larmer)		Longsleddale (Bintley)		Longsleddale (Whishaw)	
2420yd. tunnel	£ 88,935	3982yd. tunnel	£197,109	3575yd. tunnel	£176,962
cuttings	£130,410	462yd. tunnel	£ 18,480	572yd. tunnel	£ 22,880
		cuttings	£ 53,290	cuttings	£ 33,580
Total	£219,345	Total	£268,879	Total	£233,422

The Government commissioners were "appointed to enquire and report upon the relative merits, and the preference which might be given, to the respective already-surveyed and projected railways between London and the cities of Edinburgh and Glasgow following, namely via York, Newcastle-upon-Tyne and Berwick; via York, Newcastle-upon-Tyne and Hexham; via Lancaster, Whitehaven and Carlisle; and via Lancaster, Penrith and Carlisle; the said enquiry and report to include the relative merits of the two lines from London to York, by Derby and Rotherham and by Cambridge and Lincoln." It will be noted that the previous year's reference to 'manufacturing districts' had been eliminated.

The commissioners issued their report in four parts: the first, in 1840, on the Dublin communications; the second, in May 1840, on the west coast lines to Scotland; the third, in November 1840, on Grayrigg; and the fourth, in March 1841, on the east coast lines and a summary of the whole question. They began their work in the midst of general opinion that only one railway route from England to Scotland would be justifiable. Despite some northward progress being made piecemeal on both sides of the country, that had been a common idea, though it was losing some of its strength by 1840. Indeed, in February 1838 one intelligent Liverpool writer had recorded his opinion: "I do not think one line of railway from England to Scotland would be sufficient; it appears to me that two are requisite." One of the reasons why the Kendal people were so consistently energetic in their demands was just this opinion of one railway being the limit, and in his pamphlet of 1837 Cornelius Nicholson had written that before many years elapsed an English-Scottish railway would be constructed on one side of the country or the other, but: "Parliament can never be expected to sanction *two lines*." Though in general it was coming to be seen by 1841 that two lines would in the end be most likely, the commissioners ended their work by saying: "Having expressed the preference we feel bound to give to the Western route by Lockerby (*sic*) under the supposition that at present only one line of railway can be formed from the south to Edinburgh and Glasgow."

In their second report (the first one on the Scottish lines) the commissioners said that as some documents on other lines were not ready they had devoted their attention principally to London and Carlisle routes. The three projects they examined north of Lancaster were: (*a*) the West Cumberland; (*b*) the Lune valley and Orton; and (*c*) the

Kendal, Longsleddale and Hawes Water. They hardly seemed to be aware of Locke and his work. They stated: "Mr. Larmer projected and surveyed the Carlisle–Penrith line, and also that from Penrith to Kirkby Lonsdale. The line from the last-named place to Lancaster, we were informed, was laid down by persons under the direction of Mr. Locke, but the sections for the whole between Penrith and Lancaster were placed before us by Mr. Larmer."

Compliments were given to Hague and Rastrick on the way they had drawn up the plans for the coast line, the only route for which the documents presented were found at once to be sufficient, but the commissioners rejected this scheme on the ground of the difficulties of the embankments and their cost, and also because of the 'Great Way Round'. They calculated that at 20 m.p.h. average speed (and that figure alone spot-lights official thinking in 1840) the journey from Lancaster to Carlisle would take 3 hr. 20 min. the Kendal way, 3 hr. 38 min. by the Lune valley, and 4 hr. 22 min. by the coast. Moreover the coast-route fares would be 4s. higher than those of the two other lines. They calculated that Hague had underestimated his embankment costs, and with equal precision gave their estimate as £543,373 2s. 11½d., including 10 per cent for contingencies. Nevertheless, they stated that, if Hague's estimates were anywhere near correct, the embankment scheme would stand on its own without any reference to a railway, by virtue of the land reclaimed.

As put to the commissioners, the Lune valley line started from the L. & P. terminus at Lancaster and crossed the river double-fashion at lower Crook o' Lune by a three-arch bridge 60 ft. high; and from Tebay the line went through Orton Scar by a tunnel of 1 mile 30 chains, with a rock cutting 1½ miles long and 48 ft. average depth in the south approach, and one of half-a-mile in length and 36 ft. average depth to the north.

Bintley's route was to come off the L. & P. near Galgate, go through the west end of Lancaster by a 220-yd tunnel, cross the Lune by a bridge only 23 ft. above the water, and then go on to Kendal via Hest Bank and Carnforth, and thence into Longsleddale. The commissioners expressed surprise that Bintley thought he could make his summit tunnel at £50,000, a mile; but possibly Bintley had not made it clear that such a sum did not include the three deep shafts. In an analysis of the Longsleddale and Grayrigg routes published in May 1841 he gave £80,000 a mile for the whole tunnel works, and at the same time he contested the commissioners' view that Gatescarth was a porphyritic mountain and said that in commenting on his tunnel at Lancaster the commissioners seemed to be unaware that it would be only 220 yd. long. His summit tunnel would have been 2¼ miles.

Bintley continued to assert through 1841 that a Longsleddale route with a gradient somewhat flatter than 1 in 100 was preferable to any other way, and that his Lancaster proposals would have knocked £55,000 off the cost of the whole line. He must have been quite a remarkable man, for local advertisements in the 'forties show him to have been in business as a surveyor and a woollen draper; yet quantities he took out, and detailed comments he made on the Grayrigg route, show him to have been well versed in the first of his two occupations. His under-estimation of the tunnel cost, his suggestion that construction might take six years, and perhaps a glossing over the big earthworks and the two big bridges approaching Longsleddale he knew would be necessary on each side of his summit tunnel to maintain his ruling gradient, told against him when the commissioners looked over his line in 1840; but the commissioners gave no notice to Whishaw's variations.

Nevertheless, in their second report, while saying the Lune valley line must have the preference over Bintley's, the commissioners asked if it was not possible to connect the two lines together by adopting Bintley's route from Lancaster to Kendal, Larmer's from Borrow Bridge (south of Tebay) on to Penrith, and finding some connecting route between Kendal and Borrow Bridge. As far as the Lancaster–Carlisle line was concerned, these were the most pregnant few lines of their voluminous report. They had raised this question with Larmer while they were on the ground, but that engineer's view at the time had been that such a connecting line would be too expensive.

Soon after these verbal discussions the Kendal committee instructed Larmer once more, and he went into this aspect in detail. He began around Oxenholme, taking Bintley's earlier survey from Lancaster to Kendal as an established basis except in Lancaster itself and in the final approach to Kendal. It was in this survey, undertaken in the late Spring and early summer of 1840, that Larmer 'discovered' the Grayrigg route, or at least the practicability of it. Bintley subsequently claimed that it had been considered in 1837/38, and that he had gone over Grayrigg for two days in April 1840 at the behest of the Kendal committee, that is, just before Larmer started work. Though Larmer's trace from Oxenholme to Low Gill went quite close to the existing London Midland Region main line, there may have been errors in some of his sections, for he showed seven miles up at 1 in 150 from Oxenholme northward, in place of the 2½ miles of 1 in 131 and 2 miles at 1 in 106 of the line as built.

Larmer's report, dated July 3, 1840, contains also his observations on the whole line from Lancaster to Carlisle. He did not consider the inclusion of Kendal itself on the route as practicable, not for the difficulties of getting into it from the south, but for the difficulties Locke had foreseen in getting out of it to the north. Therefore he came off Bintley's southern survey two or three miles away, carried the line at a higher level through Oxenholme, nearly two miles from Kendal, then on through Grayrigg to Low Gill to join Locke's Lune valley trace. From Tebay he followed generally the route already proposed by Locke through Orton Scar, and after passing through the 1¼ mile summit tunnel came down into the valley of the Lyvennet, and so by Crosby Ravensworth, Newby, Melkenthorpe and Clifton into Penrith. The ruling gradients of this resurvey north of Tebay were 1 in 140/150 for 4¼ miles northbound and 3¾ miles southbound. Summit level would have been around 800 ft. Shap today is 915 ft.

Before their own first Scottish report was completed and printed the commissioners received from the Kendal committee a copy of this report of Larmer's, with a request to report on it. They regretted their instructions precluded them from doing so, but added a rider that if such a line was feasible and had no material increase in cost over the others already examined, then it might well be more beneficial to the public than the Lune valley line.

By the end of 1840 the commissioners' terms were extended, and in the November of that year they sent in a report on the Grayrigg line, in which they recommended it in preference to all others between Lancaster and Carlisle. This short report was not printed and published until January 1841. In their final report in March 1841 they had no longer to cover the Lancaster–Carlisle section, though they referred to the Trent Valley cut-off further south. As far as the West Coast Route was concerned they recommended north of Carlisle the Annandale way via Beattock; but they qualified this carefully by saying: "We give this opinion under the supposition that antecedently to the construction of this line, the railway shall have been formed between Lancaster and Carlisle, or that both lines should be undertaken nearly simultaneously; but should this not be the case, then we would award preference to the east coast line over the Hexham line." This final report also contains the statement: ". . . the amount of traffic which in the present state of the commercial and other relations of England and Scotland may be expected between Edinburgh and Glasgow and the South is not such as would be likely to afford an adequate return for the outlay of capital required for the construction of two distinct lines of railway."

The most astonishing thing about the commissioners' examination of the western routes was the complete absence of Locke in regard to the line south of Carlisle, though it was well known that he had been making surveys for five years, and that he had just completed construction of the L. & P. The existence of his Shap proposals, and the work he and his assistants had done on various alternatives, scarcely seems to have come within the cognisance of the commissioners. Locke was not interviewed relative to the line south of Carlisle, and one wonders whether deliberately he chose to keep quiet. He was strongly attached to his early surveys, and Shap always had an attraction for him despite its severe gradients and the tunnel on top; but to have drawn attention to this in 1840 might have revived some of the old opposition and ridicule, particularly as he was putting forward the Beattock line further north. Possibly he arranged with Larmer for that engineer to pilot the whole Lancaster–Carlisle project through the commissioners, while he himself, with Errington, dealt with the Caledonian portion. Larmer had already done much surveying for the Carlisle, Penrith and Kendal provisional committees, and knew a good deal about the whole project; and after all the business was through, and construction begun four years later, Larmer was one of the two resident engineers on the Lancaster & Carlisle Railway work.

IX

The Lancaster & Carlisle

SOME SEVEN months after publication of the commissioners' final report a public meeting was held in Carlisle on October 2, 1841, with a view to forming a company to build a line thence to Lancaster, and at this meeting representatives of the G.J.R., N.U., and L. & P. were present. Huish spoke for the G.J.R. He said he was authorised to state that if the landowners along the proposed line were willing to take the value of their property needed in shares, then his board was willing to recommend to its shareholders that the G.J.R. should subscribe for £200,000 of stock. He believed that on these terms the N.U. would also take £50,000 of stock, and possibly the L. & P. would subscribe for that amount, too. The value of the land, he thought, would be £280,000, so that £580,000 could be counted upon.

Huish also said something about the line, something which in essence sanctioned Shap and its four miles of 1 in 75. He emphasised: "the projectors of the line must above all things consider economy; they must be satisfied to go *over* the hills, not *through* them . . . The question of gradients is daily assuming less importance." Huish also stated that the line from Carlisle to Glasgow had been carefully surveyed by Locke, and that from Carlisle to Lancaster a survey had been made by Larmer. Their reports suggested that the cost of a line from Carlisle to Glasgow would cost £1,776,841 plus 10 per cent for contingencies, and that from Lancaster to Carlisle the construction cost would not exceed £1,200,000.

A second meeting followed in December 1841, at which it was stated that the G.J.R. would organise a detailed survey from Lancaster to Edinburgh and Glasgow if the money was forthcoming to pay for Mr. Locke's services. Almost at the same time a public meeting was held in Glasgow on the basis of the commissioners' report; and Col. Graham of Mossknowe said that Errington had told him a cheap line could be formed over Shap. As a result of these meetings various bodies and individuals contributed, including Glasgow Corporation (£200), Glasgow Chamber of Commerce (£100), Dumfries Burgh (£200), Govan & Polloc Railway (£300), and various citizens of Carlisle (£300). The railways south of Preston made up the necessary balance in agreed proportions.

Subsequently the provisional committee appointed from the Carlisle meeting in October reported that the route proposed by Locke was up the Lune valley through Kirkby Lonsdale and Sedbergh to Low Gill and Tebay, and then north to Orton with a tunnel through to Crosby Ravensworth, and on to Penrith. Locke was not giving up more of his ideas of 1835–36 than he could help; but this time he could no longer keep Lancaster on a branch, and began close to the L. & P. station in that town, and ran up the south bank of the Lune to join his original trace near Brookhouse and Claughton, and then via Hornby, Melling and Tunstall.

Opposition to this scheme came at once from Kendal. This time Nicholson could say that a thoroughly attractive alternative had been provided by Larmer's Grayrigg route, which had received the specific approval of the commissioners. There was an effort to combine the two conflicting views; and this time Locke had to give way. He had a check survey made in 1842 of Bintley's general route from Lancaster to Kendal, then on via Larmer's route through Grayrigg, confirming Oxenholme as the nearest practicable point to Kendal. This satisfied the Kendal people for the moment, and they gave their full support. But plans are in existence of still a further survey under Locke in 1842 to try and get a Lune valley line. From Tebay, however, Locke moved once again westward from the Orton line to Shap, proposing this time a tunnel of 850 yards, and with no gradient on Grayrigg or Shap steeper than about 1 in 100, contrasted with the 1 in 140/147 of the Lune–Orton route.

Nevertheless, promises of subscriptions from the districts concerned were not encouraging, and did not come near what the southern railways had suggested would be necessary if they themselves were to be substantial subscribers, and things dragged on through 1842. At this time the project was still being called loosely the Caledonian railway, section 1. In the same year the West Cumberland group resuscitated their ideas and had a fresh survey made, this time beginning at Carnforth so that the crossing of Morecambe Bay would be reduced to quite manageable proportions; Milnthorpe also was considered as a point of junction. This and the energy displayed on the eastern side of the country, made a composition of the differences on the western side, and a resurgence of energy, even more desirable.

Yet even as far on as March 1, 1843, at a meeting held at Liverpool of the district committees and the representatives of the railways which were interested in the matter, the conclusion was that as the district subscriptions had still not reached the stipulated amount, and as Lord Lonsdale had objected to some of the plans, further proceedings should be deferred and the district committees urged to continue their work in trying to get subscriptions.

This last work continued, even though there had to be some house-to-house canvassing in Carlisle. Eventually, at a meeting of subscribers held in Kendal on November 6, 1843, it was announced that the necessary amount from the districts had now been obtained, and a company could be promoted, as there was no doubt that the Southern railways would be ready with their subscriptions when they had summoned their respective proprietors. The objections of Lord Lonsdale had been overcome, and that nobleman himself had become a subscriber. Mr. Locke's attention had been drawn to an amended survey; and that engineer had at length found that a tunnel at Shap summit could be avoided and the earthworks materially lessened, though no one stressed that this would involve four miles at 1 in 75. Probably Locke came back to Shap and accepted the 1 in 75 without tunnel because of the G.J.R. policy of economy as outlined by Huish at Carlisle; and also to help speedy construction. From the passing of the Act the L. & C. directors were in haste, and this must have shown itself well before. It was at this time, too, that the Thrimby Grange route from Shap to Clifton was adopted. By having only a single track for the present, Locke gave his deliberate opinion that a capital of £800,000 would be sufficient for the Lancaster to Carlisle line, and would include the cost of enough land for a double track. His estimate for the Lune valley/Lowther valley route, including a tunnel at Shap, had been £1,107,000 double track.

Resolutions at this Kendal meeting were: (1) that a company be formed for a line from Lancaster to Carlisle via Kendal, Shap and Penrith: (2) that nine provisional directors be elected; (3) that the capital be £800,000 in £50 shares; (4) that Joseph Locke be appointed engineer-in-chief and Messrs. Clay & Swift the solicitors; (5) that thanks be given to Col. Graham and Cornelius Nicholson for their services in promoting the railway; and (6) that the committees at Kendal, Penrith and Carlisle continue their work in getting subscriptions. The nine directors elected comprised three each from the three towns just mentioned.

By December 1843 the London & Birmingham Railway had written confirming its offer of £100,000; the G.J.R. had verified a subscription of £250,000 (i.e. £50,000 more than the original intention); and the N.U. and L. & P. had each agreed to take £65,000. A subscription had been hoped from the L. & M., but there was no communication from that railway, though later it subscribed for £20,000. The prospectus was drawn up at the December meeting, and on it Locke and Errington are given as the engineers. The line was not merely to connect England and Scotland, but was also to bring the English Lake District within a few hours' ride of London.

An interesting light was shed by the prospectus on the traffic and methods of travel at that time to the north-west and the north. The traffic prospects were enough to suggest a return of 7 per cent on the capital, without taking account of any draw there might be from the 60,000 and more travellers who annually passed by steam boat between Liverpool and Glasgow and other ports of the south-west of Scotland. Huish had stated at the end of 1841 that the existing Anglo-Scottish traffic by sea on both coasts (east and west) could be valued at £3,000 to £4,000 a week. Around 1835–40 there were two steamship companies each giving six sailings a month in each direction between the Mersey and Whitehaven, Port Carlisle and Annan, and some ships called at Dumfries. The ships were of 350–400 tons and 180 h.p. Other vessels maintained a Liverpool–Clyde service, and still others went to Kirkcudbright and Garlieston. Fares from Liverpool to Port Carlisle or Annan were 15s. cabin and 5s. deck. From the end of 1846, when the railway was opened to Carlisle, sweeping fare reductions were made; cabin travel came down to 8s. and deck to 3s., and with a bigger and faster ship, *Royal Victoria*, of 450 tons, 200 h.p., copper-bottomed and copper-fastened.

In connection with the Solway Firth ships there was a "swift iron boat, the *Arrow*", plying on the canal between Port Carlisle and Carlisle from

1835 onwards. It was brought by teams of horses over the roads from Clydeside by the grandfather of Robert M. Thomson, the last secretary to the Carlisle Station Joint Committee. In contrast to the inner ship services, the Fleetwood–Ardrossan fares were not reduced with the coming of the railway, except for a slight reduction in second class and deck in 1847, when there were four sailings a week in each direction compared with the three in 1841.

In January 1844 a meeting was held in Liverpool with directors of the G.J.R., including Moss, Grant, Hodgson, Bold and J. Cropper, who had been co-opted on to the provisional board of the provisional L. & C. company. Cornelius Nicholson was the only representative of the district subscribers; otherwise it was a 'Grand Junction' meeting, with Capt. Huish in attendance. Here it was decided that £900,000 would be a better amount for the capital to be raised, and that was the figure put into the Bill, though different from the figure in the prospectus. The contribution of the railways, however, remained at £480,000. With the consent of the G.J.R., Huish was to act as the treasurer of the L. & C. until the Act was obtained; and he was also instructed to get rail prices at once.

Strenuous efforts were made to get the Bill prepared and presented within that session, and several of the district directors spent most of March and April 1844 in London forwarding the Bill. During this period Lord Lonsdale asked to be allowed to appoint one director to the board, to be one of the Lowther family or one of the M.P.s for Cumberland or Westmorland. This was agreed, and a clause was written into the Bill with the qualification "as long as the Lord Lonsdale for the time being holds £1,000 in shares." Lonsdale himself piloted the Bill through the House of Lords. He was William, the 3rd Earl, who, as Lord Lowther and then as Earl of Lonsdale, was Postmaster-General in Peel's Government, though not in the cabinet. He succeeded to the Lonsdale title early in 1844, and was not the Earl who had objected to some of Locke's plans a year before. Disraeli gave a pleasant picture of him as Eskdale in *Coningsby*.

After years of frustration the provisional board of the L. & C. not only showed concentration in getting the Act but made the most determined efforts to ensure construction of the line as early as possible, beginning this latter work some months before the Act was obtained. So keen were the directors, and so certain were they of obtaining the Act with little opposition, that at the end of January 1844, after Huish's price enquiries, they placed an order for 8,500 tons of rails at £5 a ton and for 2,000 tons of chairs at £4 5s. a ton. Moreover, they also invited bids for the construction of the whole line; and to assist in getting the Bill through with the least opposition, they authorised a construction contract to be signed just before the Bill went to Committee, with an over-riding clause that the contract was conditional on the Act being obtained.

Apparently the initial bids of John Stephenson and Messrs. Mackenzie & Brassey were nearly the same. With a view to getting the combined resources of those two contractors, so that the work could be done quickly and with certainty, the directors in London told those two firms on

March 7 that they were ready to contract for the whole works with one of three parties—bids to be in by March 10! The two combined at once, and on March 10 the directors resolved: "That the following tender for the whole of the works by Messrs. Brassey & Mackenzie and John Stephenson jointly for £591,605 should be accepted." Time of completion was to be within two years of the contractors being put in possession of the necessary land. All three contractors signed the offer; and an interesting condition made by them was that the terms and stipulations of the formal contract, to be drawn up and signed later, were to be in conformity with those of the Penkridge viaduct contract on the G.J.R. This had been Brassey's first contract, and the one which brought him into contact with Locke. John Stephenson also was known to Locke, for he had undertaken the Basford and Moore contracts on the G.J.R.

By May 24 the Bill had passed both Houses despite an idiotic opposition by Lord Brougham in the Lords about some gates on the line. On June 6, 1844, the Royal Assent was given to the Act, 7 & 8 Vict., cap. 37, a monumental Act with 381 clauses. Cornelia Nicholson in her book on the life of her father says: "Fortunately the Bill was not opposed in Parliament, else it must have been thrown out on Standing Orders, for so hastily were the plans prepared that one part of them was prepared from the county map." It is difficult to believe this garbled statement *in toto*. Whether opposed or not, the Bill had first to comply with Standing Orders. The whole ground had been surveyed several times; and the prospectus stated; "The intervening time since the Commissioners' report has been devoted by the engineers to a thorough survey and minute examination of the country." That was hardly a 'prospectorial' exaggeration. Another independent source dating from 1846 stated that during 1842 a Parliamentary survey of the whole line between Lancaster and Glasgow had been vigorously prosecuted by Locke and Errington; and full plans and land schedules of the 1842 and 1843 Lancaster–Carlisle surveys are still in existence today. Locke certainly would be too busy in France and elsewhere in 1842–43 to have given much time to these things personally; but Errington was well engaged, though perhaps at this time as much or more attention was paid to the surveys north of the Sark. Possibly it was some entries in the land schedule of the Parliamentary route which gave rise to Cornelia Nicholson's remark, for in the middle of March 1844 the provisional directors were urging Locke to proceed with setting out the line and preparing the landowners' plans, though there could not have been any serious errors by that time.

After the Act was obtained the first general meeting was held at Kendal on June 28. The Act stipulated 16 directors, seven of whom were to be appointed by ordinary shareholders, one by Lord Lonsdale, and eight by the four contributing railways. At this meeting the ordinary directors elected were: E. W. Hasell, Henry Howard (of Greystoke), John Wakefield, Cornelius Nicholson, H. D. Maclean, George Head Head, and John Dixon. Of these, the first two represented the Penrith area, the next two the Kendal district, and the last three the Carlisle area. Hasell was elected chairman at the ensuing board meeting. An unusual provision of the Act was that all seven of the directors elected by ordinary shareholders had to live within 20 miles of the L. & C. line; this was repealed unobtrusively by a small clause in the Lancaster deviation Act of 1845.

Directors appointed by the four shareholding railways did not necessarily have to own L. & C. shares themselves, as they were simply nominees of the shareholders. Each of the four companies could appoint one director in respect of each 1,000 shares (full £50 shares) it held; from July 1846 this was simplified in practice in that the G.J.R., L. & B. and N.U. were for all practical purposes the L.N.W.R., which company then appointed seven directors and the L. & P. one. These directors were appointed for a term of four years, but could be re-nominated. The L. & C. Act of Incorporation enforced the promised subscriptions of the four railways to the south, and gave them power to raise new capital to the amount of their L. & C. holding.

During the 15 years' independent working existence of the L. & C. the board had to suffer only one open *contretemps*, though there were internal dissensions from time to time. Dividends continued to rise until the beginning of 1855, when, due to the depression in general trade, the Crimean war, and a slight decrease in the Anglo-Scottish traffic, there was a fall in receipts and a small drop in the dividend rate. Seizing on this as an excuse, disturbed at what was said to be frequent L.N.W.R. domination, and angry that the board would not sanction or forward an amalgamation with or lease of the Little North Western Railway, a section of the shareholders led by John Barker, of Milnthorpe, made sweeping charges of defective management causing drooping dividends. Instead of moving for the adoption of the statement and accounts at the half-yearly meeting in September 1855, the board adjourned the meeting and asked for a committee of enquiry. This was, perhaps, the only case of such charges being made against a board that had been paying 8/8¼ per cent and had dropped only to 7¼ per cent, all paid out of revenue.

The tone of the letters from Barker to the chairman and directors over the preceding six months had been such as to hinder any board negotiating with even a semblance of cordiality, and the shareholders supporting Barker do not all seem to have been original holders from the district, but rather those associated with the L. & P. and pure investment. The committee appointed included James Nasmyth of steam-hammer fame, but he refused to act. Though nothing wrong was found, the committee had to justify its appointment, and made recommendations on anomalies in through bookings, development of Lake District traffic in conjunction with the Kendal & Windermere Railway, and a reduction in the number of L.N.W.R. nominees as that company now held only £350,000 of shares.

The report commended certain actions. For example, the L. & C., out of courtesy, had been sending copies of board minutes to the L.N.W.R., but had ceased this practice when controversy arose in regard to Preston station; also, in that controversy, the board had not employed its own solicitor, Swift, who was also solicitor to the L.N.W.R. The committee took what opportunities it could of condemning the L.N.W.R., in particular for sending shipments of cotton from Liverpool to the Continent via Sheffield and east coast ports instead of by L. & C. to the port of Leith as formerly; but it was on firmer ground when it drew attention to the L.N.W.R.'s seven-year agreement with the East Lancashire Railway, by which, for a payment of £3,000 a year, the E.L. undertook not to take Liverpool–Scottish traffic direct to Preston, leaving the L.N.W.R. to route it via Parkside and charge the rate for 38 miles for it, whereas prior to the agreement the L.N.W.R. had cut the rate to the equivalent of 28 miles. This was not to the advantage of the L. & C. as it tended to reduce the total traffic over that line; and half of the seven-year period was still to run.

The committee of inquiry did not think the locomotive power contract came within its province. Also it stated that as a majority of shareholders had voted at the general meeting against the absorption of the Little North Western that subject was not one for the committee. Comment was made on the forthcoming 14-year Anglo-Scottish traffic agreement; and although the L. & C. directors had expressed some dissatisfaction about it, the committee thought it was probably advisable to avoid useless competition.

Another cause of dispute at the half-yearly meeting in September 1855 was that the L.N.W.R. nominees had voted by proxy in favour of the re-election of the retiring shareholders' directors, G. H. Head and W. N. Hodgson. At the adjourned meeting in November they did not do this. Joseph Langton, an L.N.W.R. nominee, had died, and another, Wm. Rotherham, retired; in their place the L.N.W.R. nominated Head and Hodgson, and the first action of these two on formal election was to propose and second Wm. Birley and John Coulston, both of the Lancaster area, as directors, thus satisfying the Barker party. Coulston was connected with the Lancaster Banking Co. As thus constituted, the board existed until the leasing of the L. & C. to the L.N.W.R. in 1859. The L. & C. then became a holding company; the number of L.N.W.R. nominees was reduced from seven to five and that of the L. & C. increased by two. Thereupon Head and Hodgson were re-elected directors by the L. & C. ordinary shareholders. After the lease took effect, two L. & C. directors were elected to the L.N.W.R. board.

The Barker party and other shareholders at various times did not look kindly at L.N.W.R. influence, and thought the board should act with more independence. They forgot the origin of the line; as did *The Railway Times* when it inveighed on March 5, 1853, against "this valuable, prosperous but not overwell managed company (which) owes not a little of its disquietude to the constitution of the board." On the other hand, an independent shareholders' guide of 1853 stated the L. & C. "had the advantage of good management from the outset." The L. & C. only became possible when the three companies which later became the main constituents of the L.N.W.R. subscribed £415,000; and by the middle of 1848 the L.N.W.R. holding was valued at £454,373. Complaints by certain shareholders that the L.N.W.R. nominees did not even hold shares themselves were irrelevant; the Act of Incorporation stated they did not need to be shareholders. In fact, a common denominator of practically all the objectors over the years was their omission to study and appreciate the Acts by which the L. & C. was regulated.

It was hardly possible for the L. & C. not to be influenced strongly by the L.N.W.R. Their interests at first had been largely the same; but from 1847 the L.N.W.R. had quickly spread in all directions, and the L. & C. became of less proportionate importance, even though it was the key to the Anglo-Scottish route. The wonder is that the local members of the board were able to ensure as much independence as they did, for only if the Lonsdale representative and the two L. & P. nominees supported the local members could the L.N.W.R. nominees be withstood; even then the L.N.W.R. had other means at its disposal.

Apart from such things as the East Lancashire agreement, it was mainly in connection with the Ingleton branch that true L. & C. interests were made subservient to those of the L.N.W.R. A branch built by the Little North Western would have brought more traffic on to the line without any noticeable diminution of that handed over at Preston. Unfortunately, the Little North Western, already being worked by the Midland, made concurrent mistakes that roused the ire of the L. & C. board; and the absorption, or lease, of the Little North Western, insisted on so tactlessly by Barker and his supporters, was not a solution. It would have been best for the L. & C. to let the Little North Western build its Ingleton-Low Gill line without opposition, and take all the traffic it could get; but the fingers of the Midland and the Great Northern in the Little North Western pie of the day were not acceptable at Euston.

The other aspect in which the L.N.W.R. did not play square with the L. & C. was in relation to the proposals in 1854/55 to rebuild Preston station completely. The L.N.W.R. and L.Y.R., as joint lessees of the N.U., promoted a Bill for this, but did not invite the L. & C. to participate, and even sought power to take compulsorily some L. & C. ground at Preston. The L. & C. paid a big rent for its use of Preston station, even though the accommodation there was becoming archaic, and thought in the circumstances it should have been invited to be a joint owner of any new station. It petitioned against the Bill, which was defeated largely by opposition from the East Lancashire Railway.

The Barker party did not handle its case very well in 1855; and on almost the major point it brought forward, that of the Little North Western absorption, no normal shareholder was able to see any sense in his company, paying 7 to over 8 per cent dividend, becoming responsible for a company that could scarcely afford 1 to 2½ per cent and which by 1855 had no reasonable potentialities. Such a shareholder had difficulty in relating this situation, and the probability of litigation with the Midland if the Little North Western was absorbed, to Barker's statement that by this means the L. & C. would be brought into a safe and independent position.

Of the personalities mentioned above, George Head had been connected with the L. & C. from the days of the provisional committee. He had, indeed, advanced much of the early legal expense out of his own pocket. In business he had his own banking firm, and carried the L. & C.

account from the beginning. After the take-over of the L. & P. there was a move to have some of the L. & C. account given to a Lancaster bank, but this was not effected until the beginning of 1853. The reason why part of the account was then transferred to the Lancaster Banking Co. was the realisation that Head had no partner in the banking business, and that under certain circumstances the L. & C. funds thereby could be temporarily locked up. Head merged his business with a joint stock bank in 1865, and thereafter the L. & C. account, much smaller than when the company was an operator, was given entirely to the Lancaster Banking Co.

The 1855 general meeting, when the committee of enquiry was set up, enabled the directors to enunciate the policy they had followed deliberately from the beginning, and intended to follow as long as they constituted the board. As the three items of their policy were those which led directly to the financial success and stability of the L. & C., they may well be enumerated: (1) to confine their attention as much as possible to the management and conduct of their own line; (2) to keep clear of leases, extensions, branches, amalgamations and extraneous agreements; (3) to keep down capital expenditure. Differences on the last two points caused the collision with the Barker party; but apart from the Little North Western question many shareholders thought the annual payments to the L.N.W.R. for locomotive power and rolling stock were excessive, and would have preferred greater capital expenditure and a saving in operating costs. By 1859, when the L.N.W.R. lease came into effect, the L. & C. capital invested in locomotives was over £136,000, and interest on this amount at 5 per cent would have been nearly £7,000, while depreciation would have been more.

A remarkable contributory cause to the loss in passenger receipts at the end of 1854 and in 1855 was the intensification of the quarrel between those two uneasy bedfellows the Caley and the Edinburgh & Glasgow, which resulted in a certain amount of traffic being diverted from the West Coast route to the East Coast, though, because of the 'octuple' agreement and a second supplementary agreement, it was only traffic to certain stations that could influence the financial results, and not the London traffic. Falling off in goods traffic on to the L. & C. from the Birmingham area, due to the activity of the Midland, also was noticed in 1853, and for a time no through wagons came in at all, the Midland sending sundry Scottish traffic through York; and Huish (L.N.W.R.) and Chapman (N.U. section) had to be urged to reduce the Preston terminal charges to try and counteract this drop.

Another serious temporary loss to L. & C. revenue was due to the G.P.O. On differences arising as to the scale of charges, after the L. & C. had applied for £17,000 a year for four or five years for the mail contract, and on terms similar to those in force on the L.N.W.R., the P.M.G. simply withheld all payments, though the mails continued to be carried daily. Eventually, Moffatt, M.P., acting as arbitrator, very tardily made an award of 2s. a mile, a rate which brought in £5,000 a year less than the L. & C. had been budgeting. Not until the summer of 1855, when he was over 2½ years in arrears, did the P.M.G. pay £25,000 on account to the L. & C., and that was by no means all that was owing.

Though the directors desired to keep clear of all extraneous agreements, their associations with the L.N.W.R. did not enable them to do this entirely. Through those relations, and the friendly feelings towards the Caley, the L. & C. became enmeshed in a curious situation involving a railway whose nearest point was over a hundred miles away. After the disappearance of George Hudson from the railway scene some of his mania for amalgamation and control seems to have been acquired by the powerful board of the L.N.W.R., backed, or egged on, by Huish; but with the difference that the moves were considered to be defensive, to make sure no one took away what the L.N.W.R. had, or what it thought it was likely to get in future, whereas Hudson's moves were often aggressive. In a sense, Hudson set out to make an empire, the L.N.W.R. a closed ring.

On various occasions the L.N.W.R. paid large sums, or entered into heavy commitments, for lines which were supposed to have a strategic value, but which financially could never pay the commitment. In this way the L.N.W.R. really became over-capitalised and financially overloaded, though for many years it paid a good dividend. One of these moves, originating this time with the Caley, was for the L.N.W.R., L. & C. and Caley to take a joint lease of the Scottish Central Railway at a guaranteed dividend of 7 per cent on the then capital of £1,020,000. Agreements on this basis had been made between the boards first of all towards the end of 1846, and with revisions over the next two years. In 1848, when the S.C. had 45 miles of line open (from Greenhill and Falkirk to Perth), the terms of the proposed Bill to ratify these agreements came before general meetings of the three 'West Coast' companies for approval; and the interest of L. & C. shareholders was such that at the special meeting on April 28, 1848, only one shareholder turned up in addition to the chairman, though 20 others were represented by proxies; that is, the quorum was only just obtained.

The Bill to authorise the agreements failed to pass Parliament, partly owing to opposition by the Edinburgh & Glasgow Railway, which already had offered 9 per cent to the S.C. for a lease. Subsequently further terms were offered with the E. & G. included in the leasing combination, but there was a misunderstanding with that company which created a complete rupture. In any case, the fresh terms did not actually guarantee 7 per cent unless it was earned out of revenue. Litigation began; suits were promoted in the Scottish courts, and the judges decided the agreements were *ultra vires* of the contracting parties. The S.C. board appealed against this decision; and the matter was not settled until 1853, when the three 'leasing' companies agreed to pay the S.C. £9,000.

The L. & C. had for some years built up a fund to cover any legal decision against it; and as its share of the £9,000 was much less than the amount then standing in the fund, the surplus of around £7,000 was very welcome towards the cost of relaying the line with heavier rails. There were still some S.C. costs to settle between the Caley and the L. & C., and by common consent Locke was appointed arbitrator to judge the respective amounts; but on the day appointed for the hearing the Caley did not appear. The L. & C. board quickly learned its lesson from this S.C. business. The L.N.W.R. had come to a tentative arrangement in August 1848 to work the Aberdeen railway also, and offered the L. & C. an equal participation in the management; but the L. & C. had already become suspicious of the wisdom of the S.C. lease, and declined this further offer.

Though a large amount of L. & C. capital was held by the more southerly railways, the company itself also invested in the stocks of other lines. At the time the S.C. manoeuvres were in an early stage, two of the L.N.W.R. nominees on the board, Rotherham and Grant, were given authority to purchase in the company's name any number of shares in the S.C. not exceeding 1,500 at a price not to exceed £8 premium, and on the understanding that another 1,500 would be taken up by some friendly interest.

Within a month of getting their Act of Incorporation, the directors of the Caley, who seemed to spend much time in the clouds on financial matters, were inviting the L. & C.'s co-operation in the promotion of the British & Irish Union Railway. The substance of the reply was: 'of greatest interest—but no money'; a not unnatural reply when the first income from L. & C. lines was still 13 months in the future. Little matters of this kind did not trouble the original directors of the Caley, though their own line was two years away from earning its first revenue. Incidentally, the G.J.R. subscribed £100,000 to the Caley, and in 1852 the L.N.W.R. had £143,784 invested in the Caley, and though it received £2,360 from that holding in 1852, it made a loss of £2,669 after the interest payment on the loan had been met.

When the B. & I.U. *was* formed a dozen years later, the L. & C. became a subscriber for £40,000, and later engaged to increase its holding by another £60,000, but had not done so by the time it was leased to the L.N.W.R. No part of the Portpatrick, under which title the B. & I.U. became better known, was opened before this lease of the L. & C. to the L.N.W.R. There was then some friction about the L. & C. holding, and the transfer to the L.N.W.R. of the L. & C.'s right to nominate two Portpatrick directors. The first part of the question had been settled on paper in 1860; but the L. & C. had to complain often during the years of the lease that it was not being credited with the amount paid on account of the Portpatrick shares, though the L.N.W.R. was appointing the two directors. The second question was handled tactfully by appointing to the Portpatrick board two of the old L. & C. directors, Col. Maclean and W. N. Hodgson, both of whom had joined the L.N.W.R. board.

In 1864 the Caley arranged to work the Portpatrick, though the two systems were physically separated, and purchased that line's rolling stock and plant; but on January 31, 1867, the Caley and L.N.W.R. came to an agreement that the Caley should work the line for the benefit of both of them, in the proportions of two-thirds Caley and one-third L.N.W.R. either way. All traffic off the Portpatrick to places served by the L.N.W.R. was to go by that railway; all traffic off the L.N.W.R. to

Plate XXIa Low Gill station looking north in 1898; main line on left; at the low-level platform a Webb 0-6-0 engine is about to leave with the Ingleton branch freight

Plate XXIb Errington's last major work, Low Gill viaduct on the now disused Ingleton branch of the Lancaster & Carlisle Railway, completed in 1861

Plate XXIc Rebuilt Newton-class 2-4-0 on a Workington-Leeds train at Ingleton; locomotive No 1480 [LGRP

Plate XXIIa Eden Valley Junction old signalbox built in 1863 when the Eden Valley Railway made its northward projection *LGRP*

Plate XXIIb Shap cutting looking north towards the summit, 1898

Plate XXIIIa Precedent class 2-4-0 No. 1531 *Cromwell* piloting a Whale Experiment 4-6-0 No. 261 on southbound express about to leave Carlisle [*H. Gordon Tidey (RPC)*

Plate XXIIIb Precedent 2-4-0 No. 919 *Nasmyth* on an up goods between Preston and Farington [*LGRP*

Plate XXIVa Sham Gothic fireplace in the refreshment room at Carlisle Citadel (1858)
[*R. Tassell*

Plate XXIVb Exterior of Carlisle Citadel showing the plaques of the Lancaster & Carlisle Railway (left) and Caledonian (right); the two blank plaques were intended for the Maryport & Carlisle and the Newcastle & Carlisle Railways, but as they declined to contribute to the construction costs the plaques were not completed with the coats of arms [*BR, LMR*

the Port line was to be sent via the Caley. This meant taking it round over the Caley to Lockerbie and on to Dumfries by the Dumfries, Lochmaben & Lockerby Jct. Railway instead of direct from Gretna to Dumfries over the G. & S.W.R. But the once independent Castle Douglas & Dumfries Railway had been absorbed into the G. & S.W.R. by Act 28 & 29 Vict., cap. 298, of July 5, 1865; to lock up the jigsaw the Lochmaben railway was absorbed by the Caley the same day (cap. 297). This agreement of 1867 also gave the L.N.W.R. running powers over the Caley to Dumfries, and "as far as the Caledonian can grant over the intervening lines" to enable the L.N.W.R. to reach Portpatrick. It is doubtful whether the L.N.W.R. ever used these running powers; but it did send a Ramsbottom DX 0–6–0 for trial on the Port line, and subsequently sold one to the Portpatrick Railway.

The L. & C. also agreed to subscribe for £10,000 worth of shares in the South Durham & Lancashire Union Railway, which was to join the main line at Tebay; but it had not actually paid the money by the time the L.N.W.R. took over. The S.D. & L.U. was not opened until after the L. & C. had ceased to be an operator; it was that cross-country mineral railway, largely an offshoot of the Stockton & Darlington Railway, built to encourage an extensive coke, coal and mineral traffic between Cleveland and Furness, and it became one of the best-known scenic lines in England. Several of the Kendal families such as the Wakefields, Whitwells and Wilsons who had subscribed to the L. & C. and Kendal & Windermere (K. & W.) also helped to finance the S.D. & L.U., and the first chairman, John Wakefield, had been the first deputy-chairman of the L. & C. Like many of the Stockton & Darlington directors, these families were members of the Society of Friends; one of the Pease family also was on the board of the S.D. & L.U. In a sense this line did not do all that was hoped, though eventually the one-way anticipated traffic did get some reverse flow. The idea had been to get Durham coke over to the high-grade haematite ores in Furness; but while this coke cost 9s. a ton at the kilns, by the time it got to Barrow the transport charges had brought the price up to 18s. a ton, and so Barrow iron was no cheaper than Cleveland iron, which came from ore with only half the iron content of the Furness haematite.

By Act 22 and 23 Vict., cap. 124, of August 13, 1859, all the L. & C. Acts were consolidated; and the lease of the K. & W., and full amalgamation of the L. & P. with the L. & C., were finally and fully authorised. Within the next month the L. & C., including the properties which had belonged to these two other lines, was leased for 900 years to the L.N.W.R. as from August 1, 1859. Thus the L. & C. came to an end as an active operator. This lease did not require a further Act; the L. & C. Act of Incorporation itself gave power to the company to lease its property to any one of the four southern companies or to any combination of them, as long as two-thirds of the votes in each company concerned were cast; and the L. & C. Act also gave those companies power to take a lease, so they, also, did not need to take any Parliamentary action.

Naturally there was initial opposition to the lease, from both L. & C.

shareholders and from outside. Herapath considered it was just a revival of the L.N.W.R. old ruinous path of leases and extensions just as that company was beginning to recover from them. Hasell himself, while recommending the lease, said all his private feelings were against parting with the independence of the line. The reason why the recommendation was made, said Hasell, was that in view of the very large amalgamations, leases and so on by great companies on all sides, those L. & C. directors who were not nominated by the L.N.W.R. could no longer visualise permanent independence; later they might have to take worse terms from elsewhere. This view, expressed at the half-yearly meeting on September 10, 1859, was echoed at the L. & P. meeting the same day by Wm. Jackson, who said that some years earlier he had been the L. & P. representative at meetings in connection with the 'octuple' agreement, and from then on he had realised that the smaller railways were entirely at the mercy of the big companies.

As not unusual in such take-over bids, the thing was sprung upon the smaller party at short notice, though there must have been rumblings at director level. Hasell said the L.N.W.R. offer had come unexpectedly; so unexpectedly that the half-yearly meeting had already been convened for Birthwaite (Windermere) and the venue changed at the last minute to Lancaster, which the directors thought would be more suitable in view of the importance of this extra question now to be discussed. Two shareholders considered the meeting at Lancaster should be declared illegal; but Swift, the veteran and able solicitor, who had been solicitor to the G.J.R. and was then solicitor to both L.N.W.R. and L. & C., said it was not illegal, but that any shareholder could forthwith move the adjournment to Birthwaite. No shareholder did. As far as the L.N.W.R. was concerned, the chairman, the Marquis of Chandos, said they thought it would be well for them to be placed in a position of certainty and prevent some future competition at ruinous rates. Perhaps he feared a Midland take-over bid for the L. & C. Chandos also reminded his shareholders that as inheritors of the G.J.R. they had power to lease the L. & C.

Though the lease was agreed on September 10, the terms were not finally settled and a formal indenture made until December 22, 1859. The L.N.W.R. was in no hurry to look after everything, and for some months the L. & C. board took decisions and sent to Euston anything which it thought needed ratification. Then an L. & C. local committee of the L.N.W.R. took over, and dealt with all non-policy matters such as operating, signalling, goods and passenger traffic equipment, and discipline, giving six months' notice to Hinde the chimney sweep, and instant dismissal to John Longrigg, pointsman, found asleep on duty at Engine Junction, Carlisle. This committee lasted until 1879.

The lease gave the L.N.W.R. the use of the L. & C. property, to be restored at the end of the lease or sold. It did not of itself make the L.N.W.R. the owner of the physical property; and in June 1860 the L. & C. agreed that its plant and physical assets should be sold to the larger company at a price, based on values as they were at August 1, 1859, to be settled by C. E. Stewart, the L.N.W.R. secretary, and S. E. Bolden, the L. & C.

manager and secretary. Despite his name, Charles Edward Stewart had come out of Cornwall, and in his earlier days he had been an opium runner on the Chinese coast. Not all L. & C. property was sold without condition. In the short time between the receipt of the L.N.W.R. leasing proposals and the half-yearly meeting in September 1859, the L. & C. board was able to grant, as from August 1, 1859, a lease of its County Hotel at Carlisle to George Head Head for 999 years at the not exorbitant rent of £60 a year. At this precise date Head was on the board only as a nominee of the L.N.W.R., and not as a director elected by the private shareholders; but he was re-elected in the latter capacity hardly six weeks afterwards.

S. E. Bolden remained secretary of the L. & C. company until 1864, when he resigned; but two months later he was appointed a director in place of Howard of Greystoke, and remained as such until the end of the company in 1879. He was also for some years deputy-chairman of the Cambrian Railway. He had been appointed secretary of the L. & C. on the incorporation of the company in June 1844, when he was secretary of the L. & P., and was permitted to hold the dual position, though he had at once to give up all connection with the Lancaster Canal Co. He retained the two positions until the middle of 1847, when the increasing friction between the L. & C. on one hand and the L. & P. and L.C.C. on the other hand, plus his own greatly increased managerial duties on the L. & C., made his connection with the L. & P. too invidious. There must have been several occasions during the two preceding years when he was writing letters of remonstrance and defence to himself in his dual capacity.

Edward Williams Hasell, elected chairman at the first board meeting of the incorporated company on June 28, 1844, remained chairman until his death at the age of 76 in the first half of 1872. In his 28 years at the head he missed only one half-yearly meeting. He seems to have been a man of great stability and urbanity. In 1865 the shareholders presented him with a silver shield depicting three major works on the L. & C., and the heads of Locke, Stephenson and Watt. He often said he was not so skilled in railway business as some of his colleagues; but, like the Earl of Burlington on the Furness Railway, he made himself so. A pleasing occurrence was the election of his son, John Edward, to the board in 1876, to succeed another old L. & C. stalwart, W. N. Hodgson, who had died. At the end of the company in 1879, only George Head Head of the original board was still a director.

Financially, the L. & C. shareholders did quite well out of the 1859 lease; so did the holders of original L. & P. stock. (See Fig. 9). Under the stipulations the L. & C. share capital was not to exceed £2,420,333 (all of which was called up) and the borrowings £440,000, making £2,860,000 in all, without permission of the L.N.W.R. These amounts included the capital of the L. & P. The authorised capital structure at the end of 1859 was as shown in Table VII; but in 1860, for purposes of selling off several sums of money borrowed, 4,560 preference shares were created; and by an Act of July 5, 1865, L. & C. shareholders could participate *pro rata*

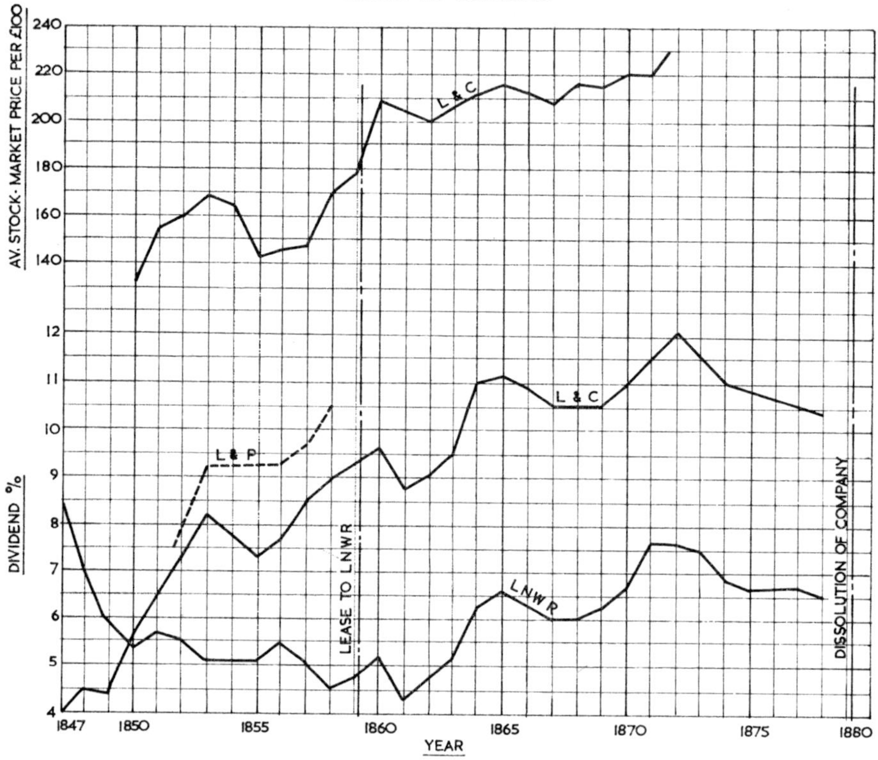

9 Financial Results, L. & C., L.N.W.R.

in any future allotment of L.N.W.R. stock. By the time the L. & C. disappeared altogether, the ordinary stock stood at the £2,420,333 plus £456,000 of 4½ per cent preference stock. Though little more than a holding company, the L. & C. did retain certain rights in some property at Carlisle, the title deeds of which it was very loathe to give up unconditionally to the L.N.W.R. Through this a certain interest in Citadel station remained, and the company was bracketed with the L.N.W.R. and the Caley in the Citadel Station Act of 1861.

Under the terms of the 1859 lease the L. & C. shareholders were in no case to receive less than 8 per cent dividend, and this rate was to be increased according to the following scale: on the L.N.W.R. paying a dividend of 4¼ per cent the L. & C. would receive 8½ per cent; when the L.N.W.R. dividend was 4½ per cent the L. & C. would get 9 per cent; at 4¾ per cent the L. & C. would get 9¼ per cent; at 5 per cent the L. & C. would get 9½ per cent; and on 6 per cent the L. & C. would receive 10½ per cent, and so on. Of course, the L.N.W.R. got some of this back by reason of its large holding of L. & C. ordinary stock.

Straight away the L. & C. began to get 9 per cent dividends; prior to 1858 those dividends had risen gradually over ten years from 4 to 8 per cent. From 1864 to 1879 the L. & C. shares received 10 to 12 per cent dividend. As a holding company paying good dividends, and with the solidity of the L.N.W.R. behind it, the L. & C. found its stocks standing high on the market, and from 1863 onwards they varied only between 205 and 240 for the equivalent of £100; up to 1858 they had stood at 140 to 180. The dividend rate and market prices over the years as shown in Fig. 9 give a good idea of the unfailing prosperity of the company, both as an operator and a holding company.

These good results did not continue to accrue to the L. & C. without determined and continuous efforts on the part of the L.N.W.R. to stop them. The Marquis of Chandos, though elected a director of the L. & C. on the lease, never attended a board meeting, and resigned in 1860. When the Richard Moon *regime*, inaugurated on the L.N.W.R. in 1861, got into its stride, the L. & C. shareholders were not long left in peace, and a remarkable suggestion was put up in September 1863 when a committee of the L. & C. directors had a meeting with Moon and three other members of the L.N.W.R. board. Moon stated that various new lines were in agitation in the interests of the Midland, and he suggested the expediency of some arrangement being made with the Midland to obviate the necessity of such lines being built. He then went on to say the L.N.W.R. would be willing to give a fixed guarantee to the L. & C. in lieu of the fluctuating dividends, and then arrange with the Midland to join such a lease; but after some discussion he proposed the L. & C. should be sold to the L.N.W.R. and Midland jointly at a fixed dividend of 9 per cent in perpetuity.

The L. & C. committee did not think its full board would entertain the offer of 9 per cent; and the board did not. It put forward 9½ per cent minimum with a graduated scale above; or, if the L.N.W.R. preferred, a flat guaranteed rate of 10 per cent. At a further meeting, Moon said he was authorised by the L.N.W.R. and Midland to offer 9½ per cent fixed dividend, and said in so many words this was their ultimatum. The L. & C. board would not agree, and simply recorded that it could not at present take further action in negotiations with the L.N.W. chairman.

This was a rebuff for Moon, and within three months he retaliated by clauses in an 'additional powers' Bill in 1864 for working arrangements with the Midland, in which the Midland would have a joint lease with the L.N.W.R. of the L. & C. These clauses were felt to be inimical to L. & C. interests, and the L. & C. board lodged a petition against them. At the next half-yearly meeting in 1864 the L.N.W.R. nominees put forward an amendment greatly to modify this petition, but they were defeated by 26 votes to 4. The L.N.W.R. withdrew the opposed clauses in 1865 and the L. & C. then withdrew the petition; but in January 1867 the L.N.W.R. tried to put back into another additional-powers Bill exactly the same clauses, and again the L. & C. petitioned. This procedure was repeated in 1868; as the proposed terms were practically to cancel the L. & C. lease and vest that company entirely in the L.N.W.R. the L. & C. again objected. In this case the L. & C. was put to some legal expense, and the board courageously told Moon and the Premier Line that if they did not foot the bill arbitration as provided by the terms of the 1859 lease would be invoked.

Table VII—Capital structure of Lancaster & Carlisle Railway after lease to L.N.W.R.

Authorised by	Stocks and Shares sanctioned	Loans sanctioned	Total
7 & 8 Vict., cap. 37, June 6, 1844[1]	£900,000[8]	£300,000; converted into shares 13/11/1845[7]	£1,200,000
9 & 10, Vict., cap. 257, July 27, 1846[2]	£100,000[6]	£433,333-6-8[10] [11]	
" "	£6,000[5]		£939,333-6-8
August 31, 1853	£400,000[9]		
20 & 21 Vict., cap. 151, August 25, 1857[3]	£300,000	£20,000	£320,000
22 & 23 Vict., cap. 124, August 13, 1859[4]	£50,000	£10,000	£60,000
" " (on L & P account)	£935,130	—	£935,130
Totals	£2,991,130	£463,333-6-8	£3,454,463-6-8

Of the above, £2,876,300 had been created in stocks and shares, plus one £1,500 loan. Subscriptions to other railways £40,875. [1] Act of Incorporation. [2] Citadel station Act [3] Ingleton branch Act. [4] Consolidation and L. & P. amalgamation Act. [5] To commute Carlisle Corporation tolls. [6] For Citadel station and approach lines. [7] By creation of 18,000 one-third shares. [8] In 18,000 shares of £50 each. [9] For capitalisation of mortgage dept by 24,000 new shares of £16-13-4. [10] Permitted under statutory powers when loan of £300,000 above was converted into one-third shares. [11] In 1860 this debt was capitalised by issue of preference shares of £100 at $4\frac{1}{2}$%.

Protests were lodged also against certain clauses in the Bill of 1873 to amalgamate the L.N.W.R. and L.Y.R., and against certain parts of the Citadel Station Bill of the same year. Four years later L. & C. opposition was raised against part of the L.N.W.R. (Joint & Various Powers) Bill; but the next year firmer discussions for the consolidation of the stock and the complete disappearance of the L. & C. as an entity took place.

As a result, in 1879 the legal existence of the L. & C. company came to an end, a full amalgamation with the L.N.W.R. being then effected under the L.N.W.R. (Additional Powers) Act, 42 & 43 Vict., cap. 142, dated July 21, after the stocks had been consolidated as from December 12, 1878. This same Act also terminated the legal existence of the Kendal & Windermere Railway, which, unlike the L. & P., had not been legally absorbed into the L. & C. in 1859.

Each holder of £100 of L. & C. 4½ per cent preference stock was then given £112½ of consolidated 4 per cent guaranteed stock of the L.N.W.R.; but the L. & C. ordinary stock, in order to secure a minimum dividend of 8 per cent, was replaced by £200 of L.N.W.R. 4 per cent guaranteed stock, plus £47½ of L.N.W.R. ordinary stock in lieu of the fluctuating dividend above 8 per cent, and to make up the £1,575 a year the L.N.W.R. had been paying for L. & C. registered office and secretary since 1859.

X

Construction of the L. & C.

WITHIN TWO months of the passing of the L. & C. Act Locke was formally appointed engineer-in-chief. He was given £1,000 for his work in preparing the contract, plans and so forth, and was to have a salary of £500 a year for the two years of the construction period. At the same time J. E. Errington was appointed engineer at £1,000 a year on the understanding that he attended a full fortnight each month. Subsequently Larmer and S. B. Worthington (an old pupil of Locke) were appointed resident engineers at £500 a year each. Larmer had the line north of Shap and Worthington the southern section. Among the assistants who laid out the line over Shap was Henry Robertson, who became a partner in Beyer, Peacock & Co. in January 1855.

Engineers and contractors wasted little time in getting to work. The first sod seems to have been cut to the north of Tebay on July 18, 1844, and 15 years later Hasell recalled he had been present. Cornelia Nicholson states her father cut the first sod—at Grayrigg. Possibly there were two first sods; such things are not unknown. This haste did not continue unbroken for long, and in early September Errington was complaining that the contractors could not get possession of the ground. In particular, the lands for Lowther viaduct and Wreay cutting were needed. In their anxiety to get going, the directors in the preceding March had asked Lord Lonsdale if they could have possession then of the ground for the viaduct, as the earth needed for Clifton embankment would have to pass over the bridge. But there was no result, perhaps because the Lonsdale succession at that time prevented the new earl, who was very favourable to the L. & C., giving the matter his attention and led him just to pass it over to his agent, who was dilatory in railway matters.

Within a month of the first sod being turned the directors took a step that in the end led to disappointment and some bad feeling. They offered to retain only 5 per cent of each month's agreed payment to the contractors on the express condition that the contractors forthwith agreed to have the line open by July 1, 1846. This offer was accepted; but that date, which corresponded approximately to the original two years from getting possession of the ground as it was hoped, could not be kept, partly through late possession of vital ground (land for Wreay cutting was not obtained until March 1845), partly through labour troubles, and partly through some bad weather causing slips. Despite the eagerness which led to this offer, the directors from time to time drew their engineers' attention to the need to prevent desecration of the Sabbath by allowing any work to be done on that day if it could possibly be avoided.

There have been repeated statements from the end of 1846 onwards that the contractors promised 18 months completion time. There is no confirmation of this in official records; and the error probably arose from a misreading of the July 1, 1846, agreement in relation to the actual date of opening the whole line.

In the construction of the line there were 72 accidents causing death, a considerable proportion of them between Oxenholme and Shap. A contemporary local account said that many were caused by the carelessness of the deceased. The average number of men employed during the whole contract was around 5,000, but at times up to 10,000 were on the pay-roll, assisted by up to 1,050 horses. One account said the navvies were better behaved than the populace had expected. In that case the populace must have expected very little, for there was constant trouble between Oxenholme and Penrith, and occasionally elsewhere. It culminated in intensity in a fracas near Penrith in which the Irish were involved, though no more to blame than others. This was in February 1846. Unluckily for the rioters the location was as close as the line went to the house of the chairman, E. W. Hasell. Being a resident magistrate, he quickly had the local yeomanry cavalry called out, and they continued on duty for about a week. In March 1846 the board authorised payments, with a rider that the company was not legally liable, to:

Mr. Galloway for soldiers	£16	6	6
Mr. Galloway for police	33	2	4
Jackson & Wickham, surgeons	5	5	0
Attendance on wounded men	3	1	0
Two men for reconnoitring	2	0	0
Other sums to total of	10	9	6

These sums paid out by the L. & C. are no true reflection of the seriousness of the riots, which drew navvies away from Shap and even Kendal to Penrith. Well over 2,000 high-tempered men seem to have been rioting and fighting around Penrith at one time. More details of this particular riot are given in Terry Coleman's book, *The Railway Navvies* (1965).

When Stephenson, Mackenzie and Brassey took on the contract for the whole line in March 1844 no other single railway contract with one firm or group had ever approached this size. When the L. & C. was finished two-and-three-quarter years later the only bigger contract placed in the meantime had also been given to the same combination, for the construction of the Caledonian Railway. When the L. & C. contract was signed the average wage of a railway labourer was still low, averaging about 2s. 6d. a day; but after the contract had been going some eight or nine months the average wage had risen to 3s. 6d. a day. This meant about £80,000 extra on the L. & C. construction, which the contractors had to make up mainly out of their own resources; and it was quite a large amount on a contract which, with all additions and extras, did not reach three-quarters of a million.

By the time the L. & C. contract was nearing its end Brassey and his partners were at their peak, and had under construction also the Caledonian (127 miles), Clydesdale Junction (15 miles), Barrhead line (30 miles), Scottish Central (50 miles), Trent Valley (50 miles), South

Midland (30 miles), Sheffield & Great Grimsby (50 miles), Oswestry & Shrewsbury (35 miles), and the Kendal & Windermere (10 miles).

Brassey and Mackenzie themselves seem to have taken no great personal part in the L. & C. work; John Stephenson was the partner who took charge, and under him was Mould as works superintendent. Mould had a journalistic type of mind; and at one of the opening banquets he recorded that in making the whole 70 miles of double-track route 4,800 barrels (or 200 tons) of gunpowder had been used for blasting; that the patent fuses used would extend for 400 miles if placed end to end; that the length of drilling into rock aggregated 200 miles; that the number of man-nights worked was 152,147 and the number of man-days over 3 million; that the temporary wheel planks used by the navvies had an end-to-end length of 35 miles; and that the number of bridges on the line was 219 and the number of culverts 230. The firm obviously kept its statistical department well up to the mark for such figures to be produced the day after opening; but in the atmosphere of conviviality and relief no one would remark on this, and Mould was loudly applauded for having departed from the back-slapping tenor of the other speeches. To assist the work, John Stephenson put up at Kendal the Lound Foundry, disposing of it in 1848 when his work in the district was finished.

There is little doubt that in the early days of promotion the district committees thought generally in terms of a double track; but in view of the difficulty in raising money, the meeting at which the company was formed decided to adopt "a single track for the present." This fitted in with the £800,000 capital then agreed; and when the capital was increased to £900,000 seven weeks later, this was not specifically to provide for double track, though the plans envisaged enough ground for two sets of rails.

Several references to the L. & C. spread over many years have stated that double track was agreed if the Caledonian Act was obtained, or was agreed after the Caledonian Act was passed, and that an increase of capital was sanctioned when doubling was undertaken. These statements are not true. Certainly the directors were keenly aware of the importance of the railway system being carried on into Scotland; and over the years the help they gave the Caley was amazingly generous and the forbearance outstanding. But the decision to put the double track in hand is recorded as early as October 4, 1844, when the directors resolved: "That viewing probable increase of traffic and the extension of the railway to Scotland . . . it is desirable that this board shall recommend to the shareholders at a special meeting to be held as early as possible, to lay down a double line of rails for the whole line or for any part that may be considered desirable."

This was nine months before the Caley Act of Incorporation (8 & 9 Vict., cap. 162, of July 31, 1845). So strongly did the L. & C. directors feel, that Errington was forthwith instructed to report at the next meeting as to the probable cost of doubling. This he did, and his estimate not being as high as the directors probably thought, and being within the company's financial resources, the board resolved at its next meeting, on November

9, 1844 "That the line be laid double from Lancaster to Carlisle . . . not doubting that the proprietors at the next meeting will approve this resolution." and "That the contractor be paid for the extra earthwork such price, not exceeding £80,000, as the engineer shall decide to be fair . . . and on the understanding that the time for completion is not extended beyond July 1, 1846." Actually when the line was opened throughout the track was still single through Wreay cutting, but the doubling of this part was completed in January 1847.

Thus the directors took time by the forelock, not waiting for Parliaments' decision on the Caley, and far anticipating the Board of Trade's power, given by the Act of Incorporation, to make the L. & C., at any time after 12 months from the public opening, lay down a second line of rails and also erect an electric telegraph along the line.

The directors were frequently about the works checking progress, riding and walking considerable distances; and as early as August 1845, after a full-scale tour, they were urging Errington to have the work speeded up so that the line could be opened by July 1, 1846. They told him of certain specific works they thought were behindhand, such as Wreay cutting, Clifton embankment, Docker Garths viaduct, the embankment near Oxenholme, and Lancaster bridge. Though the southern portion of the line was opened in September 1846, the board was disturbed that the northern section was not ready at the same time; and at the meeting in October of that year a record was made that the board "explicitly reserve their rights of penalties against the contractors, and would specially urge on the contractors the seriousness of the consequences of the delay in opening." At the same period, when Errington brought up the question of a line maintenance contract, the board intimated it "did not intend to enter into any new contract with Messrs. Stephenson whilst the present contract is in so unsatisfactory a state."

Before one judges the contractors too hardly one must appreciate the great labour difficulties they had in 1846, when the number of lines under construction was bringing a shortage of good labour. To read the accounts of 1846 is like reading the newspapers in 1968. There were repeated strikes on the L. & C. construction for higher wages and shorter hours, and these were pressed because the workers knew their employer was under bond to complete by a certain date. Eventually, to ease labour matters, the L. & C. board let it be known that it was no longer pressing for completion by a particular date. Despite some awkward late possession of land, 70 miles of double track had been completed within two-and-a-half years of the first ground being given, equal to 28 miles a year. Of the other railways on the Crewe–Carlisle route the N.U. construction progress rate was 4 miles a year, and on the L. & P., an exceptionally easy railway to make, under 5 miles a year. The L. & C. contract is a measure of the improvement made within seven or eight years in organisation, financial arrangements and technique.

Principal works on the L. & C. were the bridge over the Lune, the Docker Garths and Borrow Beck viaducts between Oxenholme and Tebay, the Lowther and Eamont viaducts further north, and the cuttings at

Shap and Wreay. The works were well and truly done. When Captain Coddington, the Government inspector, went over officially the northern section of the route from Oxenholme to Carlisle he said he had never seen handsomer or more substantial masonry on any line in the Kingdom. Looking at Docker Garths and Borrow Beck viaducts today, one can realise the pleasure they must have given Coddington more than 120 years ago when they were first built. In fact, all the works from Oxenholme to Tebay are well worth the inspection of those hundreds of railway enthusiasts who hurry north each year to Scout Green to watch a day's working up Shap, particularly as the constructional works of the M.6 motorway are making a mess of this area, even though the final result may be in harmony with this wildest and most beautiful section of the L. & C.

The original Lune bridge had seven 53-ft. stone and brick arches at the south end leading to three 120-ft. laminated timber arches over the tidal part of the river, carrying the rails 53 ft. above the water. There was a footpath to one side, a condition of the Lancaster town council's approval; a path was included in the stone-piered wrought-iron bridge that replaced the original structure in 1866; and a foot-path is found also on the present bridge erected in 1962 on the old piers, a work skilfully carried out while maintaining the full train service except at one or two critical week-ends.

The line had its own Chat Moss, a peat bog 20 ft. deep by Bolton-le-Sands, which took a good deal of filling up to make a low embankment over it. After that came the Sedgwick embankment north of the Lancaster canal, which is quarter-of-a-mile long and up to 50 ft. high. Milnthorpe station buildings for long could be recognised as those of a place more important than a wayside station such as Carnforth was at the beginning; this construction was because Milnthorpe was the old connecting point for the Ulverston and Furness coaches. It is at Milnthorpe that the ascent to Grayrigg really commences, and for 13 miles on end the line rises at 1 in 193–106, with the final two miles steadily at the steepest rate.

Near Oxenholme are big embankments and deep cuttings, of which Birkhall, where there was an excavation of around 150,000 cu. yd., was not on the original trace, but had to be made to suit the objections of E. Wakefield, brother of the L. & C.'s first vice-chairman. There have been statements that this unwanted deviation cost £3,000 extra, and they are typical of the many half-truths linked with L. & C. history. The actual facts are that after much discussion the directors, rather than go to law, instructed the engineer to modify the line at Birklands, and if necessary to spend an additional sum not exceeding £3,000 on that modification. It may well have cost less than that amount; indeed, at the half-yearly meeting in 1845 the chairman said the extra cost had been nil.

North of Benson Hall the line turns almost east, and after passing through cuttings crosses Fiddler's Gill by a viaduct, usually known as Docker Garths after an adjacent house, of six 50-ft. arches with a maximum height of 50 ft. This is some two miles short of Grayrigg summit, which is itself 26 miles north of Lancaster. The line swings round again to the north at Low Gill, where the disused viaduct of the old Ingleton branch is prominent, and runs up the Lune valley to Tebay. This four-mile section has within it Dillicar cutting, Dillicar water troughs, and the fine three-arch Borrow Beck viaduct, 65 ft. high. North of that is the embankment lying along the old bed of the Lune, the river having been diverted slightly here.

From Tebay 'Shap' is begun over the Birk Beck embankment, near where the first sod was cut. Shap cutting itself, leading to the summit, was one of the most arduous and expensive works in the whole 70 miles, for it is up to 60 ft. deep and through hard rock. Here, as early as mid-September 1844, the Vicar of Shap had to be requested to attend the magistrates for the purpose of having some special constables appointed to keep the railway labourers in order. Some 500 men were concentrated on this cutting for several months, and about 350,000 cu. yd. of earth were excavated, at least half of it being whinstone.

North of Shap the line falls continuously to Carlisle, with seven miles unbroken at 1 in 125, as shown on the gradient profile. But for southbound trains the 3¾ miles up at 1 in 131 from Carlisle to Wreay are more of a trial for the locomotives, as the start out of Carlisle has just been made when the bank is struck. Though there are one or two big embankments, such as Clifton, and cuttings like those by Shap village and at Wreay, the only substantial masonry works are the Lowther viaduct of six 60-ft. semi-circular arches carrying the rails about 100 ft. above the bed of the stream, and the adjacent Eamont viaduct of five 50-ft. arches of 70 ft. maximum height. Both of these are in the last few miles of the approach to Penrith from the south. Wreay cutting had a maximum depth of 45 ft., and 410,000 cu. yd. were excavated; because of the numerous slips this cutting was bound by timber framing.

All stations on the line except Carlisle were included in the basic contract of £591,605; and all were designed by Wm. Tite (later Sir Wm.), designer of the London Royal Exchange, but better known as the designer of many railway stations on 'Locke lines', including the original Vauxhall and Southampton stations, Carlisle, the stations generally on the Caley and the Scottish Central, and even on the Paris–Le Havre Railway. Lancaster (Castle) station was described at the time of its erection as "a beautiful building in freestone, in the Elizabethan style," but there is little of the original structure left except some buildings on the present down platform. Penrith station had some pretensions, but apart from Milnthorpe all the others were very small, and one or two quite primitive.

Only in May 1845 were the engineers asked by the board to prepare a list of all the first and second class stations they considered desirable. By the opening of the line to Carlisle those decided between the two termini were: Hest Bank, Bolton (le Sands), Carnforth, Holme, Milnthorpe, Oxenholme, Lambrigg, Loups Fell, Shap, Hackthorpe & Clifton, Penrith, Plumpton, Southwaite and Newbiggin & Wreay. The decision was not kept entirely. There was no station at Oxenholme at the beginning, only a changing point out in the open. A station was not opened to the public for booking purposes until July 1847, because the L. & C.

thought the K. & W. should provide the accommodation. Even then, buildings and shelter were not provided, and they came only after loud complaints by an L. & C. shareholder at the February 1848 meeting, and permanent buildings were not completed until 1852. Lambrigg was the original name for Low Gill; there was a station there from the start, but it was nearly three-quarters of a mile south of the Low Gill junction station that existed from 1861 to 1960; it was near the Beck Foot cross roads.

Construction of Newbiggin & Wreay was deferred, and another station three miles south of Carlisle was put in and named Brisco; but it disappeared at the end of 1852 and Wreay station was then built instead. There was no station at Grayrigg for years. It was no more than a halt location in its early days. In May 1848 it was advanced to the rank of third class station for the summer months, but even then had nothing in the way of buildings, which were not erected until 1860/61, a measure put through by the L. & C. local committee of the L.N.W.R. The name Grayrigg, of both village and station, was that of the local squire, Mr. Gray Rigge, whose legal title to certain ground needed for the railway was considered so dubious that the purchase money was paid to the Public Trustees. Nevertheless, Gray Rigge himself was a man of repute, and at a later stage the L. & C. board put him forward as a referee in some land dispute with other proprietors.

No station was actually put in at Bolton until 1850. Hest Bank many years later achieved a certain fame in being the only station between Carlisle and south of Preston to be lit by electricity, and this continued more or less to the time of the second world war, even Preston being lit by gas at that time. The reason was the independent erection of a small windmill by one of the station staff to produce a lighting current, and this mill was taken over and maintained by the staff when the erector was transferred elsewhere. It is no longer there.

Loups Fell was never anything more than a water crane and a siding and tiny engine shed for the Shap banking engine. It was about half a mile north of the present Tebay station, the embryo of which began only when some L. & C. permanent buildings were opened in 1852. Loups Fell itself is the 850-ft. hill a little to the north-west of Tebay junction; and on it was a small reservoir to give the water supply and head to the water crane. Oxenholme, too, had its engine shed before the station was built. Carnforth was a second class wayside station; its long-standing importance as a junction did not begin until the Furness group of lines reached it from the west, and the Furness–Midland joint extension from the line of the old Little North Western came in from the east.

At the half-yearly meeting in February 1847 the report stated there was every hope that the line had been built and equipped within the £1,200,000 capital, except Carlisle station, which was an extra and for which further financial powers had been obtained. The equipment included only two locomotives, but the basic construction cost may have been below the capital despite a payment of £50,000 extra to the contractors for additional work above the £591,605. By no means all the capital had been called up by the beginning of 1847, and six months later the finance committee reported simply that over half the capital had been called up, though fresh borrowing powers of £400,000 had been obtained. Actually the last call on the original £900,000 was made in November 1846, but the next £300,000 was not fully called up until 1848. When everything was settled the equipment and construction came up to the full £1,200,000, though there were only two locomotives and no carriage stock.

Although in September 1846 the board had refused to consider Errington's suggestion about maintenance of the line while the contractors were still behindhand with construction, the matter could not be delayed too long, and early in 1847 a contract was given to John Stephenson to maintain the whole L. & C. line exclusive of the L. & P. section for five years from the end of 1846 to the end of 1851 on terms reputed to be equal to £200 a mile a year. The sum was carried into the capital account and not charged to revenue. From the beginning of 1852 Worthington was deputed to take over the line maintenance on behalf of the L. & C.

Installation of the electric telegraph was sanctioned before the northern part of the line was opened, and had been extended over the whole route by the summer of 1852. It cost the company 5 guineas a mile a year. By the time the L. & C. was leased there were double-needle instruments at Preston, Broughton, Garstang, Lancaster Junction, Lancaster Castle, Carnforth, Milnthorpe, Oxenholme, Low Gill, Tebay, Shap, Penrith, Carlisle and Carlisle Loco, with bells in addition at Carnforth and Shap. There was a second double-needle instrument at Oxenholme for the K. & W. Railway, and there were K. & W. instruments at Kendal and Windermere. Electric Telegraph Co.'s clerks were in attendance from 8.0 a.m. to 8.0 p.m. at Preston, Lancaster, Oxenholme and Carlisle.

Though Locke is usually given the credit for the L. & C. line as built, and still in use today, several others made vital contributions. The whole conception was due mainly to the Grand Junction directors, and their instrument was Locke; but one must not forget Steel of Carlisle. Errington was the engineer, and there is no question he gave immense energy and thought to seeing both surveys and construction through to a successful conclusion. Very much is due to him.

In the actual course of the line, the 'west end' crossing of the Lune at Lancaster, and the westward diversion from the L. & P. line to the south, were suggested first by George Stephenson in 1837, and his trace there was followed largely by Bintley in 1837–38. It is in essence Bintley's line that is followed from Lancaster to Natland, just south of Oxenholme. From there on to near Borrow Bridge via Grayrigg it is Larmer's line; thence on through Tebay and over Shap to Penrith is pure Locke and Errington. In 1835 Locke carried his preliminary inspection on to Carlisle down the vale of the Petteril; but detail surveys were first carried out by Larmer in 1839, acting independently for the Penrith–Carlisle provisional committee, on the suggestion of Locke, who asked for someone to go over the ground and take levels before he came north to give his official opinion.

As it is today the line has some variations in gradients from the Parlia-

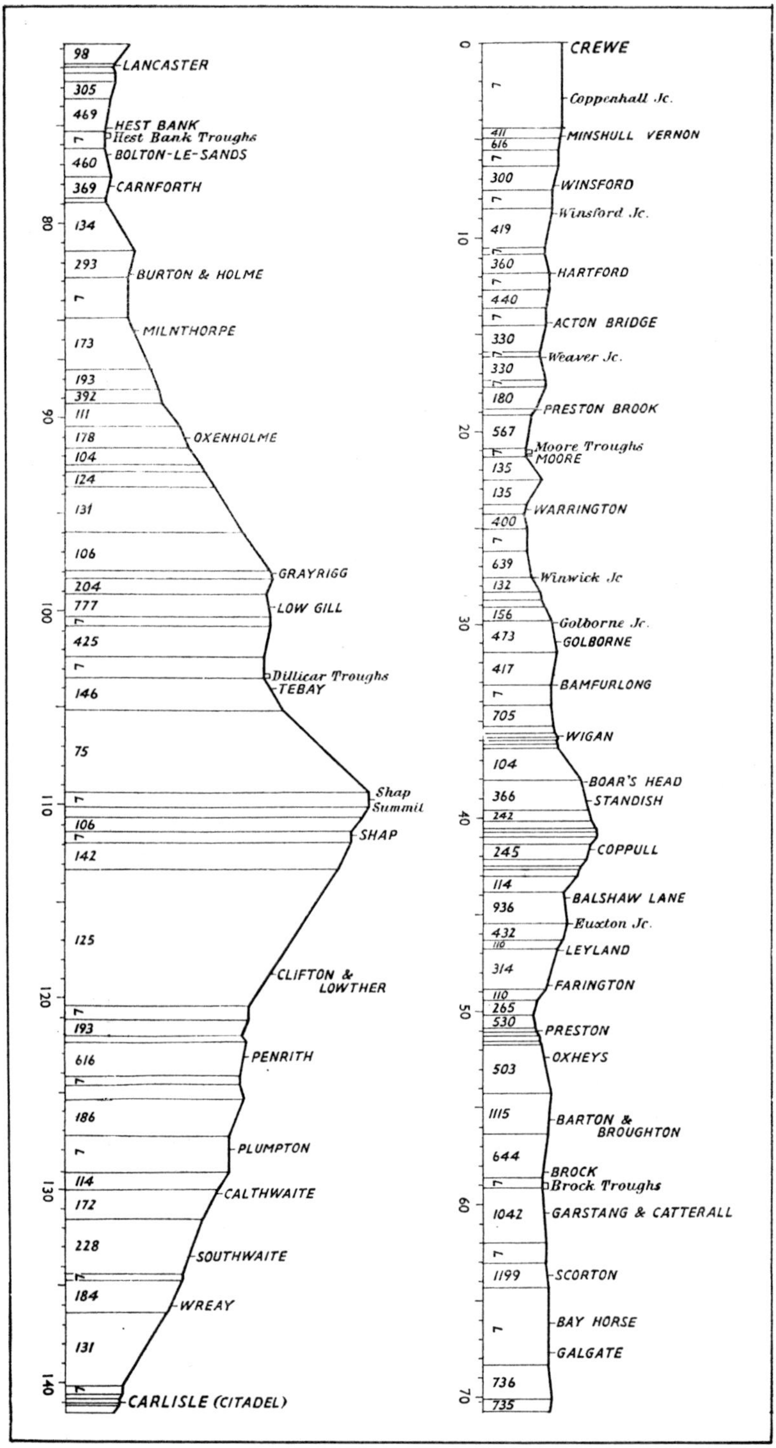

10 Gradient Profile, Crewe–Carlisle

mentary plans of Locke and Errington as drawn up and submitted at the end of 1843 and early in 1844. In particular, Grayrigg bank is steeper. Passing Oxenholme at 1 in 176, the Parliamentary line showed a full mile up at 1 in 120 followed by three-quarters of a mile at 1 in 132, then 1½ miles at 1 in 150 and 1½ miles at 1 in 110, after which there was quarter of a mile level, three-quarters of a mile down at 1 in 200, and 1¼ miles up at 1 in 660. Shap had 4¼ miles up at 1 in 75, and after Shap there was a nine-mile fall at a steady 1 in 132 through Thrimby, which may be compared with the seven miles at 1 in 125 shown on the present-day gradient profile in Fig. 10. Approaching Carlisle there was a steady fall for five miles at 1 in 140 ending exactly at the St. Nicholas crossing.

Whether Shap with its four miles of 1 in 75 was the best choice must always remain questionable. At least twice, in 1898 and in the 1930s, serious proposals were made and Parliamentary powers obtained for an 8.85-mile deviation, with a ruling gradient of 1 in 135 and including a tunnel about a mile in length. In each case the powers were allowed to lapse without more than trifling work being done. The deviation was to begin near Loups Fell and keep to the west of the existing route, going more up the line of the Birk Beck to the summit tunnel and rejoining the existing line between Shap summit and Shap station.

On the Anglo-Scottish route as a whole the south side of Beattock is a worse proposition than Shap; but to Locke's credit this was not his first choice, and he adopted it with some misgiving, and only because this one route with its steep gradient could best serve both Edinburgh and Glasgow, whereas his original 'G. & S.W.' route would have served Glasgow only. In regard to Shap one must also remember the tightness of money at the time, and the strictures of Huish in 1841. The saving of £100,000 or more compared with the alternatives, and the quicker probable time of construction, could not but tip the scales in favour of the no-tunnel 1 in 75 route.

XI

Lancaster

THE L. & C. WORKS had not gone very far, indeed only the first sod had been turned, when an important deviation was seen to be necessary. It throws a curious light on the predominance which the Lune valley route had attained in Locke's mind, and how the repeated arguments on this and the alternatives in open line had occupied the minds of all concerned almost to the exclusion of other important matters—in this case Lancaster.

At the same meeting, on August 2, 1844, that Locke and Errington were confirmed in their positions, the L. & C. board also had to consider the alteration of the line at Lancaster; and so disturbing did this seem that the directors were disposed to offer the contractors £5,000 if they would consent to the proposed deviation, pay the expenses of the necessary Act and of any claims such as might be associated with a new crossing of the Lune, and to begin putting up the new bridge at their own risk without waiting for the necessary new Act. Fortunately for themselves the contractors did not respond to this almost panic suggestion, practically the only occasion in its history when the L. & C. board was startled and disturbed, as distinct from irritated. The company had to prepare a Bill to permit of the alteration of the whole route in the Lancaster area; but opportunity was taken to include in the same Bill power for a short extension to join the Newcastle & Carlisle Railway at Carlisle, to get increased borrowing powers, and to sanction certain other details. So the rest of the year 1844 was occupied, and the Lancaster deviation Act (8 & 9 Vict., cap. 83) did not get the Royal Assent until June 21, 1845.

A principal reason given for the deviation was the receipt of a memorial signed by 228 Lancastrians asking for the line and the station to be brought nearer the easily-navigable stretch of the Lune, though this was no nearer to the centre of the town. There can be little doubt that this memorial was a blessing to Locke and Errington; and one cannot help wondering whether it was not 'engineered', for attention was drawn away from the engineers' responsibility for the unsuitability of the Parliamentary exit from Lancaster, though there were some nasty ensuing down payments.

In his Preston–Glasgow appreciation of 1835/36 Locke had by-passed Lancaster, and he had done so, as his report admitted, because of the difficulty of passing through the town and over the river except by big works and great expense. Throughout his career Locke made the greatest endeavours to avoid costly and difficult works, not just on the score of economy and maintaining the reputation the G.J.R. had given him for completing the works within the estimates, but because he saw no sense in risking his reputation as an engineer by stretching his capacities and engaging in works where there were almost bound to be unknown factors. Nor did Locke like tunnels, though he had some thrust upon him when he took over from other engineers the London & Southampton and the Sheffield–Manchester railways. There is not a single tunnel between Preston and Glasgow or Edinburgh by the West Coast Route, though one, if not two, might well have eased the line.

Lancaster was certainly a problem, though not really an onerous one even for those days; but the obvious easy continuation of the northern line up the Lune valley provided a way out of the difficulty, or rather it provided an easy way of shelving the difficulty. The ease of that passage drew Locke's attention away from a different approach to Lancaster from the south, keeping further west and at a lower level, and involving at the worst only a short tunnel, if any at all. Such a line would have been no good for a continuation up the Lune valley towards Hornby; and in his tour of 1835 Locke had not spotted the possibility of serving Kendal through Oxenholme and then going on round Grayrigg.

In a sense, Locke funked Lancaster, and seemed to continue in that way. It was probably the thought of this expensive crossing of town and river that made him return again and again to the Lune valley scheme when he was invited to try other ways; until in 1842 the Kendal interest, backed by the Government commissioners' recommendation, forced him to adopt the Carnforth–Oxenholme–Grayrigg route. As soon as it became definite that the line would go north through Carnforth, the crossing of Lancaster and the bridging of the Lune became a major problem. Bintley, writing in 1841, said that Locke even by then had stated the necessary bridge and approach embankments could not be built for less than £80,000 to £100,000. This was due to Locke having located the L. & P. terminus high up at Penny Street, because he was clinging to Lune valley and still hoped to get Lancaster on to a branch; and this despite some pretty plain speaking at the public meeting in Lancaster in 1836 in connection with the formation of the L. & P., that Lancaster was having no branch, and that the time would come when the Glasgow line would be glad to use the L. & P. Now Locke had to restart from that terminus, and it was almost equally inconvenient for going north to Hest Bank or north-east to Crook o' Lune, except that the latter route did not involve a big bridge at Lancaster.

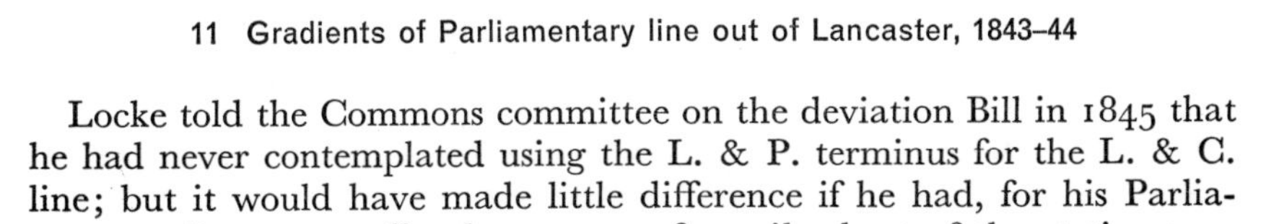

11 Gradients of Parliamentary line out of Lancaster, 1843–44

Locke told the Commons committee on the deviation Bill in 1845 that he had never contemplated using the L. & P. terminus for the L. & C. line; but it would have made little difference if he had, for his Parliamentary line came off only quarter of a mile short of the station, ran behind the L. & P. engine shed, and was only about five chains away when it passed eastward of Penny Street. Moreover, the Parliamentary powers were given for a line commencing "by a junction with the L. & P. at or near the present station in Lancaster." The Parliamentary line, as drawn up in November 1843 for the L. & C. Bill of Incorporation, shows the down gradients and skeleton of a big bridge with nearly 700 yd. of arching as indicated in Fig. 11; and this bridge and its approaches were along the line proposed by Larmer in his survey of 1840. In the end, neither Locke nor anyone else seems to have tackled the Lancaster exit courageously and realistically when the Bill for the formation of the L. & C. was being prepared and seen through the Commons.

All other surveyors from 1838 to 1842 were also in difficulty at Lancaster. (See Fig. 12). Larmer and Rastrick presumed any northward line would have to begin at Penny Street terminus; but neither of them was going up the Lune Valley; they were aiming north and north-west. Larmer proposed a long high bridge away up the river above Green Ayre; but it would have been over 600 yd. long including approach arches, and would have had a maximum height of 60 ft., with the southern approach over the eastern end of the town. Another route, suggested by Watson (probably the engineer of the Little North Western) descended from Penny Street at 1 in 100, and crossed the river by Skerton on a bridge 55 ft. high with big embankments at each end. Both of these lines then proceeded north through Slyne to Hest Bank.

The rival Great Way Round scheme also was in difficulty from the same cause. Rastrick, too, assumed he would have to begin at the L. & P. terminus; and he reported to the West Cumberland committee: "The L. & P. has so high a terminus at Lancaster above the river, and the grounds are so low on the north side of the river, and the distance between so short, that I have been obliged to adopt a steeper gradient than otherwise I would have wished." Yet he reckoned on only 1 in 220. He refrained from stating just how he did propose to cross the Lune, for he would have needed bigger embankments and a higher bridge than the other two to maintain that inclination. His trace was almost exactly the same as Larmer's, and both made use of an island then in the river for one of their piers; but Larmer came down at a steeper gradient from the 116 ft. height of Penny Street station, and was down to 30 ft. or so near Skerton after two miles, whereas Rastrick would have needed some five miles to get down to the elevation of the ground just inland from Morecambe bay.

Job Bintley would have none of this. He proposed to by-pass Penny Street station entirely (Fig. 12). His line would join the L. & P. tracks near Galgate, some 2½ miles south of the terminus. He proposed to descend northward at 1 in 133, put a short tunnel through the west end of Lancaster to a separate station suited to a northern main line, and cross the river at low height. In 1838, while making a survey of this portion for the Kendal committee, he even suggested to Locke, who was then building the L. & P., that that engineer should divert his line to the west from Galgate northwards to facilitate an eventual end-on connection with

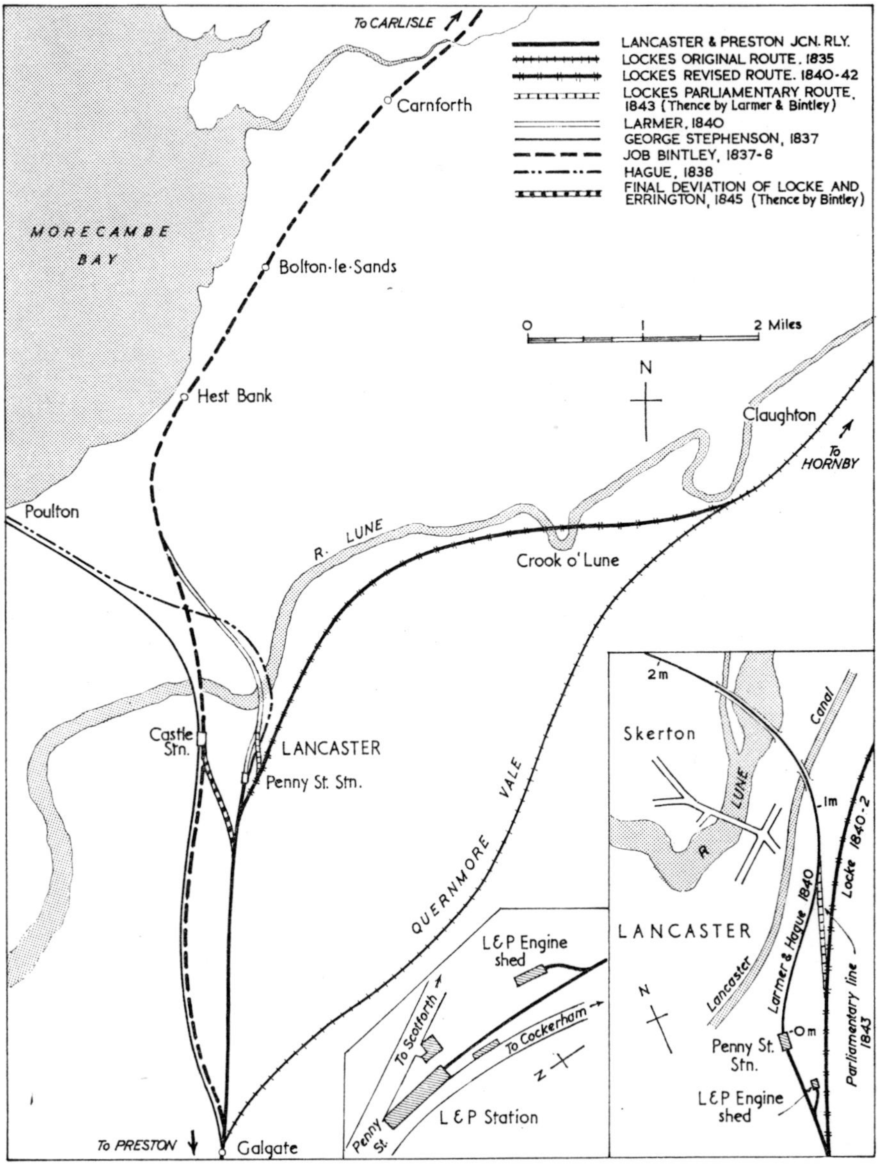

12 Ways out of Lancaster, 1835–43

any northern line. George Stephenson had suggested the same kind of deviation of the L. & P. from Galgate, with a western crossing of the Lune, in his West Cumberland report of August 1837, or, if necessary, that two lines should be built from a short distance south of the town.

Bintley was convinced that the coming main line would have to go on up the coast near Hest Bank, and then preferably on through Kendal.

He stated in 1841 that "Locke saw this to some extent"; but that engineer, with the Lune valley in his marrow, did nothing. Bintley, who had the Longsleddale route equally in *his* marrow, reckoned the southern part of his line would have lowered Galgate embankment by 8 or 10 ft. throughout its length; the tunnel would have been only 220 yd. long, and the Lune would have been crossed at a height of only 23 ft. if the Admiralty agreed. All this, he calculated, would have saved £55,000 in construction costs from Galgate to Hest Bank compared with the other schemes, though some of the saving would have accrued to the L. & P. and not to the L. & C. Francis Whishaw and some of the Kendal provisional committee in 1840 thought Lancastrians would object strongly to a 'tidal' crossing of the Lune, and went back to the Larmer–Rastrick crossing.

Despite all these studies of 1837–42, the L. & C. found after its incorporation that no very economic or well-studied way out of Lancaster had been laid out for its line. In fact, the Parliamentary sections showed more or less just what Larmer had proposed over three years earlier. But when it was seen immediately afterwards that another Act would be needed, and that a new and as yet undesigned bridge and approach to the Lune built, there was no reprimand or expression of dissatisfaction for Locke and Errington.

Called before the Commons committee in 1845, Errington said the line marked out in 1844 did not commence at the L. & P. station, but had a junction close to the engine house. That is true; but as already remarked, it was not a stone's throw away when it passed by the Penny Street station. S. E. Bolden, the L. & C. secretary, told the Commons committee that the company had contracted for the whole of the works before the Bill of the previous session had been passed, and that the L. & P. station could not be made serviceable for the present line; and the company's counsel said it was never the intention of the L. & C. to use the Lancaster station of the L. & C. The Parliamentary plans submitted with the Bill for the incorporation in 1844, have the word 'station' written on them just behind the L. & P. engine house, but no indication at all as to what buildings or platforms were suggested. But all seemed agreed that the total cost of the line would not be increased by the proposed deviation. That was logical, for the deviation did not cross over Lancaster town, and the approaches to the Lune were more favourable. Nor were Parliamentary charges for this second, or deviation, Act very heavy, for there was little opposition except that of the Lancaster Canal Co., which was easily brushed aside as being fractious, which it was. But there were expensive conditional acceptances, and the conditions were not properly settled, until the Bill had more or less passed the House and was within a couple of months of receiving the Royal Assent.

First, Lancaster town council wanted a walkway on the bridge; and the L. & C. agreed to pay £600 towards this, plus another £100 if a toll station for goods had to be removed from its site. Then, as the bridge had come into the navigable part of the river, the Tidal Harbours Commission of the Admiralty entered the picture; and, as the new bridge was to be located below the existing quay, they gave their agreement on condition of a payment of £10,000 to improve the river navigation. The L. & C. deputation charged with this matter declined to pay, but later returned to the Admiralty with an offer of £5,000. At the same time Errington was told to contact Brassey forthwith to see if he could possibly undertake to build the originally-proposed bridge higher up the river by July 1, 1846, if the company gave £5,000 for doing so instead of giving it to the Admiralty. There must have been a dubious reply, for two days afterwards Locke recommended paying the £5,000 to the Admiralty; and this suggests his view was that the 'Parliamentary' exit would cost well over £5,000 more than the deviation and would not be so good. However, the Lords Commissioners of the Admiralty 'were not having any'; and before the end of the month (May 1845) the L. & C. had agreed to pay the £10,000.

This was not all. The Lancaster Quay Commissioners entered the lists; and *their* price was £16,500 for reconstruction of quays and wharves. This was agreed in the summer of 1845, and £8,000 of it paid on account, the remainder being sent later. Part of this sum possibly was considered by the Quay Commissioners as compensation, for up to 1840, when the railway from the south reached Lancaster, there was a profitable ship service between Liverpool and Lancaster.

All this rearrangement had cost the L. & C. around £30,000, of which the directors appear to have had no inkling when they got the Act of Incorporation, and it was all due mainly to some omission on the part of the engineers. If Locke had seen the force of Bintley's argument in 1838, or Locke and Errington had looked into the matter closely in 1843 and early 1844 without bias, as they surely should have done at that time, much trouble might have been saved. No close estimate of the cost of the 'Parliamentary' Lune bridge and its embankments appears to have been made, though it was just this question that frightened Locke off Lancaster eight years earlier. The river payments could hardly have been avoided; but the contractors would have been saved time and indecision, and the line might have been opened a little nearer to the much-desired July 1, 1846.

Even so, the Lancaster bridge and deviation were designed and completed within 15 months of the second Act; but that strenuous work kept labour away from the more northerly parts of the line. In the end the junction with the L. & P. was made nearly a mile south of Penny Street, and a few hundred yards of over-grown track still remain as a storage for goods brake vans or cripples. From the actual junction at Lancaster no. 1 signalbox there is a down gradient of a mile at 1 in 98 to the L. & C. station in Meeting-House Lane, always known as Castle. North of that station the Lune was crossed by the timber-arch bridge already described.

XII

Openings and Early Services

THE L. & C. LINES from Lancaster to Kendal junction (later Oxenholme) and the two-mile section of the Kendal & Windermere Railway (K. & W.) down to Kendal were opened together, formally on September 21, 1846, and to normal passenger traffic on the 22nd. Major-General Pasley had made his Government inspection on September 18, and had given his certificate for one track, the eastern, or up track as it now is. Trains ran through between Lancaster and Kendal whether they were locals or had connections from the south. For the next three months coaches gave a road connection between Kendal and Carlisle and on into Scotland; but the Fleetwood steamer service was still in full activity, and continued for a long time after the railway was opened to Carlisle, as the whole railway route to Glasgow was not opened until February 1848. After the opening of the railway as far north as Carlisle, some of the Kendal trains were worked as a shuttle service between that town and Oxenholme junction, and this practice was extended when the K. & W. was opened throughout in 1847.

The ceremonial opening of this southern section went one better than most of such occasions. A special train headed by the engine *Dalemain*, with Errington and Worthington 'up', left Kendal at 12.30 for Lancaster, and was back in Kendal, behind the engine *Bela*, with Trevithick of Crewe upon the footplate, just before 15.00. At the "most splendid and *recherché* collation" which followed, Cornelius Nicholson, who was in the chair as mayor of Kendal and a director of the K. & W. (he had resigned from the L. & C. board in the previous July), invited those present to do their eating and drinking with speed, as they ought to do on the occasion of a railway opening, and because the train would leave again shortly for Lancaster, where another dinner would be served. At Kendal the directors of the K. & W. acted as hosts. At the Lancaster dinner the L. & C. did the honours; and here E. W. Hasell, the chairman, said their "railway was to connect London with Glasgow and even with Edinburgh, and forward to Johnny Groat's house and up into the Highlands." The carriages used that day were all built at Crewe and had "a look of great solidity combined, in the case of the first class, with old-fashioned elegance."

On the formal opening day the contractors made an early trip over the line to check that all was well. John Steel, of Carlisle, was with this party, and recorded: "6.00 a.m. saw us at the temporary wooden station quarter-of-a-mile from Kendal. The *Medusa* engine took a preliminary trip down the line (to Lancaster) and returned to Kendal after breakfast, performing the 22½ miles in 44 minutes. Then came the arrival of the train from Lancaster about 11.30, and we were off again to Lancaster about 12.00 with the engine *Dalemain*." *Medusa* was one of the contractors' engines, and for such must have been powerful and well-boilered to make the return trip to Lancaster and run at an average speed of fully 30 m.p.h.

She made two longer trips subsequently before coming to grief. On October 16, 1846, the day of an L. & C. board meeting, she was used to take the directors' train on a preliminary inspection from Oxenholme over Shap to Clifton and back; and on the return took the party on to Lancaster in a time reputed to have been 31 min. for the 19¼ miles from Oxenholme. It was on this day that the directors decided to look into the expediency of having an electric telegraph along the line. On Sunday, November 8 of the same year, some of the contractors' foremen and sub-contractors decided to have a spree over the centre part of the line with the two engines *Medusa* and *Tryo* belonging to the contractor. They had to take some rails from Oxenholme to Docker Garths, and then went on to Shap with some old wagons the contractors were transferring to the Caley works north of Carlisle. The party then crowded on the two locomotives for the return trip. *Tryo* went ahead as pilot, but stopped just short of Oxenholme, where *Medusa*, with 10 to 12 men crowded on, ran into it about 9.00 p.m. and was derailed and much damaged. One man died a week afterwards as a result of burns, and several were injured. *Medusa* and *Tryo* may have been Jones & Potts engines; for at a banquet in December 1846, when the L. & C. had hardly taken delivery of its first two engines (also by Jones & Potts) the *contractors* gave a toast to that locomotive builder.

On Friday, December 4, 1846, the L. & C. directors and engineers were able to make a thorough inspection trip over the whole 70 miles from Carlisle to Lancaster, the last rails having been put in during the final week in November. The next day they returned in the company of Capt. Coddington on his official inspection of the line, and he gave the necessary Government certificate. The line by then was double track except through Wreay cutting, and the second track there was ready for use by mid-January.

Ceremonial opening of the whole line north of Lancaster (Castle) took place on December 15, 1846, with a special train from Lancaster to Carlisle. The next day another special train ran south with returning guests; and on the 17th the public service began with two up and two down trains a day throughout the whole length, plus the others between Lancaster and Kendal which had been running since the September. At both openings—September and December—Hasell emphasised that they were going to run gently for a time and then accelerate the schedules, and ultimately "travel as quick as you like." Night trains, he said in December, would not begin before mid-February. It was for this reason that the L. & C. tried to defer the inauguration of mail trains; but the Post Office was insistent, and the company had to carry the mail from the beginning of February 1847, up to which time the coaches on the road had continued to run with the mails. But the company would promise the Post Office only that it would endeavour to perform the journey between Lancaster and Carlisle in three hours. A year later there is a minute that Huish was asking 3d. a mile for the hire of a T.P.O.

At the formal opening on December 15, 1846, the special train of nine carriages containing about 200 passengers left Lancaster shortly before 11.00 and reached Carlisle at 15.30 after a stop of 20 min. or more at Penrith, and probably a stop out in the open at Tebay if not elsewhere also. It was a cold day with light snow over all the higher ground and covering the great hills, and there was speculation as to how the engine would surmount the four miles of 1 in 75 to Shap, particularly as in Shap cutting great masses of ice were hanging from the rock. *Dalemain* was again the engine, a compliment to Hasell, as the name was that of his own residence. *Greystoke*, another Trevithick-Allan 2–2–2, named after the residence of one of the directors, ran ahead from Tebay to Shap as a pilot in case its services were needed; but they were not, and Shap was climbed at 22½ m.p.h. without assistance. A contemporary account said Locke and Errington were on the engine, and also Larmer and Worthington. The footplate of the tiny cabless 2–2–2 could hardly have held all four even if two of them were working their passage, so they probably took turns.

In the morning a second special train had run south from Carlisle to Penrith to meet the northbound train. The intention had been to combine the two and run on to Carlisle as one; but the feeling was that such a train would be too unwieldy, so the 'local' ran back separately, The Newcastle & Carlisle Railway provided some of the coaches and gave other help, though the two companies already were beginning to fear that differences might grow between them in the future. The opening train ran into the N. & C. London Road station at Carlisle.

A wide net seems to have been cast to draw in guests, and interesting guests, for the opening ceremonials. Among these present additional to the many connected in one way or another with the grand trunk route were: Wm. Wordsworth Jr.; James Thompson of Kirkhouse (agent of Lord Carlisle, lessee of the Brampton railway, and one of the real railway pioneers); John Viret Gooch, then locomotive superintendent of the L.S.W.R. and probably a friend of Locke; and A. S. Gee, engineer of the Sheffield & Manchester Railway, who had earlier acted as Locke's engineer in the construction of the L. & P. The boards of the L. & C. and G.J.R. were well represented, but Hope-Johnstone, chairman of the Caley, could not get into Carlisle from his home in Annandale because of the snowy weather. Locke and Errington were there throughout the whole proceedings; so were Larmer and Worthington, the last-named becoming eventually the L. & C. personified, for he was on the line for another 40 years in responsible positions.

Next night the contractors held a banquet, a rather more informal proceeding at which the 270 guests preceded the toasts by singing *Non Nobis Domine*. After this, John Stephenson, the contractor, made a remarkable forecast. Referring to Shap, he said of the formal opening trip the day before: "on the incline a train of nine carriages with 200 passengers went up at over 22 m.p.h. Who knows but some improvement may be made in the construction of the engines which will make it practicable to go up 1 in 75 at 30 m.p.h., or even at twice that speed." Before the end of the week he was vindicated in regard to the first, for a report dated December 19 said that an engine with six coaches had just gone up at 35 m.p.h. But 90 years elapsed before his second forecast was fulfilled—to be exact, not until November 16, 1936, when L.M.S.R. 4–6–2 no. 6201 *Princess Elizabeth* went up the south side of Shap at a minimum of 57 m.p.h. and at an average of 64.5 m.p.h. pass-to-pass from Tebay to Shap Summit box when hauling 230 tons. On that run, too, the 69.1 miles of the old L .& C. line from Castle to Citadel occupied only 58 min. 50 sec. pass-to-pass, that is, less than 33 per cent of the time the L. & C. reluctantly gave the P.M.G. two months after the opening for the Lancaster–Carlisle journey.

Despite the modest initial train service over the northern part of the line, all did not go without minor troubles and vexations. The first of these came on the first day of the public service, and was attributable directly to the secretary of the company, Samuel Edward Bolden. Apart from his secretarial duties, he had been appointed on the opening of the Lancaster–Kendal section to "the internal management of the traffic, with full powers on platforms and stations." He seems to have had no previous experience of traffic working, though plenty in secretarial duties, but he began to exercise his powers without delay. To quote the *Kendal Mercury* of December 19, 1846, two days after public service began:

> "While congratulating the L. & C. on its opening and beginning of service there are already complaints about their trains at Oxenholme. When the train which left Carlisle at 2.30 p.m. on Thursday arrived at Oxenholme junction, as soon as the Kendal passengers got out it was ordered on by the Secretary, without awaiting the arrival of the up train from Kendal which was nearly on top of the incline and was in full time. The consequence was that this train had to be sent on express to Preston, and it could only proceed there after some delay because it had to take on fuel and water supplies. In the meantime, passengers from Carlisle to Kendal were delayed in the cold and without any place to shelter, and it was not until nearly an hour elapsed that they were able to procure seats in some third-class carriages that were on the line and were taken on by an engine that happened to be on the line. The Windermere company too often have been compelled to wait for the Lancaster and Carlisle."

During the fortnight from the opening until the end of the year Worthington was directed to report every two weeks on all train delays, and to differentiate between those caused by the secretary's department and those due to the engineering department; Errington was instructed to try and buy two locomotives on reasonable terms (the L. & C. did not then own any locomotives at all); Thomas Edmondson was paid £146 8s. od. for some of his patent ticket cases; the Railway Commissioners were asked not to press the company to glaze the sides of its third class carriages as that would only take people out of the second class; and guard McMillan was fined 5s. and severely reprimanded for being in liquor.

Initial train service from December 17, 1846, was as given in Table VIII.

Table VIII—Original Lancaster & Carlisle Railway Timetable as from December 17, 1846

8.00	14.30	dep.	Carlisle	arr.	11.00	17.20
9.00	15.30	dep.	Penrith	arr.	10.00	16.20
15.20(1)	21.45	arr.	Liverpool	dep.	—	10.15
15.05	21.25	arr.	Manchester	dep.	—	10.30
—	0.36	arr.	Birmingham	dep.	1.25	6.00
—	5.32	arr.	London	dep.	20.45	—

(1) This train arrives at Liverpool in time for the express to London.
Trains between Kendal, Lancaster and south will continue as heretofore.

There was only one through service a day in each direction between Carlisle and London, and in each case the L. & C. portion of the journey was in daylight hours. The route was via Parkside, Newton and Birmingham, and the time of 14¼ hours northbound represented an average of 21.7 m.p.h. over the then 308.7 miles. When the Trent Valley line was opened about ten months later, eight miles were knocked off the distance; and in 1864 the Winwick–Golborne cut-off took away another 1.7 miles.

This was not the first time it was possible to travel all-rail from Carlisle to London in a day. From September 1, 1846, the Newcastle & Carlisle Railway remodelled its morning train timings so that the 8.00 ex London Road, after stopping at Milton, Rosehill, Haltwhistle, Haydon Bridge, Hexham, Stocksfield and Blaydon, arrived at Gateshead at 11.00 and connected with an express which left for the south at 11.15 and reached London (Euston) via Rugby at 21.00, this being over an hour quicker than the shorter West Coast route achieved on its opening four months later. At Blaydon the N. & C. train divided; one portion went to Newcastle; the other with Gateshead passengers and any for the south, ran along the south side of the River Tyne and up the 1 in 23 of 'Rabbit Banks' (which at that time had rope haulage) to connect with the south train, for the Tyne was not then bridged for north and south traffic. The London express consisted "of first class carriages for passengers and second class carriages for their servants only, and will not take either horses or private carriages." Previously there had been Tyneside-and-Rugby connections to London off the 11.00 and 19.00 trains ex London Road, but the former did not then reach Euston the same day.

One modification to the first L. & C. train service came quickly; the then morning train from Liverpool was terminated at Lancaster and in its place another was put on leaving Liverpool at 7.30 and running through to Carlisle, this alteration beginning on the first day of 1847. As the track settled down the board was anxious to redeem its promise of acceleration, and at the beginning of February the traffic sub-committee was asked to arrange for the quickening of the 8.00 southbound train from Carlisle to get it to Newton Junction in time to connect with the 13.00 from Liverpool to London. Night trains also began at this time, concurrent with the mail transport to Post Office requirements.

After the opening to Carlisle a good coach service continued along the roads into Scotland. There were two 'mails' a day in each direction between Carlisle, Dumfries and Glasgow; one coach and one 'mail' to

Edinburgh; a daily coach to Dumfries and Kilmarnock; and one a day to Dumfries and Portpatrick. Something of the precision and of the high tone and tradition of the old coach 'mails' is gleaned from the booked departure time of the Glasgow 'mail'—2.41 a.m. out of Carlisle.

Throughout 1847 and the first half of 1848 there were numerous alterations in the train service as the railway system was gradually extended into Scotland and working methods settled down. The timetables and fares at the beginning of September 1847 between Carlisle and London were as given in Table IX; this was just before the opening of the first short extension into Scotland, public service to Beattock beginning on September 10, 1847, after a formal opening on the 9th. From October 1 the departure of the 8.00 south train out of Carlisle was put back to 8.30 to connect with the first incoming Caley train, and it had to wait if that train was late, as there were through carriages from Beattock to London to attach, although the L. & C. train stopped at all stations to Lancaster.

This was a very brief arrangement. Within a couple of months or so two trains a day in each direction were being run between London and Carlisle and Beattock. The 10.00 ex Euston reached Preston at 17.35, Carlisle at 22.10, and Beattock at 24.00 but was soon accelerated by three-quarters of an hour to reach Beattock at 23.16. The 20.45 ex Euston was due into Preston at 5.35 the next morning, Carlisle at 10.00, and Beattock at 12.00 midday. In the reverse direction the 13.00 departure from Beattock left Carlisle at 15.00, Preston at 19.53, and reached Euston at 5.32 the next morning. The 22.30 out of Beattock left Carlisle at 0.30, Preston at 5.10, and reached London at 13.00. Acceleration between Carlisle and London thus was from one to 2½ hours within nine months. Coaches between Beattock and Glasgow took about 7¼ hours including the change-over time at Beattock. In November 1847 a special train for W. H. Smith & Son went from Euston to Beattock, 339 miles, at a running average of 40 m.p.h., and this showed what could be done with the little Trevithick–Allan type singles with 15 to 15½ in. cylinders, which would operate for 55 to 60 per cent of the whole distance; but it was long before regular trains maintained such a schedule speed, which was hardly exceeded until after Sir Richard Moon ceased to be chairman of the L.N.W.R. in 1891.

Acceleration was possible after the Trent Valley line was opened to full public service on December 1, 1847, five months after its formal opening; but when the Caley was opened throughout to the public, that is to Edinburgh and Glasgow, on February 15, 1848, the proper train services had not been organised, and major decisions were not taken until a meeting on March 14, 1848, between the L. & C. and Caley directors, with Mark Huish present to represent the L.N.W.R. In retrospect, the decisions taken at that meeting can be regarded as historic. The first was that the route between Edinburgh/Glasgow and London and other places in the south should be worked as one line. Here at last was the Grand Trunk Route. Each company's trains were to wait for the connecting trains from north or south; and if a decision was made in any

Table IX—Lancaster & Carlisle Railway Timetables and Fares; Bradshaw, September 1, 1847*

Sunday		Service						Station	Service						Sunday	
1st class mail	1st/2nd class	1st class mail	1st/2nd/ 3rd class	1st/2nd class	1st/2nd/ 3rd class	1st/2nd class	1st/2nd class		1st/2nd mail	1st/2nd class	1st/2nd/ 3rd class	1st/2nd class	1st/2nd mail	1st/2nd class	1st/2nd mail	1st/2nd mail
0.45	15.28	0.45		6.00	8.00	12.00	15.28	Carlisle ↑	10.04	13.48	17.30	19.50	21.55		10.04	21.55
					8.14			Brisco		13.39	17.20	19.41				
	15.43			6.18	8.32		15.43	Southwaite	9.33	13.29	17.05	19.31			9.23	
					8.55			Plumpton		13.13	16.44	19.15				
1.31	16.14	1.31		6.47	9.18	12.45	16.14	Penrith	9.13	13.00	16.24	19.03	21.04		9.13	21.04
					9.35			Clifton		12.45	16.08	18.49				
2.08	16.51	2.08		7.20	10.02	13.17	16.51	Shap	8.36	12.26	15.43	18.30	20.27		8.36	20.27
	17.10			7.40	10.30		17.10	Tebay		12.03	15.15	18.07	20.00			20.00
	17.25			7.54	10.50		17.25	Low Gill		11.51	14.55	17.56				
3.06	17.49	3.06		8.24	11.25	14.09	17.49	Kendal Jct.	7.38	11.30	14.25	17.35	19.29		7.38	19.29
	(17.30)			(8.15)	(11.10)	(13.55)	(17.30)	(dep.) Kendal (dep.)		11.10	13.55	17.20	19.15			17.30
3.25	18.08	3.25		8.41	11.40	14.27	18.08	Milnthorpe	7.19	11.11	14.00	17.15	19.10		7.19	19.10
3.37	18.20	3.37		8.51	11.50		18.20	Burton & Holme	7.07	11.01	13.50	17.05	18.58		7.07	18.58
				9.02	11.59			Carnforth		10.48	13.36	16.53				
				9.12	12.13			Hest Bank		10.39	13.23	16.44				
4.08	18.48	4.08	6.30	9.30	12.30	14.50	18.48	Lancaster	6.39	10.30	13.13	16.35	18.30	21.45	6.39	18.30
5.10	19.53	5.10	7.25	10.30	1.25	15.50	19.53	Preston	5.35	9.35	12.15	15.40	17.35	21.00	5.35	17.35
		9.30		16.00		19.50	0.55	Birmingham	1.25			11.15	13.45		1.25	13.45
		13.00		20.45		23.00	5.18	↓ London (Euston)	20.45			6.15	10.00		20.45	10.00

Extra trains on Saturdays: 8.00 ex-Penrith for Carlisle; 16.00 ex Carlisle for Penrith. *Converted to 24-hr. clock.

Fares: Carlisle to Kendal: 10s. 6d. first, 7s. 3d. second. Carlisle to Lancaster: 14s. first, 9s. 9d. second.
Carlisle to Preston: 18s. first, 12s. 6d. second. Lancaster to Preston: 4s. first, 2s. 9d. second.
Carlisle to London: 66s. first class express; 57s. first class mixed; 41s. second class mixed; no third class through bookings.
Kendal to London: 52s. first class express; 45s. first class mixed; 34s. 3d. second class mixed; 21s. 6½d. third class mixed.

particular case not to wait, then the ordinary train was to be sent on at that company's expense as soon as it arrived.

Another decision which began a long West Coast tradition was that 15 min. were to be allowed for all trains at Carlisle for refreshment; followed by a resolution: "That the expression of this Committee be conveyed to the lessees of the North Union that the up north trains should refresh at Preston." Here, then, was the genesis of the 20 min. stop at Preston so famous in late Victorian days, though fortunately for travellers it did not become a frequent or regular practice for years (not until March 1863) after the Committee's suggestion, though a few trains did begin to 'refresh'. Good feeding at the notoriously inadequate N.U. station would have been impossible. Even in the 1860s "a hot and perspiring woman stood at the top of the table to do the carving"; but that was before the big island platform we know today, to which the dining room was transferred when the great station rebuilding was opened around 1880. The immediate attempts to carry into effect the suggestion of the inter-allied Committee of 1848 seem to have met with indifferent results both as to eating and train remarshalling; for from the beginning of 1853 the principal up express of the day was altered to have a long stop at Carlisle to dine and remarshal instead of at Preston.

At the time of the meeting in March 1848 the daily through trains between London and Glasgow were leaving each city at 9.00 and reaching their destinations at 22.00, a throughout average of 31 m.p.h.; but from May 1, partly as a result of the March meeting, the overall time was reduced by 20 min., and then, from July 1, 1848, by another 30 min. to 12 hr. 10 min. overall, equivalent to $33\frac{1}{4}$ m.p.h. average. In each direction the trains were first class only, but took private carriages; but from May 1 the L. & C. had run a third class train from Carlisle at 11.45 which the the L.N.W.R. agreed to take forward from Preston at 16.00 as far as

Table X.—London–Carlisle–Scotland Service. January 1853, Bradshaw

1st/2nd class express	1st/2nd class express	Express	1st/2nd class Express /Mail				1st/2nd	1stclass Express (1)	Express Mail
9.15	10.00	17.00	20.45	dep.	Euston	arr.	11.00	23.25	4.50
15.45	17.16	23.25	4.15	arr.	Preston	dep.	3.44	16.50	20.37
16.18	17.59	0.09	4.57	arr.	Lancaster	dep.	2.49	16.15	19.25
18.25	21.01	2.50	7.55	arr.	Carlisle	dep.	0.20	14.13	16.33
18.45	21.16	3.15	8.16	dep.		arr.	0.03	13.53	16.18
21.45	1.15	7.25	12.35	arr.	Edinburgh	dep.	20.25	10.45	12.00
22.05	1.30	7.40	12.40	arr.	Glasgow	dep.	20.17	10.40	11.50
Stops 10 min. at Crewe and 20 min. at Carlisle for refreshment								Stops 20 min. at Carlisle and 10 min. at Rugby for refreshments(2)	

(1) Marked in Bradshaw: Edinburgh and Holyhead; 1st/2nd express from Preston and Chester.
(2) Rugby stop was from 21.00 to 21.10.

Liverpool. In the reverse direction a third class train left Liverpool at 7.45 for Glasgow.

There was a deceleration to 12½ hr. in 1849, and the 'octuple' agreement of 1851 brought another slowing, and for some years the London–Glasgow times were above 12¾ hr. by day trains and 14 hr. or more by night trains. Table X shows the timings in January 1853. By July of the same year the down day express had been slowed by 15 min. to Carlisle and by 25 min. to Glasgow. On the other hand, to meet the requirements of the P.M.G. the night mails in each direction were accelerated over the L. & C. section, the down mail taking 3 hr. Preston to Carlisle instead of the 3 hr. 40 min. in January; and the up mail being quickened from 4 hr. 4 min. to 2 hr. 52 min. over the same 90 miles. In neither case was the new schedule as quick as those of the day expresses. Not until the L. & C. had been leased to the L.N.W.R. did the London–Glasgow time again get back to around 12 hr., in fact not until 1862 when a schedule of 12 hr. 10 min. was introduced, and then, with the institution of the celebrated 10.00 departure out of Euston a month or two later, cut further to 11½ hr. to Glasgow and 11 hr. 10 min. to Edinburgh. By then the number of trains had increased greatly. From the two up and two down trains between Preston and Carlisle at the end of 1846, there were 14 long-distance main-line trains through Lancaster by the time of the L. & C. lease in 1859; but the fastest Preston–Carlisle time in 1859 was 146 min., only 12 min. quicker than the best time just after the whole Caledonian line was opened in 1848. The first class express fare from Lancaster to Carlisle was 17s. in 1859 as against 14s. a dozen years before.

The so-called 'octuple' agreement arose late in 1850 when the large railways north of London were considering the traffic flow probable for the Great Exhibition of 1851. As from the beginning of the latter year a five-year agreement came into force, signed by the eight companies concerned, for the pooling of all revenue, except that from mails and minerals, for traffic both ways between London and Edinburgh by East Coast and West Coast routes, and also between London and places north of York and short of Edinburgh on the York, Newcastle & Berwick Railway and on the North British Railway. The last-named provision was to cover the Midland and its route from Rugby to York when the Great Northern Railway direct route was opened. The signatories were: L.N.W.R., L. & C., Caley, Great Northern, Y.N. & B.R., N.B.R., York & North Midland, and the Midland.

Efforts were to be made to apportion the through traffic equally between the two routes, but in any case the gross receipts were to be divided equally between East Coast and West Coast companies. Basis for the further division of these moieties among the individual companies had to be recognised by the Railway Clearing House. Whatever the route, the gross fares or charges from point to point had to be the same, and as determined by the common consent of at least six of the eight signatories; once adopted they had to be kept strictly.

For the same period a supplementary agreement for non-octuple traffic over the same general routes was made between the L.N.W.R.,

Plate XXVa The last stage in he life of the old Lancaster & Carlisle signal box at Yealand o the north of Carnforth

[*Clapham Museum of Transport*

Plate XXVb Whale 5ft 3in -6-0 No 1512 leaving Oxenholme on a northbound freight. The double-track junction from the Windermere branch on to the main ine was removed in 1968, leaving only the connection with the island platform

[*H. Gordon Tidey (RPC)*

Plate XXVIa John Hick class 2-2-2-2 No. 1559 *William Siemens* takes a miscellaneous collection of six-wheelers and bogie coaches unassisted up the south side of Shap
[*British Rail*

Plate XXVIb Down train of coke empties near Shap hauled by a Webb 4ft 3in coal engine
[*LGRP*

Plate XXVIIa Webb 2-2-2-0 "Experiment" class three-cylinder compound on train of North Eastern Railway carriages at Tebay [*Rixon Bucknall collection*

Plate XXVIIb Webb class "A" three-cylinder compound 0-8-0 built at Crewe in 1897 passing Upperby Junction in 1898 on a northbound freight. Note the old head-code board in front of the chimney [*Rixon Bucknall collection*

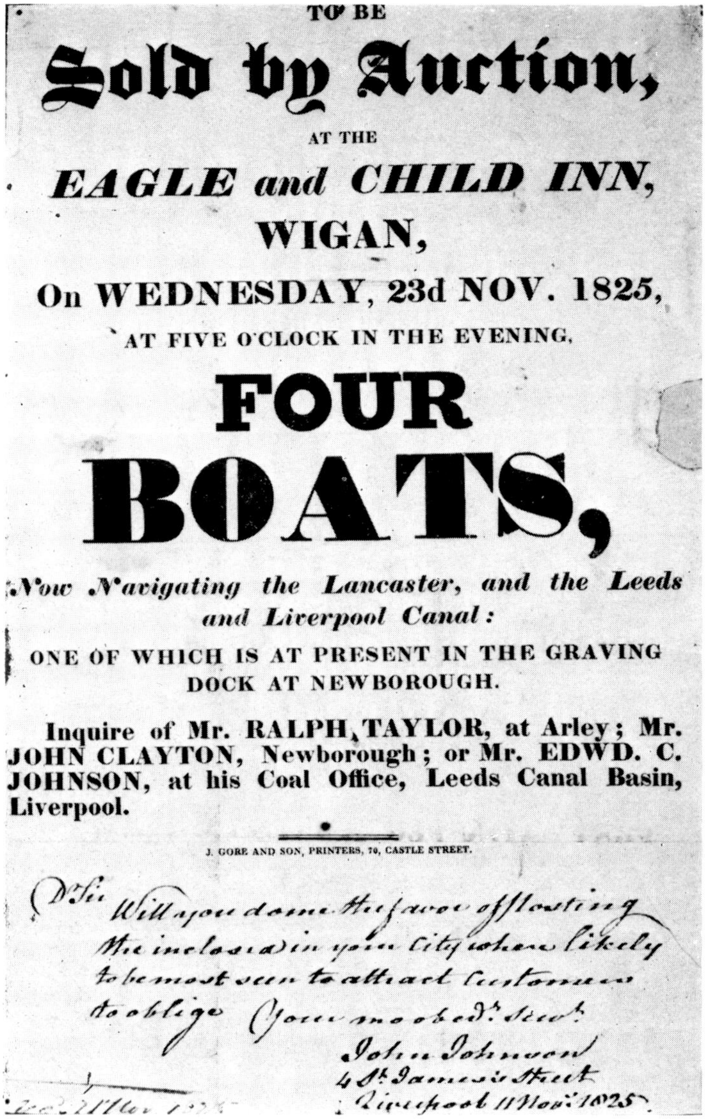

Plate XXVIIIa A relic of the very early days of the old Lancaster Canal Company

[Clapham Museum of Transport

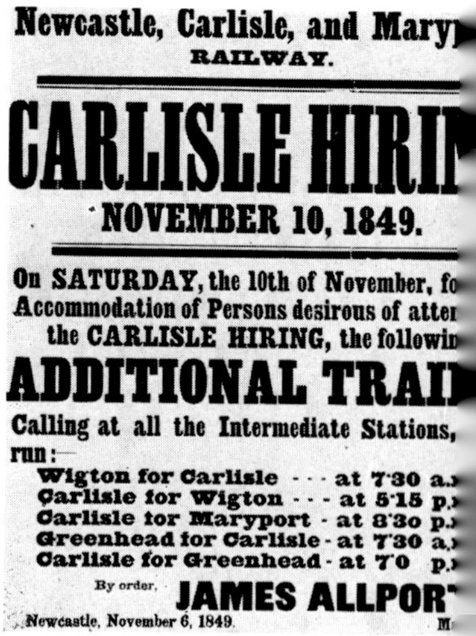

Plate XXVIIIb This notice is of interest as being from the time when George Hudson had a personal lease of both the N&CR and the M&CR, and tried to work them as one system under James Allport

[Clapham Museum of Transport

L. & C., Caley, Midland, Y.N. & B.R., and North British. As far as the L. & C. was concerned its principal terms were that all London–Glasgow traffic should go West Coast; that Leeds and Bradford to Glasgow traffic should go West Coast, via the Little North Western; that any traffic from Normanton or any Midland station south thereof to any station on the Edinburgh & Glasgow Railway except Glasgow should go East Coast; and that any traffic from any Midland station north of Normanton to any Scottish station should go West Coast. This agreement bore the same date as the 'octuple' agreement itself, that is April 17, 1851; but both agreements took effect as from January 1, 1851.

From the end of the 'octuple' at the close of 1855 a new 14-year Anglo-Scottish traffic agreement came into force, and brought some acceleration; but after 1869 that agreement was not renewed, and for nearly 30 years the rival routes were free to develop and, within the law, to charge what they liked. The signatories of the 'English & Scotch Traffic Agreement' dated January 1, 1856, were the L.N.W.R., L. & C., Caley, G.N.R., N.E.R., N.B.R. and Midland. An unusual provision reflecting the then existing war between two Scottish companies was that the Edinburgh & Glasgow Railway should be admitted as soon as its difference with the Caledonian would allow. The Anglo-Scottish committee that framed the regulations had 18 meetings; the members were charged additionally to tender their good offices as mediators in the Caley–E. & G. quarrel, but in the end had to record their failure and to state it "was useless to try and continue their mediation." Actually the E. & G. supplementary agreement was not signed until January 13, 1859.

A principal provision of the '14-year' was in relation to traffic to the north of Scotland; and 'the north of Scotland' here meant all places lying north of the Edinburgh & Glasgow Railway, both Greenhill Junction and Falkirk being named specifically as coming within this definition. The Scottish Central was a party to the early meetings, but withdrew, so no subdivision of traffic south of Perth could be recommended by the committee. The 14-year agreement included all passenger, coaching and freight traffic except mails, coal and coke. The broad terms of the traffic division were as given in Table XI.

In the 'octuple' and 14-year agreements the L. & C. helped friend and foe alike, for its Act of Incorporation whilst laying down fares not exceeding 1½d. and 2d. a mile by ordinary passenger trains, gave permission for the company to "charge any sum they think fit in respect of passengers conveyed by first class trains at a speed appointed to be not less than 25 m.p.h. including stoppages." The L. & C. was not diffident in taking advantage of this clause, and was an expensive line for such travellers. In fixing the 'octuple' fares account would certainly have to be taken of the L. & C. fares, and these would influence the overall fares agreed between the signatories. In 1847 first class express fare Carlisle to London was 66s.; in 1853 it was 70s. In the latter year first class day express fare from London to Glasgow or Edinburgh was 87s., but by the night mails the charges were 79s. to Glasgow and 77s. 6d. to Edinburgh. The full fares list as it was in 1853 is given in Table XII.

Table XI—Traffic Division under 14 Year English & Scotch Traffic Agreement, 1856-69

THE SCHEDULE or Tabular Statement of proportions of Traffic, and Receipts therefrom, mentioned or referred to in the foregoing Agreement, shewing the proportions and manner in which the same are agreed to be divided or apportioned, except where otherwise provided by, and subject to the notes, rules, and directions appended hereto, and which are considered as forming part of this schedule.

Column 1 Traffic from or to the undermentioned Towns or places in England, to or from the respective places named or referred to in Columns 2, 3, or 4.	Column 2 From or to Edinburgh, including all places lying east of Falkirk, to or from the respective Places named or referred to in Column 1.				Column 3 From or to Places in the North of Scotland, including Falkirk and Greenhill Junction, to or from the respective Places named or referred to Column 1.				Column 4 From or to Glasgow, including all places lying west of Greenhill Junction, to or from the respective Places named or referred to in Column 1.			
	West Coast Route		East Coast Route		West Coast Route		East Coast Route		West Coast Route		East Coast Route	
	Passengers	Goods	Passengers	Goods	Passengers	Goods	Passengers	Goods	Passengers	Goods	Passengers	Goods
	Per cent.	Per cent.	Per cent.	Per cent.	Per cent.	Per cent.	Per cent.	Per cent.	Per cent.	Per cent.	Per cent.	Per cent.
London	40	50	60	50	50	50	50	50	80	60	20	40
Liverpool	all	all	nil	nil	all	all	nil	nil	all	all	nil	nil
Manchester	all	60	nil	40	all	60	nil	40	all	all	nil	nil
Leeds.......................	$33\frac{1}{3}$	50	$66\frac{2}{3}$	50	50	50	50	50	$66\frac{2}{3}$	60	$33\frac{1}{3}$	40
Places between Manchester and Leeds, except Bradford	$33\frac{1}{3}$	60	$66\frac{2}{3}$	40	50	60	50	40	80	60	20	40
Bradford	$66\frac{2}{3}$	60	$33\frac{1}{3}$	40	$66\frac{2}{3}$	60	$33\frac{1}{3}$	40	75	70	25	30
Hull and Great Grimsby	No booking through	$33\frac{1}{3}$	All, and booked by East Coast	$66\frac{2}{3}$	No booking through	$33\frac{1}{3}$	No booking through	$66\frac{2}{3}$	No booking through	$33\frac{1}{3}$	No booking through	$66\frac{2}{3}$
Birmingham...........	75	$66\frac{2}{3}$	25	$33\frac{1}{3}$	90	$66\frac{2}{3}$	10	$33\frac{1}{3}$	all	all	nil	nil
Sheffield .... Nottingham	50	50	50	50	50	50	50	50	50	50	50	50
Hitchin .... Peterboro' .... Stamford .... Newark .... Lincoln .... Doncaster............... Retford	5	20	95	80	5	20	95	80	20	$33\frac{1}{3}$	80	$66\frac{2}{3}$
Stations on the Midland Railway not above named, or otherwise provided for	$33\frac{1}{3}$	50	$66\frac{2}{3}$	50	all	all	nil	nil	all	all	nil	nil

Table XII—Anglo-Scottish Fares List, January 1853 (Bradshaw)

Miles from London(1)	From London to	Express 1st class	1st class; and 2nd class express	2nd class	Express night mails		3rd class	1st class express fare per mile d.
					1st class	2nd class		
231½	Lancaster	53s.	43s.	30s. 9d.	47s. 6d.	35s. 3d.	19s. 2½d.	2.75
252¾	Kendal	59s.	48s. 6d.	34s. 9d.	53s.	39s. 3d.	21s. 0½d.	2.85
300½	Carlisle	70s.	58s. 6d.	41s. 6d.	63s.	46s.	25s. 0½d.	2.8
401½	Edinburgh	87s.	77s. 6d.	56s. 6d.	77s. 6d.	56s. 6d.	30s.	2.6
403	Glasgow	87s.	79s. 6d.	58s.	79s. 6d.	58s.	30s.	2.58

(1) Via Newton and Parkside west curve.

The L. & C. was not much attracted by third class passengers. It did have its Parliamentaries, but kept the third class carriages as primitive as it could. Nor did those carriages run off their own line, and third class passengers were not booked through to stations on other railways for some years. Thus in 1847–49 a third class passenger from Carlisle to London had to change and rebook at Preston. In August 1849 the L. & C. agreed to the suggestion of Mark Huish that the three companies (Caley, L. & C. and L.N.W.R.) should try as an experiment a third class through train between Glasgow and London on Fridays only, under conditions and times much restricted. In 1852 strict instructions were issued that no long-distance excursionists from Scotland and Carlisle to London to see the Duke of Wellington's funeral were to be allowed to travel by any mail train. The through third class train from Liverpool to Glasgow introduced in 1848 did not have any L. & C. stock in its formation.

The L. & C. directors had never intended to work their own traffic in the normal sense of the word. As early as 1845 they had come to an arrangement with the G.J.R. to supply engines, carriages, wagons and engine-men at agreed rates, as is told in more detail in Chapter XV. They had also seen fit to get this arrangement, when transferred to the L.N.W.R., to cover the working of the L. & P. section, any temporary services that might have to be provided for the Caley, and to work any excursions over the lines of other companies.

Nor had the directors proposed to work their own goods traffic, and the power agreement with the L.N.W.R. covered freight-train haulage. When the southern section from Lancaster to Oxenholme and Kendal was opened in September 1846 Hargreaves and Marshall had the right to operate the goods trains on toll; but a few weeks later those contractors gave notice to terminate their carrying trade unless they were given £400 to continue until the end of March 1847, and given liberty to increase the rates. This was not directed specially against the L. & C.; the time had come when Hargreaves felt it was no longer profitable to be in the carrying business, and at the end of the year he gave up his carrying trade on all the other Lancashire railways with which he was connected. The L. & C. board thereupon determined to look after its own freight traffic from the date of the opening to Carlisle. Forthwith Errington was told to order 100 coal wagons and erect temporary goods sheds at Lancaster, Penrith and Carlisle. The L.N.W.R. engines would work the trains at the charges already agreed; but before the end of 1846 a decision was made to work the coal trade north of Shap with L. & C. engines. As the company had none, Errington had to procure two.

Using L.N.W.R. motive power and stock, a goods and cattle train began to run between Carlisle and Preston on December 21, 1846; it ran south three days a week and returned north on alternate days. Probably the freight traffic grew more quickly than had been anticipated, and in the six and a half months from the Carlisle opening until June 30, 1847, it brought in a revenue of £11,681 compared with £37,571 from passenger traffic. According to Hasell at the general meeting in February 1848, there were then five or six trains a day regularly conveying cattle to Manchester and other large towns. The need for a considerable number of wagons became urgent, and borrowing of £100,000 to finance purchase was sanctioned. By the summer of 1851 the company owned 454 wagons, of which 50 were coal hoppers and 14 were guards' brake vans. In 1855 the wagon total was 689; but when the L. & C. lease to the L.N.W.R. was effected in 1859 the latter company took over 825 wagons plus, as the late S. S. Scott used to put it quaintly, "16 horses and 580 sheets."

From 1857 much additional mineral tonnage accrued to the L. & C. from the opening of the Carnforth–Ulverston line, but it was mainly short-haul. Promotion of the short branch from Hest Bank to Morecambe in 1859 was specifically to cater for coal and ore traffic which might come over the new Barnard Castle and Tebay railway, some of which it was hoped might go to Morecambe harbour for shipment; but traffic from this direction, whether for Morecambe or Furness, did not develop until after the L.N.W.R. began to work the L. & C.

In 1856 the company began the collection and delivery of goods in Lancaster with its own horses, carts and men; and at the end of the year extended the idea to Kendal, and then in 1857 to Carlisle. The Kendal delivery was done from Oxenholme, which thus became an early railhead; but it led to friction with the K. & W., as it lost that company its previous haulage charges over the two miles between Oxenholme and Kendal. As the working of the K. & W. was taken over in 1858 that cause of friction soon disappeared.

XIII

'Merrie' Carlisle

IF THERE was one place above all others the L. & C. directors wanted to reach it was Carlisle; but if there was one place from which soon they prayed to be delivered it was this same city. Certainly it, and the railways in it, caused far more trouble, expense and vexation than did Lancaster at the other end of the system. Yet in many ways Carlisle showed the L. & C. board at its best: firm, determined, tenacious, even audacious, but departing only occasionally from courtesy. Though the powerful L.N.W.R. interest was ever present, the mixture of county gentlemen and hard-headed business men, mainly from the 'Liverpool party', that made up the L. & C. board from 1844 to 1859 proved very effective for the line and its general reputation, and for the financial return to the shareholders, though it was called all kinds of names by the Barker party and *The Railway Times*.

Because these men had appreciated the importance of the great Anglo-Scottish trunk route since 1835–36, and were fully aware of the vital place in it occupied by their own railway, they always attached particular importance to Carlisle. Especially did they regard a single large joint station as essential, to be shared by all companies running into the Border city. Even at the time of the incorporation of the L. & C. there were two railways already in Carlisle; and while its own Bill was still in the Committee stage in March 1844, the L. & C. board sought an interview with one of the two, the Maryport & Carlisle, on the subject of Carlisle station, as the M. & C. was in the lists with a Bill for a short extension to a permanent station of its own in Crown Street, to replace its existing shanty in Bog Street.

As the M. & C. had gone so far, it proposed that its Bill should proceed, but undertook to put up at first no permanent buildings in Crown Street, and merely transfer there its existing wooden structure from Bog Street; and promised that within 12 months it would be ready to make arrangements with the L. & C. for the joint use of this station and the M. & C. land to the south-west of it; and that the third railway, the Newcastle & Carlisle, should be at liberty to join in. Already the M. & C. and N. & C. had had conversations on the possibility of a common station on M. & C. ground.

Next month the L. & C. countered with a proposal that if the M. & C. station Bill was withdrawn, the L. & C., N. & C., and the Caledonian company under formation would share the M. & C. Parliamentary expenses among them, and that the four companies should then form a joint station committee to decide on the best site and other matters; the M. & C. under such a scheme was to be paid for its seven acres of ground if that was used, and, if it were not, then the land would continue to belong absolutely to the M. & C. if that company raised no objection to the L. & C. and Caley tracks crossing the land to gain access to any joint station.

The N. & C. gave this idea approval in principle, but the M. & C. declined. Thereupon the L. & C. considered the matter closed as a specific proposal, but it assented to the M. & C. Bill as long as clauses were inserted to give the L. & C. land to cross, and to prevent the M. & C. encroaching upon land the L. & C. had already scheduled for its northern extension to meet the Caley. At this time, long before the Caley Bill was presented, and 15 months before its Act of Incorporation, that railway was regarded as a certainty, and loose engagements were being made on its behalf.

Maybe at this early stage the L. & C. made a fundamental mistake. The M. & C. original proposal, plus the ground the L. & C. had already earmarked for access lines from south and north, would have given all the ground later occupied by Citadel station and its southern approaches; and there seems no evidence that at that stage the M. & C. would not have kept its word or not come into a general station scheme. Adoption of the M. & C. scheme might also have stopped some of the questionable proceedings of the M. & C. directors along other avenues in the subsequent years, as exposed in 1850. However, by the time of the L. & C. Act of Incorporation the ground had been cleared not for a joint station but for a long series of petty and often nonsensical actions.

In July 1844 Locke presented a short report on the whole question of Carlisle station, but it did not appear to the L. & C. directors that a joint station would be agreed and erected by the time they hoped their line would reach the city; and so in the summer of 1845 amicable arrangements were made with the N. & C. for the temporary use of London Road station from when the L. & C. reached Carlisle until such time as a joint station was completed. London Road was reached by a short extension on a 1 in 140 gradient down from Upperby, which was also on a 10-chain curve, authorised in the 'Lancaster deviation' Act of 1845; this spur still exists despite the complete transformation of the L. & C./L.N.W.R. other lines in the vicinity.

After Locke's report had been considered Hasell was empowered to raise once again with the other railways the question of a joint station. Discussions took place as to the possibility of continuing the L. & C. line on from London Road round the east part of the city to a joint station near the centre; but within a couple of months this idea became abortive by reason of M. & C. opposition, and the engineers of the various lines were told to draw up a plan for another site more to the west, the M. & C. agreeing to give up at cost what land it had already bought. Before the end of the year, 1844, the decision was that things could not be brought to a proper conclusion until a company had actually been incorporated to carry the railway system on into Scotland.

There the station problem remained until May 1845, when once again the L. & C. circularised the three other companies, but this time asked specifically for agreement as to Court House Square being the most suitable common site for all four railways to meet, assuming that the *extra* cost of making a station there instead of at Crown Street did not exceed £40,000. At a joint meeting of the four companies in July two resolutions were passed unanimously: (1) that a joint station was most desirable; (2) that the site at Court House Square was the most eligible, and was adopted. But the M. & C. declined to be party to a third resolution: (3) That the respective sums to be paid by each company, the management rules of the station, and all other connected matters be referred to the Board of Trade or whomsoever they may appoint, though within a couple of months the M. & C. did offer to contribute up to £4,000 towards the cost of the station construction. The L. & C. and Caley deputations had full powers from their respective companies; the N. & C. deputation agreed to recommend to its board the adoption of these resolutions.

That board, however, did not forthwith agree. It was anxious to be given accommodation at any joint station for its growing mineral traffic; and it acquiesced in the Board of Trade as referee only if the terms took cognizance of the money the N. & C. had spent on its London Road station in the previous ten years. The L. & C. would agree to neither of these points; and by the end of 1845 had written to the N. & C. to say it was unwilling to give that company the trouble of further meetings, and that in any case it might be more convenient if the joint station was confined to passenger traffic and each company made its own arrangements for goods. This, in fact, is what *did* happen, and gave rise to the array of goods and avoiding lines at a much later stage, and to the half-dozen separate goods yards spread round the city.

It is of little interest today to record the almost incessant approaches, discussions, differences and squabbles that went on from that time for years. Suffice it that from the beginning of 1846 the L. & C. was fully determined to have one common station at Carlisle, even if it had to provide all the money itself. A Bill for the station had already gone forward, and the Act (9 & 10 Vict., cap 257 of July 27, 1846) gave powers for the L. & C. to enlarge its station and to raise another £100,000 plus one-third borrowing powers. This was the practical beginning of Citadel station, though the first recorded mention of that name was in February 1847, in a report from Errington.

This Act also gave the L. & C. power to extend its railway from near the junction with the N. & C. and M. & C. lines to Borough Street, which lay to the north-west of Crown Street. This was the origin of the L. & C.'s peculiar S-curve by means of which M. & C. trains were fouled twice. On the same day as the station Act, July 27, 1846, Royal Assent was also given to an Act (9 & 10 Vict., cap. 249) enabling the Caley to deviate its scheduled line from near the Eden bridge to Crown Street. L. & C. and Caley powers thus overlapped, as it were, over the short distance from Crown Street to Borough Street. Citadel station lay between the two streets, with its frontage facing out on to Court House Square.

In September 1846 a joint meeting of the L. & C., Caley and M. & C. (the N. & C. had been invited but did not attend) resolved that the offer of Messrs. John Stephenson to erect the station for £37,982 should be accepted under the conditions that the arches, platforms and shed should be ready for traffic by January 1, 1847 (an almost impossible condition), and the whole building completed by October 1847. That these dates were not kept was scarcely the fault of the contractor, for with the breakdown in the arrangements between the four companies the L. & C. had to reduce the rate of its expenditure, and Tite, the architect, was told in July 1847 to suspend all work on the west side of the station except the platforms and approaches, and to suspend work on the portico at the east side. Not until the end of May 1848 was work resumed on the portico, and even then construction of the tower was deferred.

At the L. & C. half-yearly meeting in February 1847 the chairman's statement again repeated that the cost of the station was to be defrayed by the four railways. That was the last time such a statement could be made, though in the succeeding months there were fresh efforts to reach agreement. The L. & C. board considered the M. & C. had bound itself by a signed and sealed agreement dated June 20, 1846, to contribute towards the cost of construction; the N. & C. had not bound itself. A month or two before the completion of the first part of the general station, at an expenditure then amounting to over £60,000 provided entirely by the L. & C., that company formally suggested on May 24, 1847, to the other railways that the respective construction payments towards the cost of the station and the land purchased should be: L. & C. $\frac{3}{9}$, Caley $\frac{3}{9}$, N. & C. $\frac{2}{9}$, M. & C. $\frac{1}{9}$; and, as the L. & C. had already laid out such a large sum on the project, that £45,000 should be contributed in those proportions within the ensuing seven days, that another £15,000 in the same proportions should be paid by July 1, and a further £15,000 on August 1; also, that the interest payments the L. & C. had incurred on the borrowed money should be shared in the same proportions.

This brought matters to a definite point. Understandably, the L. & C. directors were worried about the money they had had to find and expend, and now saw dubious prospects of the other companies paying a share. They also had to face their shareholders. After some consideration, the N. & C. two months after this notice did send a cheque for part of the amount claimed to Col. Maclean, chairman of the joint station committee and a member of the L. & C. board. This was returned from the L. & C. with a note to the effect that its board had reluctantly come to the conclusion that the N. & C. could no longer be treated as parties to the construction, but that if in the future the N. & C. should desire accommodation as tenants in the new station a satisfactory solution would doubtless be found. The N. & C. not unnaturally took umbrage at this, and never again made an endeavour to share the cost. But year by year discussions were renewed as to the possibility of a tenancy of part of the station, until 1854, when the N. & C. board was so horrified at the L. & C. asking a rental as high as £1,050 a year plus a proportion of working expenses that no further negotiations took place for over two years.

Previous offers of the N. & C. had gone up as far as £500 rental plus up to £300 a year as the maximum proportion of working expenses. In 1856 further discussions were abortive, the N. & C. again offering only £500 plus £300, with a review only of the latter after 5, 7 or 10 years; but the L. & C. wanted adjustments every three years and more money. Relations of the N. & C. at the other end of its line, where it was about to get its own accommodation in Newcastle joint station, were not at all unhappy with the Newcastle & Berwick, and then the York, Newcastle & Berwick, Railways, though those relations were just beginning to develop at the time of the vital discussions in Carlisle. The N. & C. always felt that if it shared in the cost of Citadel it should have its own section of the station, as it did a few years later with the Y. N. & B.; this the L. & C. was not willing to give.

The N. & C. never became a tenant at Citadel, and for many years through passengers had to find their own way between London Road and that station, though a direct rail connection between the N. & C. and Citadel had been inserted in 1849 at the suggestion of the Railway Commissioners. Only when the North Eastern Railway took over the N. & C. as from July 17, 1862, was a change in attitude discernible; and as from January 1, 1863, it became a tenant at Citadel under an agreement dated May 14, 1862; and in practice it did have its own section of the station after the 1880 enlargement. The N.E.R. paid £1,000 a year plus a contribution to working expenses, and undertook to use no other passenger station within two miles of Citadel. The N. & C. always ran on the right-hand track and this was continued into N.E.R. days; as long as there were no daily workings into Citadel this caused little trouble, but in 1864 the N.E.R. changed the running to normal, and to suit this some signal alterations had to be made around St. Nicholas crossing and junction. London Road station was never a major establishment, and in 1857 the passenger portion of it was whitewashed at a cost of no more than £9.

The case of the M. & C. was different from that of the N. & C. In the view of the L. & C. board, the M. & C. had gone back on a definite agreement, and the matter was complicated by the seven acres of M. & C. land, much of it just where the L. & C. needed it for station extensions and approach lines. Also, the direction of the M. & C. at the time was in a peculiar state, and in 1850, following a shareholders' committee of investigation, an almost completely new board was elected and the whole management put on a better footing. A tenancy agreement for accommodation in Citadel was then made; but in the intervening years there had been much tumult and affright.

From the end of 1847 the L. & C. was no longer much concerned about the refusal of the M. & C. to become joint proprietors of Citadel; it was willing to let that company come into the station as a tenant whenever reasonable terms—on the L. & C. definition of 'reasonable'—could be fixed. The vital matter was the seven-acre Naboth's vineyard which the M. & C. had purchased early in 1844, for (*a*) it contained much ground needed for joint-station extensions and approach lines from the south, and (*b*) the L. & C. was determined to prevent the M. & C. making a

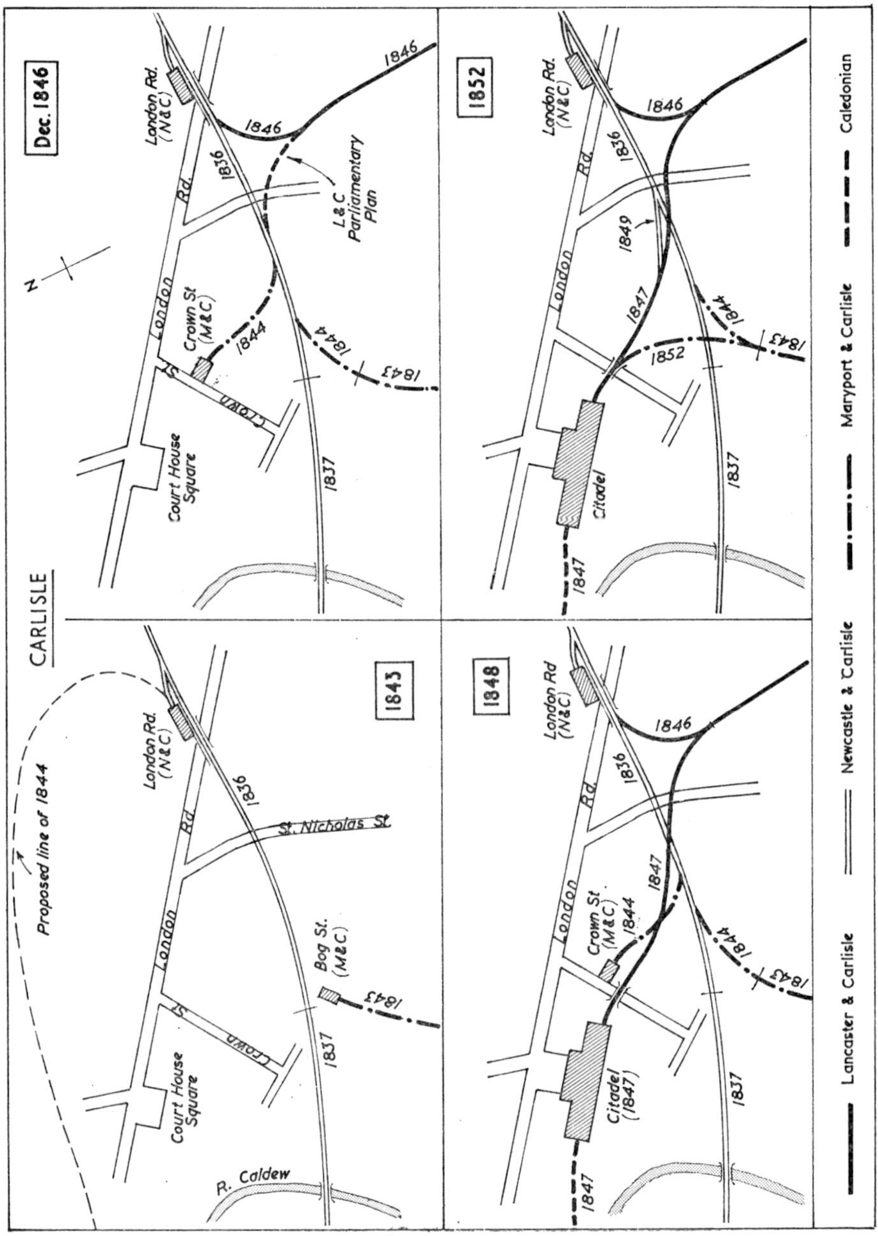

13 Quadruple map of Carlisle layout

level crossing to get to Crown Street direct from the Bog Street area. The M. & C. in 1846 had come to an agreement with the N. & C. to cross over that company's Canal branch with a direct approach to Crown Street.

Already there was a most bizarre arrangement of lines, as can be seen from the 1848 section of Fig. 13. The M. & C. temporary station at Crown Street, as promised by that railway to the L. & C. at the very first conversations in March 1844, was opened on December 30 of that year, but no direct extension to it from Bog Street had been made. Instead a short curve was laid down to the N. & C., and another reverse curve led off that line to Crown Street. Thus an arriving M. & C. train ran over the N. & C. for a few hundred yards, and then backed up to Crown Street. In the reverse direction the train backed down to the N. & C. There was not much trouble about this until in the summer of 1847 the L. & C. began to approach Citadel, and crossed the existing Crown Street branch on the level. Worse, it also crossed the N. & C. Canal branch on the level at St. Nicholas. From that time on a city-bound M. & C. train fouled the St. Nicholas level crossing of the L. & C. before it had got far enough to back the tail on to its own line; and then, when it did get on to its own branch, the L. & C. crossed over it again. The L. & C. track at that time was a little east of the present-day L. & M. Region main line. Simplification of movement might have been gained by the M. & C. going direct from Bog Street to Crown Street at the end of 1844, but this route required an embankment and money was short. Moreover, at that time the M. & C. *did* consider Crown Street as a station that might be temporary. But if the direct spur had been put in then the M. & C. would have established clear priority.

It is difficult to understand why the L. & C. laid its track on just the trace it did. Its 'Parliamentary' line is shown paralleling the M. & C. track at the southern end, and in such fashion that only the St. Nicholas crossing would foul either M. & C. or N. & C. trains. As the company had to go to Parliament in any case for an Act to finance and construct the large common station, there must be regret that a complete first class scheme was not brought up in the bill. Certainly there would have been opposition, but the cost of overcoming that would not have borne so hardly on L. & C. finance as did the actual happenings of 1846–51; the Commons would have been inclined to look favourably on such a scheme; and the shocking and dangerous layout of lines which existed for so long to the south of Citadel might have been obviated.

As a result of the tangle, the L. & C. in 1849 resorted to law to get possession of the M. & C. ground, after an agreement with the Caley to offer the M. & C. £7,005 for the area, which was in line with the M. & C.'s own suggestion made in the summer of 1845 of £1,000 an acre. The legal process was hurried on when it was found that the M. & C. and N. & C. were thinking of going to Parliament with a Bill to join tracks and make a joint station of their own on M. & C. land at Princess Street, just short of Crown Street. Errington was instructed to make sure the rails at the M. & C. station were taken up as soon as the sheriff gave possession of the land, to prevent any further level crossing being put in by the M. & C. as part of a direct line to Crown Street.

The under-sheriff of the county gave possession on March 17, 1849, after a jury had awarded £7,171 4s. 3d. as the value of the land and the L. & C. had paid the money in. Errington's men not only took up some of the rails but removed the station buildings, and the M. & C. had to make hurried arrangements with the N. & C. for the use of London Road station at £250 a year until such time as a way could be found out of the impasse. Legal proceedings in the January had been complicated by the presence of George Hudson, who at the time had a personal lease of both M. & C. and N. & C. The kaleidoscopic atmosphere enshrouding Carlisle is further lighted by the fact that in the same month, April 1848, that Hudson made his first offer to the N. & C., that company also had a leasing offer from Hope-Johnstone on behalf of the Caley, unknown to the L. & C. Only the bare bones of the M. & C. Crown Street story have been set out here; the body corporeal in all its unhealthiness was dissected in G. O. Holt's article 'The Battle of Crown Street' in *The Railway Magazine* for August 1963.

After the reconstitution of the M. & C. board a permanent tenancy at Citadel was arranged, with rent fixed by arbitration under an agreement dated April 2, 1851; and from June 1, 1851, the M. & C. trains used that station, at first by reversal off the N. & C. on to the L. & C., but from August 8, 1852, up the new direct spur from Bog Street. The tenancy terms did not go uncriticised by M. & C. shareholders, for at times the amount paid rose to £600 a year. That was one of the real sources of all the troubles with the M. & C. and N. & C. in relation to the joint station; they were small companies unaccustomed to the amounts which big main-line railways thought normal; they were not to get their own accommodation, and felt the L. & C./Caley combination would always put its own traffic interests first, a feeling shared to the full by the four other larger companies that became tenants at the station in later years.

One wry reminder of the quarrels over Naboth's vineyard remained. When all the land was taken and occupied it was found that not all of the seven acres was needed by the L. & C./Caley combination. Therefore under a conveyance dated April 2, 1851, an area at the corner of Crown Street and Currock Street was leased back to the M. & C. for 999 years at a peppercorn rent after the M. & C. had paid £1,300 an acre to get the ground back; and this formed the inner end of the ground on which the M. & C. Crown Street (or Bog) goods depot and sidings were formed. In the same area some excess land also was given later to Iredale's brewery in part payment of other land acquired for the station enlargement over the years 1876–80. The M. & C. depot was further west in Crown Street than the original M. & C. station; the site of the latter in later years was occupied by the L.N.W.R. St. Nicholas depot.

With the defection of the M. & C. and N. & C. the Caley and the L. & C. came to an easy agreement in principle to share the cost of Citadel, but the L. & C. was led into much deeper financial waters than previously because the Caley would not pay up. In early days the financial direction of the Caley was most inexperienced, and the L. & C. had to carry much of the financial burden at Carlisle for several years. That company took drastic action against the N. & C. when the suggested proportion of the initial £45,000 was not paid promptly in July 1847; but it gave immense rope to the Caley when that railway paid only £5,000 instead of £15,000 due, and made no further payment for many a long month.

At that time the L. & C. had advanced £56,490 on the station and adjacent ground, and the Caley's £5,000 was all it had got in. The Caley was told a month or so later that the L. & C. had laid out £62,000, and as the two other railways had backed out the Caley was asked to pay half the total and to concur in going on with the whole station on a 50-50 basis. The Caley, then within a month of wanting to start using the station, quickly agreed to the second question; but as its fluid cash was short it asked if the L. & C. would accept a debenture as payment. This the L. & C. would not do, though it seems eventually to have taken a bill; but so determined were the L. & C. directors to clear up the position and find out just where they did stand that they told the Caley it could back out if it liked, and come in later as a tenant.

At once the Caley intimated its wish to continue as joint owner; but time and time again had to be reminded that it was not paying up. As late as April 1848, after the Caley had been using Citadel for nearly seven months, the L. & C. board had to minute: "that it is really and absolutely essential for the L. & C. interests that the balance of £21,885 13s. 0d. due from the Caledonian be at once paid, and that the Caledonian board is urgently called upon to make payment accordingly." Again in the August there was pressure for £30,000 then due. Even in July 1849 there was still £10,000 outstanding, but by that time the Caley was having to pay 5 per cent interest on its non-payments. Well over £100,000 had then been expended on the station and land, of which the Caley had contributed only £30,000. After that matters improved; the total cost of the station works at the beginning of 1854 was £178,324, but the Caley had then paid £85,391 as its portion.

This great leniency of the L. & C. over a long and difficult period was the practical expression of the minute of the provisional L. & C. board on January 25, 1844: "That this company will co-operate with the promoters of the extension of the railway from Carlisle to Edinburgh and Glasgow to the utmost of their power;" and of the statement at the general meeting on January 15, 1845: "that of the three Scottish schemes the Caledonian should be actively and cordially supported as it offers superior means of communication."

That leniency was by no means confined to joint-station finance; for just at the time the Caley was so tardy in its payments it did not hesitate to approach its neighbour for more positive help, on grounds that today seem sheer effrontery considering the circumstances at the time, though reflecting the financial mess into which the Caley had already begun to drift. As soon as the line from Carlisle to Beattock was opened in September 1847 a most novel proposal was put up. Because of the L. & C.

board's consistent friendly feelings and helpful attitude towards the Caley, despite that railway's financial misdemeanours in regard to Citadel, it concurred with the Caley suggestions, and agreed that: "If the Caledonian makes any new arrangement to expedite the opening of the remainder of its line (i.e. Beattock to Edinburgh and Glasgow) the L. & C. would be prepared to assume that its passenger receipts above £1,000 a week between such opening and the hitherto assumed date of March 1, 1848, are due to that earlier opening, and in such case the L. & C. would be prepared to pay half of that excess to the Caledonian towards the extra payment to the contractors." This decision was not made without great dissension in the L. & C. board. Fortunately, the actual opening date of the Caley was only a fortnight before the date mentioned, and not in the December as the Caley had hoped.

Financial expenses in connection with Citadel did not end with the full payment of the constructional and land costs, even though the L. & C. proportion of these was over £20,000 more than the company had expected when the four-company proposals were initiated. Carlisle Corporation also needed its rights observed, despite the great benefits the north-south railway would bring to the city. It had certain medieval toll rights on stock and goods coming into the county; these it was prepared to waive as far as traffic over the L. & C. was concerned for a yearly payment of £240, less £40 a year as long as the M. & C. and N. & C. did not have a permanent interest in the joint station. At the option of the Corporation, this annual payment could be commuted by a down payment of £6,000, which was legalised in the station Act of July 27, 1846 (9 & 10 Vict., cap. 257).

The Corporation exercised that right almost at once; but according to the Act, until such time as the M. & C. and N. & C. acquired a permanent interest in the station, the Corporation had to pay the L. & C. £40 a year. Long years after the passing of the L. & C. as an operator, some one in Carlisle realised the Corporation had been paying unnecessarily £40 a year to the L. & C. and L.N.W.R., as the M. & C. and the N. & C.'s successor, the North Eastern Railway, had for a long time had a permanent interest in the station, even though just as tenants and not as joint owners. Not until 1882 did the case finally arrive at the higher courts, and the L.N.W.R. had to pay Carlisle Corporation £540 plus costs which would be several times that sum. As to the toll rights, Carlisle city holds them still, and any traveller who cares to venture 60 yd. outside the Citadel portico will find the 1967 scale pasted up.

On August 23, 1848, traffic from Dumfries off the Glasgow, Dumfries & Carlisle Railway began to come into Citadel, before any proper arrangements had been made for it, or any tolls and charges fixed by the L. & C.; and the directors' station committee of the time had at once to consider the question. This traffic was just from Dumfries; the line from that burgh to Kilmarnock was not opened until 1850. The Caley at once began to claim that the Dumfries traffic, which travelled over the Caley between Gretna junction and Carlisle, should be considered as Caley traffic, doubtless hoping to come to some private remunerative arrangement with the Dumfries company; but the L. & C. was adamant that this should not be so, and that the Dumfries company must pay a reasonable share of the station's working expenses. After the Glasgow & South Western Railway Act took effect, from the opening of the last section of line from Cumnock to Dumfries on October 28, 1850, new arrangements were made; and from March 1, 1851, under an agreement of that date, the G. & S.W.R. became a 999-year tenant at Citadel at a rent of £500 p.a. the first year, £750 the second year, and £1,000 a year for all succeeding years, though after 1853 the actual rents paid were between £825 and £900 a year. This reduction was coincident with a traffic arrangement made with the Caley, following the promotion by the South-West of a Bill to build a line from Gretna to Brampton, and so get an alternative route to the south via the N. & C., for the G. & S.W.R. felt it was being excluded from much of the traffic to and from the south of Carlisle by the strong alliance between the L.N.W.R., L. & C. and Caley. Some years before the Caley itself had proposed to build such a competing line.

After the L. & C. had been leased to the L.N.W.R., the North British Railway in 1860 was given in one of its own Acts running powers over a short length of Caley track into Carlisle, and authority to use Citadel. An agreement dated January 8, 1861, called for the rental to be settled by arbitration, and the L.N.W.R./Caley agreed to apply for an Act to enlarge the station. The N.B.R. began to use Citadel on August 1, 1862, for trains off the Waverley route, and from July 1, 1864, for trains on the Port Carlisle and Silloth railways, which in their private days had terminated at the Canal basin, though they had running powers over the N. & C. Canal branch. In due time the Midland was admitted, following the completion of the Settle and Carlisle line; as and from May 1, 1876, it ran through Anglo-Scottish expresses with the N.B.R. and G. & S.W.R., though this was before the remodelling of the station and approach and goods lines had been completed. The Midland had running powers over the N.E.R. from the junction near London Road.

In February 1849 Errington had stressed that the positions of the parties occupying Citadel should be settled by legal contract, and that full rules and regulations for the working of the station should be drawn up, for he considered the then existing state of affairs as dangerous. A month later he presented draft regulations; and a secretary was appointed to have the superintendence of the station and charge of the accounts and statistics connected with the traffic, being responsible to the four directors of the L. & C. and Caley who sat as a station committee. Previous to this Bolden had acted as secretary to the station committee.

Not until July 22, 1861, under Act 24 & 25 Vict., cap. 166, were statutory powers granted for the better regulation of the station. The management then came under the Carlisle Citadel Station Joint Committee, which more or less had the autonomy of a separate railway, with jurisdiction over the station and its traffic and the approach lines in each direction. It was composed of two L.N.W.R. and two Caley directors. Existing agreements with the M. & C., G. & S.W.R. and N.B.R. were confirmed by the Act, new works and further land purchase authorised, and power also given to raise another £25,000. A fairly substantial enlargement of the station was made in 1861–62 at a cost said to have been £39,000. Before that time there was a through platform line with a bay at each end, and a second through face. By 1848 there was an underground connecting passage between the two platforms, and this must have been a very early example. There was also one goods avoiding track running past the west side. These facilities handled up to 50 trains in 24 hr. From about 1860 a ticket-collecting platform was in use to the south of Citadel, just where the loop from the N. & C. came in; and there was a similar platform just north of the bridge over the River Caldew where tickets were collected from incoming Caley and G.S.W. trains.

In 1871 the N.B.R., only a tenant, took the extraordinary step of promoting a Bill for powers to enlarge the station, but this was rejected. The next year the L.N.W.R. brought forward a Bill for the same purpose, and this, too, was rejected, but on the grounds that the joint owners had not gone before an arbitrator as required by the 1866 Act (29 & 30 Vict., cap. 223), dated July 16 of that year, for the Midland Railway's Settle and Carlisle line. In conformity with the terms of that Act, the Board of Trade then appointed an arbitrator to approve of a plan for the enlargement of the station, as some of the tenant companies were opposing the plan submitted by the L.N.W.R. and Caley. Joseph Cubitt was selected, but died before he could make any award. Therefore the two owning companies and the Midland came to an agreement on December 16, 1872, as to what additional accommodation was needed for the last-named railway, and how it should be paid for. This was sanctioned by Act 36 & 37 Vict., cap. 187, of July 21, 1873, which gave authority for the complete remodelling of the station and the approach lines, and for the construction of a series of goods avoiding lines.

In August 1877 the goods avoiding lines, by-passing Citadel well to the west, were brought into use. They were worked by a goods traffic committee composed of two directors each from the L.N.W.R., Caley, G. & S.W.R. and Midland, all of which had contributed to the cost of construction. A year or two later the Dentonholme Joint Committee of the Midland, N.B.R. and G. & S.W.R. built another shorter joint loop line for freight traffic; but the N.B.R. had to abandon, by terms of the 1873 Act, its own proposed full loop round to relief lines south of Citadel which had been authorised by an N.B.R. Act, 28 & 29 Vict., cap. 204, of July 5, 1865.

The enlargement of the station itself was completed in 1880, at a cost, including that of altering the approach lines and building the avoiding lines, stated to be £379,135. Since that time no additions or improvements of any moment have been made to the platforms or to the tracks within the Station Joint Committee's jurisdiction; but electric light was installed in 1898–99 at a cost of £9,568; and there is a record that the whole station roof was reglazed in 1901 at the relatively enormous expense of £12,367. Until January 1, 1916, the maintenance of Citadel was undertaken in five-year periods alternately by the L.N.W.R. and the Caley; from that date until the Grouping the maintenance of buildings, roofing,

Plate XXIXa The 12.40 ex-Carlisle stops at Shap Summit to detach the pilot; both engines are Webb "Jumbos" [*LGRP*

Plate XXIXb Main southbound platform (now No. 4) at Carlisle Citadel about 1919, showing G&SWR coal-eater 4-4-0 No. 327, a Midland compound on train alongside present platform No. 3, and an LNWR "Claughton" 4-6-0 on the centre road [*Rixon Bucknall collection*

Plate XXXa Caledonian 4-6-0 *Cardean* between Preston and Wigan during the interchange trials in July 1909 [British Rail

Plate XXXb Bowen Cooke 4-6-2T and Webb 0-6-0 hauling freight train through Shap cutting

Plate XXXIa Stanier Pacific No. 46238 *City of Carlisle* leaving Penrith in a snow storm with an up special [*Alec Fraser*

Plate XXXIb The Lune bridge at Lancaster as renewed in 1962-63 using the old piers. Compare with view of the original bridge taken from the same spot in Plate Xa. In foreground is a catenary of the Lancaster-Heysham electrified line [*courtesy, C. L. Parkinson*

Plate XXXIIa English Electric Type 4 diesel No. 376 enters Borrow Beck viaduct south of Tebay with the up day Perth-Euston express [*Derek Cross*

Plate XXXIIb English Electric gas-turbine mechanical-drive locomotive built up on the chassis of a "Black Five" hauling test train up Shap; trailing load 370 tons [*Derek Cross*

platforms and electric lighting was done by the Caley, and that of the permanent-way and signals in the Joint Committee area by the L.N.W.R.

The extent and complexity of the lines adjacent to the station had grown gradually up to the time of the 1873 Bill. Some of the extremely awkward features of the 1848/49 layout remained for a long time, in particular around St. Nicholas. By 1852 the arrangement had been simplified through the elimination of the M. & C. Crown Street terminus and its back shunt, and by the construction of the loop from Bogfield direct to Citadel; but the L. & C./N. & C. level crossing at St. Nicholas remained, and also within a few yards of it a busy road, St. Nicholas Street, crossed both lines on the level. From the opening of Citadel there were many proposals to abolish the road crossing; but despite memorials from Carlisle Corporation and recommendations from the Railway Commissioners, it was 1852 before the two railways could agree on the design of the bridge and their proportionate contributions to the cost.

The rail crossing survived, but had its inconveniences, and also its troubles for, among others, Hall Pearson, L. & C. engine-driver, who in 1859 ran into a train at the crossing "and damaged two ladies", his bad manners costing him 5s. fine plus loss of wages while suspended. But the rail crossing itself remained—until on the night of July 9/10, 1870, a North Eastern goods train cut through an up Anglo-Scottish express and killed six persons. The goods train driver and his young and inexperienced fireman had been drinking along at the London Road end of the Canal branch, and the train was taken from there to Canal by the fireman alone, the driver remaining behind. On the return journey, with 27 loaded wagons behind a 0–6–0 tender engine, neither the lights of the converging express nor the light of the crossing signal seemed to register with the fireman. Saxby's interlocking was by then installed at the crossing, but of course could make no difference with complete disregard of signals. The distant signal between Canal Junction and St. Nicholas crossing stop signal was defective, and its lamp was unlit; on the other hand the crossing stop signal and the stop signal beyond (also visible) were both showing red. A most astonishing tale of laxity in regard to rules by all at the Carlisle end of the N.E.R. was revealed.

Even then the crossing itself remained inviolate until the complete rearrangement of all the lines south of Citadel between 1873 and 1877. The wonder is that no serious accident had happened before. From 1862 the L.N.W.R. pointsman at the crossing had simple gong communication with his colleague 250 yd. to the south where the L.N.W.R. yard and depot tracks debouched; but the latter, in addition to keeping the tracks set for main-line trains, had also to look after another 42 pairs of points in the yards. In the 1860s the L.N.W.R. main line from Upperby inwards was moved over a little to the west, and the curves thereby eased; about that time the present double-track connection from the N.E.R. to Citadel was put in, but for some years it was single where it came off the N.E.R. Canal branch and became double after a few yards. The L.N.W.R. branch to the St. Nicholas goods station, on the site of the old M. & C. Crown Street station, was laid down in 1870–71 and taken up in 1968.

L

Because of the complexity and amount of traffic about, an L.N.W.R. general manager's rule of April 1889 laid down that Citadel was to be considered a terminal station by entering trains, and so extra care had to be taken. This supplemented long-standing rules of great clarity about the slow approach to be made by main-line trains. Despite this, and another instruction by F. W. Webb in May 1889 warning drivers to test their automatic vacuum brakes fully, a down express on March 4, 1890, ran right through Citadel from the south before colliding with a Caledonian engine, No. 62, at the northern end. The accident took place about 3.30, and the train involved was the 20.00 ex Euston the previous evening, composed of 13 vehicles including three sleepers and headed by compound engine No. 515.

This mishap has been referred to as the second 'frozen vacuum brake accident'; but though some half-pint of water was found in the belly of the pipe between engine and tender it had nothing to do with the accident. The real cause was mismanagement by the driver, but a contributory cause was Webb's disinclination to give up entirely the simple vacuum brake. The train was fully braked on the automatic system; so was the engine, but there was also a device on the driver's brake valve which enabled him to change over to simple vacuum working.

When stopping to detach the pilot at Shap the train driver shut off his small ejector, as was common practice on the Premier Line at the time, but he forgot to open it again. He ran all the way down to Carlisle under clear signals, during which time the brake was leaking on, unnoticed because the engine was being steamed hard, despite the falling gradient, to make up lost time. When the driver tested his vacuum on approaching Carlisle there was little or no vacuum in the pipe and he felt no further check to the train. Trying to blow up his vacuum by the use of the large ejector, he then became anxious and confused, omitted to whistle for guards' brakes, took out the pin in the driver's brake valve and altered the lever to simple vacuum. He also apparently took off the steam brake at the time he first tried to get automatic braking power by turning on the large ejector. Also he pulled his brake lever only to the notch in the slide instead of pulling it right over; he thus took the brake off the engine and off every vehicle in the train, so that only the hand screw brakes applied on two vehicles by the guards near Upperby were giving any retarding force. The guards had opened their release valves to put on the automatic brake, but at that time the driver was pulling it off by the use of his large ejector.

An attempt was made at the enquiry to show that the water in the belly of the pipe would be frozen in the cold early hours; but the inspector, Col. Rich, pointed out that a plug of ice would have caused the automatic brake to leak on and that it could not have been taken off by the driver as long as the ice remained. The inspector criticised this combination of simple and automatic braking, and also the arrangement of it whereby the simple vacuum was applied by pulling a lever and the automatic system by pushing the same lever. Moreover, he considered the L.N.W.R. practice of working with only 17 in. of vacuum quite insufficient, and said they should never go below 20 in. The coroner had summoned a jury of 18 men; *they* went beyond the inspector, and added a rider: "We are further of the opinion that the L.N.W.R. are incurring a very grave responsibility by using a brake of such uncertain and unreliable character."

Curiously this accident was paralleled by another over 20 years before, when, about 6.30 on Saturday morning of August 13, 1870, a down Anglo-Scottish express ran at too high a speed through the station and collided at the north end with the stock for a Caley local train which was being marshalled. An even closer parallel, the 'first frozen vacuum brake accident', occurred on December 21, 1885, when a north-bound express of 14 vehicles, fitted throughout with the simple vacuum system, ran through Citadel and struck a Midland engine; plugs of ice were found in the droops at all pipe connections.

Brakes were ever a trouble at Carlisle in the good old days. On July 7, 1880, the 5.0 p.m. up express out of Glasgow on the G. & S.W.R. ran into the 8.0 p.m. N.B.R. train from Carlisle to Silloth just north of Citadel at a time when signalling alterations were under way. The inquiry showed that though the Westinghouse air brake was operating on the locomotive the automatic brake was not functioning on the train, because at Dumfries an unbraked fish van had been put into the train just behind the engine, this location being chosen to obviate too much shunting at Carlisle, where the van had to go on to an L.N.W.R. train! Thus the train was running without continuous brakes over the last 33 miles, and the driver knew it. The other curious aspect was that G. & S.W.R. and N.B.R. trains were involved on track that belonged to the Caledonian.

In the very early years at Carlisle there was a primitive L. & C. shed with accommodation for three engines just south of St. Nicholas crossing but a move was soon made a little further south to Upperby. The Caledonian had a locomotive shed under West Walls, and this was on ground owned by the L. & C. for which a rent was paid. When the G. & S.W.R. began to run into Carlisle its engines were given stabling room alongside the Caley locomotives below the Walls. Under the 1873 Act the Caley had to provide similar accommodation at its new shed to be built at Kingmoor, but this was not taken up, and the Sou' West came to an arrangement with the Midland for accommodation to the south, at Durran Hill sheds. This lasted until 1896 when the G. & S.W.R. opened new sheds of its own at Currock, reached by running powers over the M. & C., for which it had to pay a minimum of £750 a year. Some time after Grouping these sheds were converted to a goods depot, and the G. & S.W.R. engines then went to Kingmoor. The Caley shed was moved from West Walls to Kingmoor in 1880, but the original timber-framed shed there was replaced by another building on the same site in 1901. Under the 1873 Act the Station Committee had to erect a two-engine shed for the M. & C. on Committee ground to the north east of the N.E.R., and another shed for the same railway in the Bog Street area, each to be complete with turntable and water tank.

The route layout at Carlisle as it existed in 1921–22 just prior to Grouping is shown in Fig. 14; and it was at this time, as from January 1,

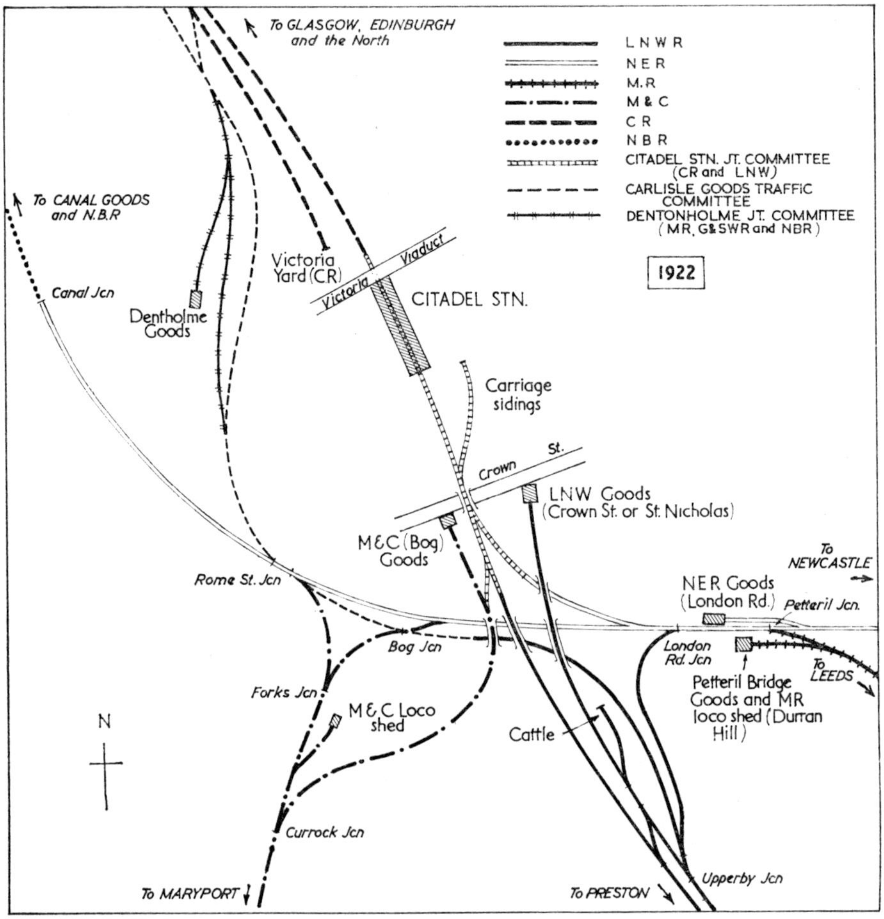

14 Carlisle layout, 1922

1923, that the Citadel Station Joint Committee came to an end, as both L.N.W.R. and Caley were merged in the L.M.S.R. Since that time the Viaduct yard of the Caley has disappeared; it was uplifted when the new marshalling yard north of Etterby was opened. The G. & S.W.R. shed at Currock was closed after Grouping, and the Durran Hill shed of the Midland after Beeching. Otherwise the tracks remain more or less as in 1922, except that many of them are much less used.

A surprising feature of the last 88 years in Citadel's history is that no attempt has ever been made to get the best use out of the tracks, platforms and space. There is not so much need for that now, but over the half-century from the middle 90s to the end of the second world war considerable improvement in working could have been effected at very moderate cost. On the west side were, and are, five carriage roads under the roof, and nothing like full use has ever been required from these. At

between Green Ayre and Poulton Lane (Morecambe) comprised 11 trains each way in 1853, and seven each way on Sundays. In the 1859 timetables a special through train by the Green Ayre loop is shown as running from Leeds and Bradford to Ulverston and Whitehaven, with a time of 4¼ hr. from Leeds to Ulverston.

Coincident with the initiation of the Morecambe works there came into the ken of the L. & C. that magnificent project for a direct line from York to Carlisle. As a preventive measure the directors of the L. & C. thought first of getting powers to build a branch from near Clifton to Appleby and Brough; but the York & Carlisle at once suggested that if the L. & C. gave up this idea it would build a branch to link up at Penrith, and let the L. & C. take up one-third of the capital. There the matter rested for some months, in which time the name was changed to the Northern Counties Union, and an Act of Incorporation (9 & 10 Vict., cap. 260) obtained on July 27, 1846, for a company with a capital of £3,000,000 to make a south-east/north-west line from Thirsk or Northallerton to Penrith, crossed at Kirkby Stephen by an east-west line from Bishop Auckland to Tebay. These proposals did not disturb the L. & C. directors; and after some approaches by the N.C.U. they said they were not undisposed to take a lease for a limited time, in a way of a guarantee on the cost, of the section between Tebay and Kirkby Stephen, or even to Brough, as long as the other parts of the N.C.U. were put in hand at once. However, the whole N.C.U. project fizzled out, and the Tebay line came into being over a dozen years later under quite different sponsors.

In the same years, 1845–46, interest was being shown in the possibility of a railway to link Ulverston with the L. & C. in the Carnforth–Milnthorpe area; and the L. & C. had some surveys made of an eastward extension into the Craven area of Yorkshire, so as "to complete in the most direct manner the railway communication from the port of Whitehaven to Yorkshire." This was probably just to let the Little North Western promoters know there was such an entity as the L. & C., even if it had no line open. The Ulverstone & Lancaster Railway was not incorporated until July 24, 1851 (14 & 15 Vict., cap. 102); it ran only to Carnforth and never had any intention of making a separate line from that town on to the second place mentioned in its title. The line from Ulverston to Carnforth was opened to goods traffic on August 10, 1857, and to passenger traffic on August 16. Though the tonnage brought on to the L. & C. was substantial, the ton-mileage was not. Nevertheless this line was of considerable importance to the industrial development of Furness and West Cumberland. The Carnforth–Wennington joint line of the Furness and Midland Railways was opened on April 10, 1867 (goods) and on June 6, 1867 (passengers). At that time Carnforth station was enlarged and became L.N.W.R./Furness joint; the Midland used the station as a tenant. Yet by a peculiar arrangement the whole station was not joint; the up main platform and its bay remained wholly L.N.W.R., and was maintained by that company.

By the end of 1849 the Little North Western had completed its 'main' line from Skipton to Ingleton, and at the latter place it remained. In 1855, when it was realised that the powers for construction had lapsed, at a time when the Midland and also the Great Northern were showing some interest in the line's possibilities as a means of them getting a long-distance service through to Carlisle, the scheme for the line on to Low Gill was resuscitated. But after the friction with the Little North Western, and the Barker party's efforts, the atmosphere at Euston and Lancaster was now somewhat different to what it had been a decade earlier, and led to the L.N.W.R. and L. & C. taking action, because of the threat to Scottish traffic. The Little North Western by that time was in close association with the Midland, and had actually been worked by that railway since June 1852. Therefore the L. & C. promoted a rival Bill to build a line from near Tebay to Ingleton, a move possibly enforced by the L.N.W.R. nominees on the board as part of the Huish anti-Midland policy, and as a counter to the wish of Barker and some other L. & C. shareholders to amalgamate with the N.W.R., as related in Chapter IX.

By control of such a line the L.N.W.R./L. & C. combine hoped to prevent the branch, and the existing end-on line from Ingleton to Skipton, ever being used by the Midland; but it was defeated (on paper) in this object, not by the Little North Western or the Midland, but by the House of Commons Committee that examined the two rival Bills. After 15 days of hearing counsels' argument and the evidence of others, the Committee announced:

> "We have come to an unanimous decision, first of all, to fill up the gap between Tebay and Ingleton with one or other of these lines, giving the preference to the L. & C. project, but propose to introduce into the preamble of the Bill, to be followed by clauses corresponding to them, words to this effect: 'Whereas for the purposes as well of local and other traffic, as of through traffic from Carlisle to the Southern, Midland, Eastern and other parts of England, the construction of a railway communication between the L. & C. line and the North Western at Ingleton is necessary.' We make that a condition precedent, and we will not grant the line without it."

The L. & C. consented to make the line under those conditions; the words above were inserted in the preamble of the Bill, and a clause put in to secure to the public the proper use of the railway for all purposes of through traffic. The L. & C. also had to purchase from the Little North Western, within six months of the passing of the Act, all the lands acquired north of Ingleton and any works which might have been done thereon, at prices to be determined by arbitration. Another Act (20 & 21 Vict., cap. 134, of 1857) passed at the same time to enable the Little North Western to abandon the project north of Ingleton also confirmed the powers given to that company under Act 12 Vict., cap. 19, of May 24, 1849, to lease or sell at any time in the future the whole or any part of its line to the Midland and L. & C. or to one of them. The N.W.R. was actually leased to the Midland in perpetuity as from January 1, 1859.

In its earlier years the N.W.R. had various proposals for the northern end of its line. First it was to join the L. & C. by Low Gill; then a junction was proposed at Dillicar, which would have involved a big viaduct; and yet another idea was to go further up the east bank of the Lune and cross over the river to the north of Borrow Beck to join the L. & C. Though the L. & C., or L.N.W.R., had to buy land acquired by the N.W.R., the line as built did not follow strictly any of the routes mapped out by the N.W.R. between Sedbergh and the Anglo-Scottish main line.

Authorisation for the L. & C. to build its line to Ingleton was contained in Act 20 & 21 Vict., cap. 151, of August 25, 1857; the additional capital permitted was £300,000 plus the usual one-third borrowing powers; but calls were not to be more than 20 per cent and not more than three-fifths per annum. Length of line authorised was 18.8 miles plus a branch of 1.25 miles, which branch was to be a south-facing curve near Low Gill and ending near Grayrigg. Completion of the works and line was to be within four years, and ruling gradient was to be 1 in 100. Locke and Errington were appointed engineers at £300 a mile.

The L. & C., and L.N.W.R. after the summer of 1859, took their time, and the line was not opened until August 24, 1861, for freight and September 16 of the same year for passenger trains, the former date being the last day within the statutory period. The L.N.W.R. had to complete the works, which had really been initiated at its own wish. A change in detail was made by a second Act (21 & 22 Vict., cap. 128) of July 23, 1858, which permitted the south-facing curve at Low Gill to be abandoned, and the sharp north curve at the same location to be eased considerably as it joined the main line. It was this easing or diversion that resulted in the fine 11-arch stone viaduct which was, and still is, though abandoned, such a visible feature when rounding the curve from Grayrigg to Low Gill on the main line to Glasgow. Though now 107 years old, this viaduct, one of Errington's last works, is still in fine condition. Peter Baughan in his book *North of Leeds* gives a diagram of the various junctions and connections proposed at Low Gill over the years 1842–61.

Despite the special terms of the Commons Committee in acceding to the Bill, the L.N.W.R. took all steps to prevent through traffic. Passengers had to change at Ingleton, where there were two stations, although the service was such that passengers did not have to change stations—only trains. There was never any reasonable connection at Tebay, and no Midland carriages to or from Scotland were permitted for a long time. Speed limit over the line was 45 m.p.h., and 15 m.p.h. over the viaduct into Low Gill.

How the L.N.W.R. got away with this performance must remain an unanswered question; but in large measure it led to the construction of the Midland main line from Settle Junction to Carlisle, whereby the L.N.W.R. lost much more revenue than it would have done by co-operating with the Midland from the beginning. The 'Premier Line' realised this too late; overtures were made to the Midland, and eventually that railway sought powers to abandon construction of the Settle to Carlisle line, but the legislature would not give permission. The whole Clapham Junction to Low Gill line never really had a purpose other than as a through railway, and the Commons Committee showed more than usual prescience in its addition to the preamble. Even under Beeching and Raymond it would have been far better to keep this line and use it, closing the Midland from Settle to Appleby if not through to Carlisle, for with the altered traffic pattern today the Low Gill to Carlisle section is easily capable of taking what traffic could come off the Midland, and that traffic would be a useful feed to justify electrification.

From Ingleton the L. & C. branch, after the closure of Middleton station many years ago, had the unusual distinction of each successive station being in a different county: Ingleton in Yorkshire, Kirkby Lonsdale in Lancashire, Barbon in Westmorland, Sedbergh in Yorkshire, and Low Gill in Westmorland. Moreover, Kirkby Lonsdale town is in Westmoreland, though the station, a mile-and-a-half away, is in Lancashire. A curiosity was that though trains began and ended at Tebay, the junction points at Low Gill came off the main line north of that station, so that a second set of platforms had to be provided alongside the main-line pair, but they were at a slightly lower level. The original L. & C. main-line station at Low Gill, half-a-mile to the south of the last one, was built specifically for Sedbergh traffic, and it got what there was through a connecting omnibus service.

After the 1870s, when there was a connection from Leeds at 14.50 off the 8.55 ex St. Pancras which joined at Tebay the 10.10 out of Euston, and a return service due into Leeds at 17.10, the only regular through train services to the north seem to have been a Midland Leeds–Keswick train for a few summers before the 1914–19 war and for a while afterwards; and one Midland Anglo–Scottish express for a season or two beginning in July 1910. The latter was the 10.00 ex Leeds, and the return working left Carlisle at 13.17. Perhaps the most curious passenger train service ever to use the L. & C. Ingleton branch was an evening train between the two world wars, which ran through from Kendal to Ingleton, with reversals both at Oxenholme and Low Gill in the course of the 35-mile journey. This train had a Saturdays-only predecessor up to 1914 which took 79 min. including seven intermediate stops and the two reversals.

Only one other branch was promoted by the L. & C. during its independent working days; that was the short loop from Hest Bank to a road level crossing on the Little North Western line at Bare Lane, on the outskirts of Morecambe. Powers for this branch were contained in the general Act 22 & 23 Vict., cap. 124, which was concerned mainly with the consolidation of the various L. & C. Acts, the amalgamation of the L. & P., and the lease of the K. & W. As the Royal Assent was dated August 13, 1859, only a month before the decision to lease the L. & C., the branch was actually built by the L.N.W.R., and worked by that company from its opening on August 8, 1864. Originally the branch was double track, but was soon singled.

When promoting the Bill in 1858 the L. & C. proposed to go further into Morecambe, and to have full use of the N.W.R. and its Morecambe harbour. The N.W.R. countered with a proposal to build a short connecting line to link the L. & C. main line with the Lancaster–Morecambe branch just north of the Lune. In the end, the N.W.R., still a legal entity though leased to the Midland, dropped this proposal in return for the L. & C. dropping the harbour part and certain running powers from its Bill.

The reason for this Hest Bank–Morecambe branch was to try and develop an export trade from Morecambe Harbour of coke and other minerals coming from Durham and Cleveland cross-country to Tebay, over a line being projected at the same time by other interests to bring coke to the developing Furness haematite industry. What traffic of this type there ever was over the Morecambe branch eventually reversed after Heysham harbour and the Carnforth ironworks were built; and L.N.W.R. working books prior to the first world war had special regulations for the handling of laden mineral trains from Heysham to Carnforth,

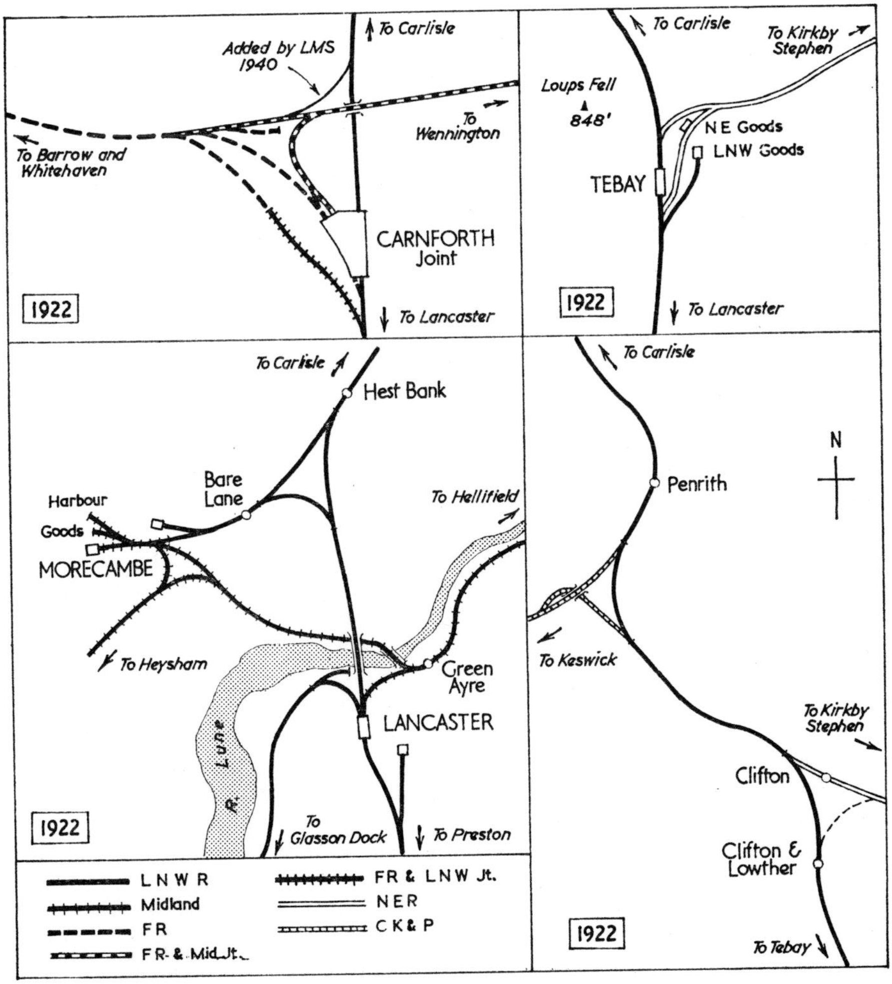

15 Four junction diagrams

and mineral empties in the other direction, as these were worked by Midland engines and men.

The only branches subsequently built by the L.N.W.R. off the 70-mile L. & C. main line were the double-track direct, or south, curve from the Lancaster direction leading to the Hest Bank branch near Bare Lane, authorised under Act of July 19, 1887, and opened on May 19, 1888; and the five-mile Glasson Dock branch from Lancaster, opened for goods traffic in April 1883 and for passenger trains on July 9, 1883. The idea of this second line had been put up to the L.N.W.R. by the Lancaster Port Commissioners, who agreed to make some quay improvements. Authority was given for the line by 41 & 42 Vict., cap. 182, of July 22, 1878, which Act charged the L.N.W.R. "for ever afterwards to maintain the said railway"; but the successor of that company withdrew passenger services on July 5, 1930, and the successor once removed closed the line altogether on September 7, 1964, except within the confines of Lancaster. This was the only railway line with which the Lancaster Canal Co. made contact without causing trouble, but the L.N.W.R. by that time had been lessee of the L.C.C. waterways for 20 years, and was about to buy the property outright. There was from the main canal at Galgate a branch waterway to Glasson running parallel to the River Conder.

The first connection of any sort off the L. & C. was the Kendal & Windermere Railway. Its two-mile section from Oxenholme to Kendal was opened to passenger traffic with the southern section of the L. & C. on September 22, 1846, but goods traffic did not begin until January 4, 1847. The project arose from the early strong desires of the Kendal inhabitants to have a railway; and when the nearest approach of the L. & C. was finally settled at Oxenholme, meetings were called to form a local company, and again Cornelius Nicholson was a leading spirit. He was at that time still a director of the L. & C., an office he resigned in the summer of 1846 preparatory to being appointed managing director of the East Lancashire Railway.

On June 30, 1845, an Act (8 & 9 Vict., cap. 32) was obtained for the incorporation of a company to build a line from Oxenholme to Birthwaite, which at that time was the name for the houses around what is now known as Windermere town, to distinguish it from Bowness down on the lake side. The original idea was to have single track between Kendal and Windermere, but this was soon changed to one for double track, though it was hoped still to build the railway within the statutory finance of £125,000 capital plus £40,000 borrowing powers. The Kendal to Windermere section was opened on April 20, 1847; and at the banquet Cornelius Nicholson said they thought nothing nowadays of travelling 400 miles and having 14 to 20 meals a day. Until the summer of 1850 the locomotives and rolling stock were provided and worked by the L.N.W.R. as part of the L. & C. pool, and then until the end of 1851 by E. B. Wilson & Co. under contract. At this time there were five trains a day in each direction between Kendal and Windermere and extra trips to Oxenholme; but by the summer of 1853 there were six trains each way between Kendal and Winderemere and nine pairs between Kendal and Oxenholme.

A passenger carriage was also attached to the 16.00 goods train out of Windermere. On special holidays a cheap day return ticket from Kendal to Windermere cost 6d.

It was the projection and construction of this small line that led to Wordsworth's poem against railways. There were two rejoinders. One, from Monckton Milnes, famous father of the equally famous and less notorious first Marquess of Crewe, was also in the form of a poem. The second, concocted by the L.N.W.R. and L. & C., was to name *Wordsworth* one of the Crewe-built 2–4–0 engines (L.N.W.R. no. 82) drafted to the L. & C. in 1846, a principle followed half-a-century later by F. W. Webb with *Argus*.

The small K. & W. was ever in trouble, both on its own account and in relation to its big neighbour the L. & C. Early good relations began to fade as soon as the line was opened and Cornelius Nicholson left the district; and by 1848 the K. & W. was making approaches to the L. & C. to lease or buy the line. Throughout the next ten years there was constant bickering; but in relation to the Grand Trunk Route the only influence of the K. & W. was that its trains were often late in arriving at Oxenholme, and main-line trains were held for them until the L. & C. grew impatient, told the K. & W. to get its trains to the junction ten minutes earlier, and instructed Bolden that L. & C. trains were no longer to be held at Oxenholme to wait for trains off the branch.

After a remarkable arbitration case, the award in which the K. & W., perhaps with some justification, put aside, the system was leased in perpetuity to the L. & C. Possession was taken in 1858, but the legal angle being in some doubt, the terms had to be included in the L. & C. general Act of 1859. As this came at the same time as the leasing of the L. & C. to the L.N.W.R., the latter company guaranteed the K. & W. 3 per cent on its ordinary shares and 6 per cent on the preference shares. As a company the K. & W. disappeared in 1879 along with the L. & C., a fitting end, for the two companies had really begun together and had some common original directors.

Cornelius Nicholson lasted another ten years after the end of the K. & W., though from 1846 he was no longer living in the Westmorland area. After a few years with the East Lancashire Railway he was until 1859 the London manager and secretary of the Great Indian Peninsula Railway, and one of his first jobs was to persuade 'John Company' to take £500,000 of shares, or guarantee the interest on the first half-million. His great-grandson today is one of the oldest members of the Stephenson Locomotive Society.

Lines which eventually made junction with the L. & C. main line at Carnforth, Hincaster, Tebay, Clifton and Penrith belonged to other companies. Those at Carnforth have already been mentioned. At Hincaster the joining route was that of the Furness Railway from Arnside, opened on June 26, 1876, to provide a shorter route, and one without reversal, for the mineral trains to Furness coming off the N.E.R. at Tebay. The L.N.W.R. had running powers over this line, and an agreement made at the time of the Bill gave the Furness running powers from Hincaster to Tebay, but not for local traffic.

The incoming line at Tebay was that of the South Durham & Lancashire Union Railway, an associate of the Stockton & Darlington Railway, as already recorded in Chapter IX. The S.D. & L.U. was opened in 1861 to an enlarged station at Tebay, which began to take freight trains on July 4 and passenger trains on August 8. The enlarged station was a joint effort, the two companies (L.N.W.R. and S.D. & L.U.) agreeing to a 50-50 division of an expenditure not to exceed £13,000. Arrangements for the eventual working at Tebay had been largely agreed before the L. & C. was leased, and were completed by the L. & C. local committee of the L.N.W.R. One provision was that if trains from the two railways arrived simultaneously the staff was to give priority in handling to the one on the L. & C. line. Another stipulation, made at the insistence of the L.N.W.R., was that the S.D. & L.U. should never transfer any of its rights at Tebay to any railway other than the S. & D.R. or its successor.

At Clifton the Eden Valley Railway from Kirkby Stephen originally made a south-facing curve to join the L.N.W.R., an unusual direction in view of the existing Kirkby Stephen to Tebay line, and of use only for taking away any Shap granite traffic to the east. This railway was opened to mineral traffic on April 10 and to passenger traffic on June 7, 1862; at the end of June the railway was taken over by the S. & D.R. A Bill had already been lodged to give a deviation towards Penrith, and the Act received Royal Assent on July 7, 1862. In August 1863 traffic began to pass over this deviation, and passenger trains terminated at Penrith. The goods loop to the Keswick line at Redhills was built for the anticipated mineral traffic, and this lasted until 1937. The old south loop from the Eden Valley to the L. & C. station at Clifton was abandoned in 1874 having been little used during the preceding ten years. The Eden Valley line and its connection to the C.K. & P. resulted in a certain amount of coke traffic from Durham to Workington, and so helped in some degree to increase the competition in the steel-making industries in West Cumberland and Furness, and its construction with the help of the S. & D.R. party brought friction on the S.D. & L.U. with the Furness group that had supported that line.

In the second railway that came in just south of Penrith the L.N.W.R. subsequently became a joint owner. This was the Cockermouth, Keswick & Penrith Railway, incorporated on August 1, 1861 (24 & 25 Vict., cap. 203), which had Thomas Bouch of Tay Bridge fame as its first engineer. Proposals for this line had been made at least 16 years earlier, and in 1845, the L. & C. board recorded that while it did not look unfavourably on a line from Penrith to Keswick it was not prepared to subscribe. By a further Act of 1864 the L.N.W.R. was permitted to subscribe £25,000 and to nominate two directors to the C.K. & P. The L. & C. itself was never involved in any joint lines; and the only one promoted by the L.N.W.R. which touched the erstwhile L. & C. system was that of the Goods Committee at Carlisle.

XV

L. & C. Locomotive Power

FROM THE beginning the L. & C. had no intention of working the line itself. The locomotive committee of the board met for the first time on Boxing Day 1844, though there is no prior board minute establishing the committee. Its members were all G.J.R. nominees, viz. John Moss, T. W. Rathbone, D. Hodgson, George Grant, J. Cropper and N. D. Bold. They decided it would be best if one of the companies south of Preston supplied the motive power and stock, *i.e.* one of the three railways owning large blocks of L. & C. shares. In essence this meant the G.J.R. The L. & B. was too far away; the N.U., though well-established by that time, was nevertheless small beer, and had experienced enough difficulty already in trying to supply locomotive power to the P. & W. and L. & P. By March 1845 the G.J.R. had agreed in principle to supply all that was necessary for a five-year period, and Locke was left to fix numbers and terms. For the sake of form, Bury, Curtis & Co. sent in a tender for making locomotives, and Beattie one for making carriages. The G.J.R. contract for the supply of engines, engine-men, carriages and wagons was formally signed on February 11, 1846.

By the time the first section of the L. & C. was opened in September of that year the G.J.R. had ceased to exist, and a new contract had been drawn up with the L.N.W.R. dated August 11, 1846. Its terms and conditions were practically those of the G.J.R. agreement, but a new paragraph was added for the provision of power and stock sufficient for working also over the L. & P. section, and there was an option for the L. & C. to bring this part of the contract to an end before the expiration of the main contract, possibly in case the L. & C. was to come into possession of the weedy locomotives and archaic stock of the L. & P. Even before the original agreement was signed the G.J.R. had put in hand at Crewe an extra batch of Trevithick–Allan standard Crewe-type locomotives, both 2–2–2 and 2–4–0, specifically to work the L. & C., and was also building some passenger coaches for the same purpose. In January 1846 Errington reported he had inspected both under construction.

The four 2–2–2 and eight 2–4–0 locomotives built and drafted to the L. & C. in 1846 for the initial and full openings were as given in Table XIII; another four engines were sent soon afterwards. For the first opening to Kendal only four engines were sent. Construction of these represented a goodly proportion of Crewe's capacity at that time, and did not contribute to the efficiency of the G.J.R.-section motive power, which even in 1846 included a number of old and effete locomotives. The measure of the L. & C. locomotive-supply agreement is to be found not in any financial profit to the L.N.W.R., but in the riveting of part of a new link in the Anglo-Scottish west coast communication chain, and in setting main-line standards on the L. & C. from the start. But the growing traffic on the L. & C. began to put a strain on the G.J.R.-section stock of the L.N.W.R., and towards the end of 1847 the locomotive committee of the L.N.W.R. had to record that 30 engines were then allocated to the L. & C., instead of 16 contemplated; and that as working of the Trent Valley line had been given to the Northern Division, it might not be possible for Crewe to provide power for the forthcoming opening of the Chester & Holyhead Railway unless some engines were transferred back from the Southern Division.

Table XIII—Crewe-built Trevithick-Allan Locomotives Drafted to the L. & C. for the openings up to the end of 1846

L.N.W.R. Running No.	Name	Type	First of later L.N.W.R. re-numberings	Year built	Year scrapped
79	Belted Will	2–2–2	1835	2/1846	1877
80	Dalemain	,,	1836	3/1846	1874
84	Saddleback	,,	1837	4/1846	1874
94	Helvellyn	,,	1912	11/1846	1878
78	Lonsdale	2–4–0	1967	2/1846	1884
81	Greystoke	,,		4/1846	1865
82	Wordsworth	,,	1969	4/1846	1880
83	Windermere	,,	1978	4/1846	1886
87	Eden	,,	Became Earlestown works shunter		
88	Lune	,,	1861	8/1846	1881
89	Bela	,,	1973	8/1846	1886
90	Lowther	,,		9/1846	1874

The L.N.W.R. contract with the L. & C. was for the supply of proper engines, tenders, carriages of every class, trucks, vans, horseboxes, cattle, goods and merchandise wagons, which the L.N.W.R. was to keep in good repair and travelling order, including cleaning and repainting, for a period of five years from the opening of the L. & C. Any improvements in the locomotives found desirable by the L. & C. could be made at that company's expense if the L.N.W.R. had not already adopted the particular modification. For passenger traffic the contract was based on trains up to 11 vehicles hauled by one engine; for any additional number up to 13 the L.N.W.R. had the option of double-heading. Schedule speed of all mail and express trains was to be based on 30 m.p.h. overall between Lancaster and Carlisle, including any stops, and 22 m.p.h. for other passenger trains. Terms were to be 1s. 0d. a train-mile for each engine used. First class carriages were to be charged 0.55d. a mile; and second and third class vehicles, including carriage trucks, vans and horseboxes, were to be charged 0.35d. a mile.

Freight trains were to be based on trailing loads up to 130 tons behind one engine, the L.N.W.R. having the option to put on a second engine between that weight and a maximum of 150 tons. Goods train speed was to be based on 12 m.p.h. average; but for both passenger and goods trains the speed rates were to be increased if found expedient. Terms for freight trains were to be 1s. 2d. per train-mile for each engine used, and charge for goods wagons was to be 0.25d. a mile. The whole agreement was to be for five years' in the first instance, and whenever it ended the L. & C. was to have the option of taking over at a price to be fixed the average number of engines, tenders and carriages used during the last year.

Drawn up with care under the aegis of Locke, this arrangement gave satisfaction for a year or two, but by the end of 1848 was creating some dissent about the accounting and the need or otherwise for double-heading; and in the summer of 1849 the extra charges and basic weights were terminated. Instead, an addition of 1 per cent was made to the actual passenger-train mileage, and this was to cover the use of any second engine. For freight trains an addition of 12½ per cent was made to the actual train mileage to cover any double-heading or engines running back light, together with shunting and marshalling. Because of the general inconvenience of freight working at Carlisle, the goods traffic and shunting there were to be considered distinct, and paid for at 3s. 6d. an hour as before. Whether these modified terms saved the L. & C. money is questionable, but they eased the paper work and smoothed out various points. One matter of dissent had been the supply of some engines insufficiently powerful for the L. & C. line, and £225 5s. 10d. was deducted from the loco-power account in 1849 to compensate this.

Service by the engine-men from the G.J.R. seems to have been a success, and Errington reported: "The exact attention of the engine-drivers on the road is more creditable to them because they have been removed from an old-established and finished railway to one where of necessity much more attention is required." After the southern section to Kendal was in operation, and the northern section within a week or two of being opened, difficulties in obtaining accommodation for the increased number of G.J.R. engine-men came to the fore; and Errington was authorised to pay the lodgings at the nearest farmhouses until proper houses could be built.

Actual yearly sums paid to the L.N.W.R. rose to £40,000 in 1850 and £47,000 in 1851; and at the time the first five years were drawing to a close the L. & C. directors were able to renew the contract on rather more favourable terms, which, if existing mileage was maintained, were hoped to save £7,000 a year. The first half-year under the new scale cost £23,041 whereas perpetuation of the modified first contract would have cost £27,000. Basic terms in the new contract of 1852 were 10d. a mile per locomotive on passenger trains and 1s. 0d. a mile per engine on goods trains.

Renewal of the contract was decided only after much discussion and investigation. Serious consideration was paid to setting up an L. & C. locomotive department, and enquiries were made for a suitable locomotive superintendent. Among the applicants was David Joy, who recorded in his diary: ". . . obtained information as to directors, line, gradients, plant, engines (all big Crewe engines); and went to Liverpool to see directors, then to Penrith to see chairman—a seven-mile drive out towards Ullswater, with Saddleback and Skiddaw to the right."

Despite the lower rates, increased traffic and services caused the gross payments to rise within three or four years to the level of £56,000 to £60,000 a year, and they were the subject of much comment by shareholders at general meetings. The directors agreed that the payments were greater than the direct cost if the company worked its own trains, but emphasised that capital outlay, interest and depreciation charges were less, and that no additional department and equipment were necessary.

The board wished to continue the contract; but as 1857 approached it was the L.N.W.R. that gave notice to terminate. One objection that

Table XIV—Engines bought by L. & C. from L.N.W.R. in 1857 and returned on lease of L. & C. by L.N.W.R. in 1859

L.N.W.R. No. in 1857	L. & C. No.	L.N.W.R. name perpetuated by L. & C.	Wheel arrgt.	Crewe type	First L.N.W.R renumbering	Year built at Crewe	Year scrapped
369	26	Banshee	2–2–2	LFB	489	1855	
259	27	Windermere	2–2–2	,,	490	1855	
313	28	Prince Ernest(1)	2–2–2	,,	491	1853	
150	29	Linnet	2–2–2	,,	492	1856	
285	30	Sefton	2–2–2	SFB	493	1852	
179	31	Nun	2–2–2	,,	494	1849	
178	32	Friar	2–2–2	,,	495	1849	1880
217	33	Emperor	2–2–2	,,	496	1848	1878
223	34	Rose	2–2–2	,,	497	1848	1878
193	35	Pearl	2–2–2	,,	498	1848	1861
195	36	Emerald	2–2–2	,,	499	1848	1871
169	37	Huskisson	2–2–2	,,	500	1847	
40	38	Jason	2–2–2	,,	501	1848	
110	39	Canning	2–2–2	,,	502	1857	1873
355	40	Hardman	2–4–0	LFB	503	1855	
357	41	Terrier	2–4–0	,,	504	1855	
359	42	Glow-worm	2–4–0	,,	505	1855	
358	43	Falstaff	2–4–0	,,	506	1855	
20	44	Eagle	2–4–0	,,	507	1857	
373	45	Snake	2–4–0	,,	508	1853	
353	46	St. Arnaud	2–4–0	,,	509	1854	
152	47	Bullfinch	2–4–0	,,	510		
156	48	Redstart	2–4–0	,,	511	1846	
18	49	Cerberus	2–4–0	,,	512	1855	
154	50	Starling	2–4–0	,,	513		
151	51	Goldfinch	2–4–0	,,	514		
333	52	Hardinge	2–4–0	,,	515	1854	
311	53	Ida	2–4–0	,,	516	1853	
321	54	Autocrat	2–4–0	,,	517	1853	
304	55	Hector	2–4–0	SFB	518	1853	
308	56	Booth	2–4–0	,,	519	1853	
309	57	Huish	2–4–0	,,	520	1853	
295	58	Penmaenmawr	2–4–0	,,	521	1852	
276	59	Pluto	2–4–0	,,	522	1851	
275	60	Vulcan	2–4–0	,,	523	1851	
271	61	Minotaur	2–4–0	,,	524	1851	
199	62	Castor	2–4–0	,,	525	1848	1878
200	63	Pollux	2–4–0	,,	526	1848	1878
209	64	Envoy	2–4–0	,,	527	1848	1883
210	65	Alchymist	2–4–0	,,	528	1848	1877

(1) Renamed *Blenheim* after re-acquisition by L.N.W.R.

railway had was the capital outlay on stock for the L. & C. After Col. Maclean had interviewed the Marquis of Chandos and Mr. Hardman Earle of the L.N.W.R. board in January 1856, the L. & C. asked if the contract could continue if that railway made a capital investment of £100,000 on new motive power and stock for the L.N.W.R. to work, but this suggestion was not acceptable. There were, of course, other reasons. The L.N.W.R. was expanding both in mileage and in density of traffic, and a concentration on its own needs was desirable. It has been suggested the withdrawal may also have marked a hint of displeasure at the proposals and wrangles regarding the Little North Western Railway that had occupied much of the year 1855, but this is doubtful. The influence of the L.N.W.R. over the L. & C. was in no way decreased as a result of the withdrawal of L.N.W.R. operation, because the financial holding and nominees on the board remained the same.

Thus in 1856 the L. & C. began to make arrangements to work the line by its own power as from August 1, 1857. As early as April 1856 new engine repair shops at Carlisle were sanctioned, and Edward Woods, earlier well-known on the L. & M. and G.J.R., was engaged to plan them. In July 1856 a contract was given to Rothwell & Co. for 20 goods engines of 2–4–0 type at £2,000 apiece; and in November of the same year Rothwell was given another order for five 2–2–2 passenger engines and tenders at £2,100 each, to be delivered by July 1, 1857. All these engines were of Trevithick–Allan pattern; they were constructed to the inspection of Robert Sinclair, chief engineer of the Eastern Counties Railway, but well-known to the L. & C. directors in his former position of manager and engineer of the Caley.

The L. & C. then proceeded to the business of the engines to be obtained from the L.N.W.R., and 40 was the number agreed, all, of course, used engines and ones which had been at work on the L. & C. Worthington, who had to take charge of the locomotive side while continuing as chief of the civil engineering, went to Crewe and agreed with Trevithick which 40 were to be taken over. The engines acquired are listed in Table XIV, and it is sad to record that the original 2–2–2 *Dalemain* (L.N.W.R. no. 80 in 1846) was not among them, but it would then be 13 years old. The name was used by the L. & C. in 1857 for one of the new Rothwell 2–2–2 engines, no. 22, and this engine had a mishap two miles south of Penrith on December 27, 1859, and the driver died of injuries. John Kennedy of Liverpool (old partner of the then deceased Edward Bury) was asked to make a valuation of the Crewe-built locomotives on behalf of the L. & C.; his price, agreed with Harrison as the L.N.W.R. referee, for the 40 was £54,750, and this sum was paid. Among the 40 was L.N.W.R. no 313 *Prince Ernest* (L. & C. no. 28) built in 1853 as the first Trevithick–Allan 2–2–2 with large firebox (LFB).

Increased traffic led to an order early in 1859 to Fairbairn for five 2–2–2 and seven 2–4–0 engines, these again being of the Trevithick–Allan type; price was £2,600 apiece. Eight of these were delivered before the L. & C. was leased to the L.N.W.R. in August 1859, and the other four came in the autumn. All 37 engines by Rothwell and Fairbairn were somewhat larger, heavier and more powerful than the similar locomotives built at Crewe up to 1856. The 2–4–0 type had 17 in. by 20 in. cylinders (Rothwell) and 17 in. by 24 in. (Fairbairn), and 5 ft. wheels, contrasted with the 15 in. and 15¼ in. cylinders of Crewe-built locomotives, so most of the double-heading would disappear. The 2–2–2 engines built outside all had 16 in. cylinders, but with 20 in. stroke (Rothwell) and 24 in. (Fairbairn). Boiler mountings of the L. & C. engines were different from

Table XV
Locomotives built for L. & C. in 1857 and 1859

L. & C. No.	L. & C. Name	Wheel Arrgt.	Builder	Delivery Year	First L.N.W.R. Number after 1859
1	Rickerby	2–4–0	Rothwell	1856	377
2	Newby	,,	,,	1856	378
3	Sedgwick	,,	,,	1857	379
4	Quernmore	,,	,,	1857	380
5	Patterdale	,,	,,	1857	381
6	Lune	,,	,,	1857	382
7	Eden	,,	,,	1857	383
8	Luck of Edenhall	,,	,,	1857	384
9	Skiddaw	,,	,,	1857	385
10	Saddleback	,,	,,	1857	386
11	Lonsdale	,,	,,	1857	387
12	Petteril	,,	,,	1857	388
13	Inglewood	,,	,,	1857	389
14	Ingleboro	,,	,,	1857	390
15	Levens	,,	,,	1857	391
16	Fylde	,,	,,	1857	392
17	Brougham	,,	,,	1857	393
18	Eamont	,,	,,	1857	394
19	Ribble	,,	,,	1857	395
20	Shap	,,	,,	1857	396
21	Lowther	2–2–2	,,	1857	397
22	Dalemain	,,	,,	1857	398
23	Greystoke	,,	,,	1857	399
24	Belted Will	,,	,,	1857	400
25	Lazonby	,,	,,	1857	488
70	Wennington	,,	Fairbairn	1859	533
71	Duchess of Lancaster	,,	,,	1879	534
72	Merrie Carlisle	,,	,,	1859	535
73	Lang Meg	,,	,,	1859	536
74	John o' Gaunt	,,	,,	1859	537
75	Penrith Beacon	2–4–0	,,	1859	538
76	Preston	,,	,,	1859	539
77	Kendal	,,	,,	1859	540
78	Sedbergh	,,	,,	1859	541
79	Tebay	,,	,,	1859	542
80	Cross Fell	,,	,,	1859	543
81	Ulleswater	,,	,,	1859	544
82	Morecambe	0–4–2	Robt. Stephenson	1859	545
83	Underley	0–4–2	,,	1859	546
	From Kendal & Windermere Railway Stock				
66	Langdale	T	E. B. Wilson	1850	529
67	Windermere	2–4–0		1850/51	530
68	Lady of the Lake			1850/51	531
69	Grasmere	2–2–2T	Carrett, Marshall		532

those of Crewe products; the dome, with Salter spring-balance safety valves, was above the firebox. All engines built for the L. & C. in 1857–59 are listed in Table XV.

After being absorbed, or re-absorbed, into the L.N.W.R. stock in 1859, many of the L. & C. engines had a long life and drifted to other parts of the system, such as the Manchester–Buxton line with its 1 in 60 gradients. The six Rothwell 2–2–2 engines also wandered away from the L. & C. lines except no. 24, which, renamed *Ingleboro*, and renumbered 1191 and later 1284 and 1898, was recorded by Ahrons to have operated the Tebay–Ingleton service until it was scrapped in 1884. Rothwell-built 2–4–0s nos. 1 and 8 were sold to the Eastern & Midlands Railway in 1883, but departed with McConnell six-wheel tenders attached; they became E. & M. nos. 29 and 30, and later were Midland & Great Northern Joint Railway nos. 42 and 43; they were scrapped around 1895. No. 110 *Canning* (L. & C. no. 39) rebuilt into *Engineer Lancaster* lasted in that capacity until 1903. A summary of the 40 Crewe-built engines taken over again by the L.N.W.R. in 1859 is given in Table XVI.

Table XVI—Summary of L.N.W.R. Engines Re-absorbed by that company from L. & C. in 1859

L. & C. Nos.	First L.N.W.R. re-numbering	Type of Crewe Locomotive
26—29	484—492	6 ft. 2-2-2 LFB
30—39	493—502	6 ft. 2-2-2 SFB
40—54	503—517	5 ft. 2-4-0 LFB
55—65	518—528	5 ft. 2-4-0 SFB

Some of the Rothwell and Fairbairn engines built for the L. & C. bore names the same as those of some of the original 12 L.N.W.R. engines which took up the first working in 1846. Also, some of the engines, both Crewe-built and from the two private builders, taken over from the L. & C. in 1859 had the same names as others then running on the L.N.W.R. In general, these were not renamed until 1862–64; and during that period the L.N.W.R. had examples of two engines bearing the same name concurrently.

The first two locomotives ever owned by the L. & C. were bought off the Jones & Potts shelf for £2,350 the pair in December 1846, with the idea of working coal trains between Carlisle and Shap. Errington was authorised at the same time to purchase another two if any were available suitable for conversion to coal-train haulage, but apparently there was nothing to hand. Technical details of the two set to work no longer exist. By the summer of 1849 the entry 'engines and waggons' in the half-yearly capital accounts had been replaced by 'waggons' only, and these two engines seem to have been sold to the L.N.W.R. at the end of 1847. On that railway they were no. 214 *Shap* and 215 *Spitfire*, and were the first two engines of those numbers. As no. 214A the former was sold out of service in 1860 after, according to one account, having been rebuilt by

Ramsbottom at Longsight in 1856/57 into what became a prototype for the celebrated DX class.

At the very end of the L. & C. working existence two 0–4–2 tender engines were obtained from Robt. Stephenson & Co. They were completely different from anything else on the L. & C., and probably were the only ones available off any builder's shelf to meet some immediate need for motive power. They had 17 in. by 24 in. cylinders and 5 ft. wheels; builder's works nos. were 1199 and 1200. They had some patent of Beattie's incorporated, probably the firebox, and in L.N.W.R. locomotive lists were simply stated as 'Beatties'. They disappeared from the capital list of the L.N.W.R. in 1866, becoming duplicate nos. 1184 and 1223 (later 1866); they were scrapped respectively in 1870 and 1873.

Four small engines were also absorbed into the L. & C. stock from the Kendal & Windermere Railway in 1858, and were taken through into the L.N.W.R. list the next year. Three of them, at least, did not have a long L.N.W.R. life; but one detail of K. & W. locomotives did remain for many a long year, for that company's 2–4–0 engine which became L. & C. no. 68 bore the name *Lady of the Lake*, presumably in connection with Windermere. It was the first engine of this name on the L.N.W.R., and after it was sold in 1860 the name was adopted a year or two later for a Ramsbottom Problem-class 2–2–2. The K. & W. engine which did have a longer life on the L.N.W.R. was a 2–2–2 well tank built by Carrett Marshall about 1850, named *Grasmere*. It was renamed *Dwarf* on the L.N.W.R., and lasted until 1873. S.S. Scott stated it spent its last years at Stafford as the saloon engine of Woodhouse, the engineer there; the *S.L.S. Bulletin* of 1955 (p. 350) states it was on *Engineer Salford*.

After August 1857, when the L. & C. had its own motive power and department, the running expenses exclusive of interest and depreciation were around £40,000 a year, and the figures for the last half-year of the L. & C. as a working company are given in Table XVII. In 1858–59 the board also transferred £18,000 from capital to the credit of the loco-

Table XVII—Details of L. & C. Locomotive Dept. Expenses, Six months to July 31, 1859

Engine-men's wages				£4,596	6	11
Cleaners' and coke-men's wages				1,348	14	4¾
Oil and tallow				728	1	8¾
Sundry small stores				538	9	10
Repairs to coke wagons				37	9	8¾
Clothing, stationery, etc.				159	12	10
Rates and taxes				61	10	5
Building repairs				144	15	11
Gas				255	2	3
Water				214	4	6
Salaries				612	1	6
Coke and coal: 12,869 tons 14 cwt.				6,109	14	4
Repairs of engines:						
Wages:	£2,589	6	1			
Materials:	2,605	0	8¼	5,194	6	9¼
Total:				£20,001	1	1½

motive account to make up the equivalent of a full stock of new engines, as the 40 units from the L.N.W.R. were secondhand, instead of drawing sums from the general capital as new engines became necessary. Another £2,000 was transferred in the same way in respect of K. & W. engines after that system came into the possession of the L. & C. in May 1858. The motive power contract with the L.N.W.R. came to an end in the summer of 1857 for locomotives only; that company still continued to hire passenger coaches to the L. & C.

Carlisle repair shops and an L. & C. engine shed at Preston had been completed by the autumn of 1857. A number of the engines taken over from the L.N.W.R. were given heavy repairs or were rebuilt at Carlisle; and in the last half-year before the L. & C. was leased to the L.N.W.R. the cost of this work amounted to £3,018. Engines so dealt with were: *Emperor*, *Emerald*, *Huskisson*, *Jason*, *Canning*, *Castor*, *Pollux*, *Envoy* and *Alchymist*. Worthington began to make experiments in 1858 for a change over from coke to coal as a fuel, beginning with some modifications to suit a mixture of the two fuels, and by the end of August had eight or nine engines so running. At the time the L. & C. was leased, its investment in locomotives stood at £136,474. By that time, too, the heavier engines were contributing to a higher cost of permanent-way maintenance, and in 1858 the timber viaduct over the Lune had to be strengthened to withstand them, so the construction of that bridge must have been cut fairly fine in the first instance.

After the working absorption of the L. & C. into the L.N.W.R. its engines continued to form the backbone of power between Preston and Carlisle for a few more years, with incomings from and outgoings to the normal stock of L.N.W.R. Northern Division engines, until in the late 1860s Ramsbottom's 2–4–0 'Newton' class with 6 ft. 7½ in. wheels and 17 in. by 24 in. cylinders began to handle the main Anglo-Scottish expresses. Crewe shedded a considerable number of these engines; Preston and Carlisle a handful each. Ahrons recorded that at one time *Cornwall* had a period of working the mail between Crewe and Carlisle. This must have been in the early 1860s before the 'Newton' class came on the scene. *Cornwall* at that time had £5,182 10s. charged against it in the capital account; this would include its various six-wheel, eight-wheel and six-wheel stages, and so it had been an expensive proposition.

In the mid-1870s the 'Newtons' were largely replaced on the main Crewe–Carlisle services by Webb's 'Precursor' 2–4–0 class with 5 ft. 6 in. wheels, though some of the Ramsbottoms continued on secondary services for years. The 'Precursors' had the same size of cylinders as the 'Newtons', and were some three tons heavier, but the boiler was only nominally larger. Despite the small wheels they could run fast, but the timings of the principal expresses in the late 1870s were not exciting, the 10.00 out of Euston, for example, being allowed 130 min. for the 90 miles from Preston to Carlisle, and the 20.50 night mail 135 min. including a 3-min. postal stop at Carnforth.

Webb 'Precedents' with 6 ft. 7½ in. wheels took the main duties from the 'Precursors' before 1880, though many of the small-wheeled engines remained on the Crewe–Carlisle section. Both types were sometimes piloted by a 'Newton' in the up direction from Carlisle to Shap, and the 'Precedents' (including the Ramsbottom engines after 'conversion') not only formed the main-line power into the 1890s but could be seen on humbler duties on the L. & C. section and connecting lines until after the formation of the L.M.S.R. They also did the Crewe-Carlisle work in the Races of 1888 and 1895, though more powerful engines were on the line in the shape of Webb's compounds of the 'Dreadnought' and 'Greater Britain' classes. The 'John Hick' 2–2–2–2 compounds with 6 ft. 3 in. wheels were also used on the Carlisle line, but after the first one came out in 1894 another three years and more went by before the other nine appeared. Full details of the two Races in 1888 and 1895 have been given in O. S. Nock's *The Railway Race to the North*, and no repetition is called for here. Similarly, the locomotive work of the 20th Century over the Crewe–Carlisle division has been covered with adequacy in several railway and engineering periodicals.

XVI

Later Days

FOR MANY years after the fusion of the L. & C. with the L.N.W.R. in 1859 the route north of Crewe, and especially north of Preston, kept its individuality. Some of this was due to the perpetuation of the Lancaster & Carlisle local committee. On the locomotive side, the so-called 'Northern Division', with which the L. & C. had always been closely connected, did not lose its identity overnight when the two locomotive divisions of the L.N.W.R. were combined under John Ramsbottom in 1862. Moreover, V.I.P.s were not so numerous north of Crewe; and working was more homely, with less of the strict discipline which extended down the main line from the Euston Road side of the Doric Arch to the hither side of the fly-over at Bird's Wood fox covert, which was the proper name for Weaver Junction. Lancaster was the headquarters of a district extending thence to Carlisle, and staffed by many old L. & C. individuals and families.

The ginger of this tradition was well recognised by J. Pearson Pattinson in 1893 (*British Railways*): "Between Crewe and Preston speed falls off and averages only about 45 m.p.h. . . . The other Scotch trains are slower over this length, and have to make up for it between Preston and Carlisle, where the timing is of the most extraordinary description . . . quite surpassing, in our opinion, anything performed elsewhere on the iron road." He quotes the average timing of the 1888 Race trains start-to-stop over the 90 miles from Preston to Carlisle over the whole period as 96½ min., with a 'best' (by no. 275 *Vulcan*) of 89 min., with a load of four 8-wheelers averaging 78/80 tons every night except one, when there were five. Engines used were all of the 'Newton' class. Pattinson gave a summary of the express train services at 45 m.p.h. or faster as reproduced in Table XVIII; again he refers with delight and appreciation to the work of the Newtons, Precursors, Precedents and compounds over the years 1888–93.

Table XVIII—Summary of Fastest Passenger Trains, Preston–Carlisle, 1892-93

Down Express Preston dep.	Miles	Time, min.	Speed m.p.h.	Up Express Carlisle dep.	Miles	Time, min.	Speed m.p.h.
12.20 a.m. (from Wigan)	105	130	48·5	12.05 a.m.	90	117	46·2
2.25 a.m.	90	115	47·0	12.01 p.m.	90	106	50·9
10.50 a.m.	90	120 (incl. 2 stops)	45·0	12.23 p.m.	90	102	52·9
11.00 a.m.	90	120 (incl. 2 stops)	45·0	12.34 p.m.	90	105	51·4
2.40 p.m.	90	105	51·4	4.20 p.m.	90	115 (incl. 1 stop)	47·0
6.42 p.m.	90	113 (incl. 1 stop)	47·8	4.30 p.m.	90	115 (incl. 1 stop)	47·0
3.30 p.m.	90	122 (incl. 2 stops)	44·4	8.41 p.m.	90	121 (incl. 1 stop)	44·7

By the beginning of the first world war the L.N.W.R. control system had been extended from Crewe to Lancaster. There were four control offices dealing with the 71 miles. They were: (1) *Crewe*, which in the northerly direction covered the line only as far as Weaver Junction; (2) *Warrington*, extending from Weaver Junction to Winwick Junction, and certain connecting lines; (3) *Springs Branch*, from Winwick Junction to Euxton Junction, plus many connecting lines; and (4) *Preston*, from Euxton Junction to Lancaster, plus the Longridge and Ribble Docks branches. Crewe office was open continuously, the others from 6.00 on Mondays to 6.00 on Sundays. The whole 141 miles of route from Crewe to Carlisle was worked on the absolute block system with three-wire instruments, and the block posts over the 90 miles of the L. & C. system were as shown in Table XIX.

Table XIX—Block Posts, Preston to Carlisle, 1913–14

Distance		Block Posts (Absolute Block, 3-wire Instruments)	Closed
Miles	Yards		
		Preston No. 2 (Station box)	
	378	,, No. 4 (Dock Street)	
	389	,, No. 5 (Maudlands Jct.)	
	778	Greenbank Siding box	
	811	Oxheys station	
3	371	Barton & Broughton station	5.0 a.m. Sunday to 6.0 a.m. Monday
2	1547	Brock station	
1	1694	Garstang & Catterall station	12.0 noon Sunday to 6.0 a.m. Monday
3	563	Scorton station	5.0 a.m. Sunday to 7.0 a.m. Monday
2	761	Bay Horse station	
2	1668	Oubeck box	5.0 a.m. Sunday to 7.0 a.m. Monday
1	1338	Lancaster No. 1 (Old Jct.)	
	1383	,, No. 2	
	338	,, No. 3 } [1]	5.0 a.m. to 6.0 a.m. Monday; 9.30 a.m. Sunday to 5.0 p.m. Sunday
	530	,, No. 4 } [1]	
		,, No. 4 } [1]	} Single line instructions
	900	,, *Green Ayre (Midland)*	
1	1041	Morecambe South Jct.	5.0 a.m. to 6.0 p.m. Sunday; 8.15 p.m. Sunday to 5.20 a.m. Monday
		Morecambe South Junction	
	1210	*Bare Lane*	
1	232	Hest Bank station	
2	1365	Carnforth No. 1 Jct. box [2]	
	615	,, No. 2 station box	
		Carnforth (No. 2) station box	
		,, ,, ,, (F. & M. Jct. box)	
	960	Carnforth No. 3 box (Iron Works)	8.30 p.m. to 6.30 a.m. weekdays; 8.30 p.m. Saturday to 6.30 a.m. Monday
1	1529	Yealand box	5.15 to 7.30 a.m., 5.30 to 7.15 p.m. weekdays, and 5.15 a.m. Sunday to 8 a.m. Monday
2	476	Burton & Holme station	5.00 a.m. Sunday to 6.45 a.m. Monday
2	996	Milnthorpe station	
2	41	Hincaster Jct. box	5.00 a.m. Sunday to 6.45 a.m. Monday
		Hincaster Jct. box } *Furness Rly. instruments*	
		Heversham } *Furness Rly. instruments*	
1	837	Sedgwick box	Closed at present
1	1191	Oxenholme No. 1, south box [3]	5.00 a.m. Sunday to 7.00 a.m. Monday
	644	,, No. 3, yard box	
	346	,, No. 3, junction box	6.00 a.m. to 5.30 p.m. Sunday, and from 7.45 p.m. Sunday to 6.00 a.m. Monday
1	917	Peat Lane box	5.00 a.m. Sunday to 11.00 p.m. Sunday
1	1488	Hay Fell box	5.00 to 9.00 weekdays; 5.00 a.m. Sunday to 9.00 a.m. Monday
1	223	Lambrigg Crossing box	
1	364	Mosedale Hall Crossing box	4.00 a.m. Sunday to 7.00 a.m. Monday

	1417	Grayrigg station	5.00 a.m. Sunday to 7.15 Monday
1	1431	Lowgill junction	
2	128	Dillicar box	4.00 a.m. Sunday to 7.00 a.m. Monday
1	1533	Tebay No. 1, south box	6.00 a.m. to 8.30 a.m. Sunday; 8.00 p.m. Sunday to 4.00 a.m. Monday
	294	Tebay No. 2, junction box	
		South box, No. 1 *Junction box, No. 2* *N.E. yard box, No. 3*	N.E. passenger single line between Nos. 1, 2 and 3 cabins is worked absolute block with L.N.W.R. 2-wire instruments and N.E. train staff between Nos. 2 and 3 cabins
2	1700	Scout Green Crossing box	
2	958	Shap Summit box	
2	27	Shap station	6.00 a.m. Sunday to 6.40 a.m. Monday
3	1330	Thrimby Grange box	6.00 a.m. to 11.00 p.m. Sunday
3	869	Clifton & Lowther station	
1	70	Eden Valley junction (5)	4.00 a.m. to 3.00 p.m. Sundays;
		Eden Valley junction box	4.30 p.m. Sunday to 7.00 a.m. Monday
		Clifton N.E.R. box	
2	288	Eamont Junction	5.30 a.m. to 11.00 p.m. Sunday; 6.00 a.m. to 9.00 a.m. Monday
		Eamont Junction box *Redhills box (C.K.&P.)*	Permissive working; 3-wire tell-tale instruments
		Goods loops { *Eamont Junction box* *Keswick Junction box (No. 1)* }	Permissive working; 3-wire tell-tale instruments
	1240	Penrith, Keswick Jct., No. 1	
		Keswick Jct. box, No. 1 *Redhills box, C.K.& P.* } (4)	
	463	Penrith No. 2, yard box	9.30 p.m. to 6.30 a.m. weekdays; 9.30 p.m. Saturday to 6.30 a.m. Sunday; 7.30 a.m. Sunday to 6.30 a.m. Monday
	360	Penrith No. 3, north box	10.00 p.m. to 6.30 a.m. weekdays; 10.00 p.m. Saturday to 4.45 a.m. Sunday; 6.00 a.m. to 7.10 p.m. Sunday; 8.00 p.m. Sunday to 4.45 a.m. Monday
2	934	Kitchen Hill box	Closed at present
2	427	Plumpton station	6.00 a.m. Sunday to 5.00 a.m. Monday
2	506	Calthwaite station	4.00 a.m. Sunday to 7.30 a.m. Monday
3	599	Southwaite station	
2	672	Wreay station	4.00 a.m. Sunday to 7.00 a.m. Monday
3	1116	Carlisle No. 13 Upperby Bridge Jct.	
	684	" No. 12 box	
	1320	" No. 5 box (Crown Street)	
		" *No. 5 box (Crown Street)*	Permissive working; 3-wire tell-tale instruments
	266	" *No. 4a box (Platform cabin)*	
	316	" *No. 4 box*	
		" *No. 5 box, Crown Street*	Absolute block; 3-wire instruments. No. 6 M. &. C box is closed from 9.00 p.m. to 6.00 a.m. weekdays, and from 9.00 p.m. Saturday to 6.00 a.m. Monday
	315	" *No. 6 box (M. & C. box)*	
		" *No. 5 box, Crown Street*	
	751	" *No. 7 box, London Road Jct.*	
		" *No. 13 box, Upperby Bridge Jct.*	Goods lines Permissive working; 3-wire tell-tale instruments Electric bell code between No. 12 and and sorting sidings boxes for old upline rly.
	684	" *No. 12 box*	
	1090	" *No. 10 box (Bog Jct. box)*	
		" *Bog Jct., No. 10 box*	
	390	" *Rome Street Jct., No. 11 box*	
	343	" *Dentonholme South Jct. No. 14 box*	
	750	" Dentonholme North Jct.	
	420	" No. 3 box	
		" Bog Jct. No, 10 box	
	927	" Currock Jct., No. 8 box	
		" No. 12 box	
	470	" Sorting Sidings box	
	360	" London Road Jct. No. 7 (N.E.) box	
		" No. 12 box	Electric bell code. Elevated box and sorting sidings box arc closed after finish of work on Sunday night until 0.00 a.m. Monday
	315	" Elevated box	

(1) *Lancaster*: All lines between Nos. 3 and 4 cabins worked on absolute block; up and down main lines between Nos. 2 and 3 boxes on absolute block, and up goods loop between same boxes on permissive system. (2) *Carnforth*: Up and down loops worked on permissive system with tell-tale instruments; used for goods trains only. (3) *Oxenholme*: Platform loop line between Nos. 2 and 3 boxes worked as single line with 3-wire instruments. (4) *Penrith*: Down loops from Eamont Jct. to C.K.P. Jct. for goods trains only. (5) *Eden Valley*: Up loop from Eden Valley Jct. to Clifton & Lowther on absolute block, and used for goods trains only.

Of all places it is Crewe that has changed most, from the wayside station out in the country to the hub of the L.N.W.R. and then of the L.M.S.R. Though improvements and enlargements were made from time to time, the situation had become chaotic in the early 1890s; it had been only temporarily relieved, and then intensified, by the quadrupling of the 24 miles south from Crewe to Stafford, completed as early as 1876. After the retirement of Sir Richard Moon in 1891, and the accession to the general managership of Frederick Harrison in 1893, a scheme for complete 'modernisation' was studied in 1893–94, and authority given in 1896 for reconstruction. From that year until 1906 work was carried on steadily,

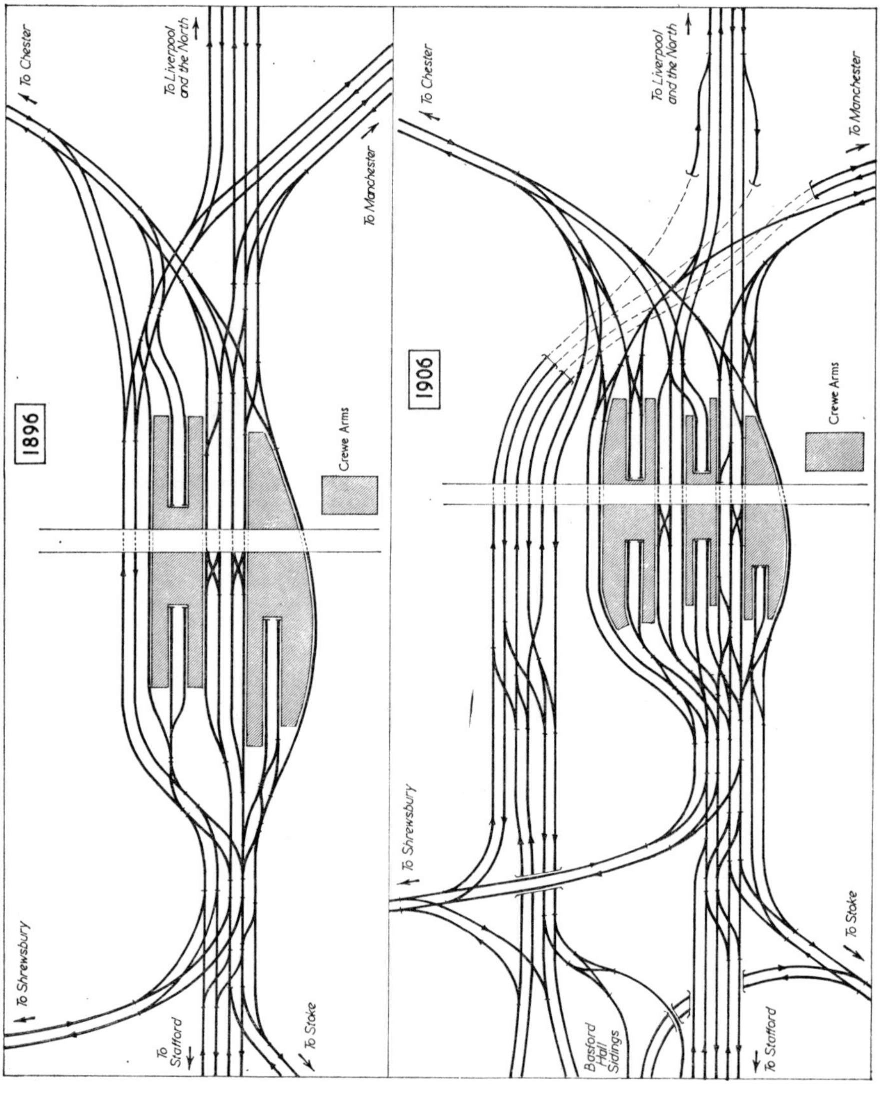

16a Layout at Crewe, 1896

16b Layout at Crewe, 1906

not merely to improve passenger facilities in Crewe station but, above all, to keep goods trains away from it. Prior to 1896 there had been only one up freight track and one down which did not go through the platform area, and anything to or from Manchester had to cross the main-line tracks. North Staffordshire freights had to go through the station, though a long time before there had been a scheme to take a lead from the N.S. to near Coppenhall, crossing the Manchester line but avoiding Crewe station.

By means of a series of burrowing junctions, entirely new goods relief lines, and the great array of sorting sidings at Basford Hall, totalling 35 track miles in all, the old Crewe arrangement was remodelled into that indicated in Fig. 16b, which in all essentials is what Crewe is still today. The last job in the station reconstruction was the new island platform, now nos. 1 and 2; the old nos. 1 and 2 were renumbered 3 and 4, and became the main up platform, though no. 3 face is still used for down trains also. This reconstruction almost doubled the platform area.

North of Crewe, quadrupling of tracks began before the end of last century. Warrington to Winwick was undertaken in 1880–81; Golborne and Bamfurlong to Wigan (Springs Branch Junction) in stages from 1888 to 1895; and Standish junction to Euxton junction, with a second pair of tracks on a separate alignment for a mile or so, from 1888 to 1895 under Act 51 & 52 Vict., cap. 176. Euxton junction to Preston was already four-track, the work being done in 1879–81 along with the widening of the Ribble bridge; but the section from Wigan through Boar's Head cutting to Standish remains double to this day, as does the Winwick–Golborne cut-off.

Beyond Preston little in the way of quadrupling was ever attempted; but in 1903 goods loops were put in over the four miles north of Preston (Greenbank) to Barton & Broughton, these following the remodelling of the curves immediately north of Preston station after the smash in 1896. Early in the present century further goods loops were put in at Garstang, Oubeck, Burton, Shap summit, Clifton and Southwaite; and the old Grayrigg down loop, dating from 1849 and lengthened by a hundred yards in 1854, was extended. Slight deviations were also made towards the end of last century at Wreay and between Grayrigg and Low Gill under Act 51 & 52 Vict., cap. 176. In 1889 came powers for a deviation between Clifton and Penrith, whereby the old main line became the goods loop, and the slight deviation the main line; this was opened on July 27, 1892. One operating disadvantage never removed while the railways were in private hands was the long block section from Upperby to Wreay on the up line, a $3\frac{1}{2}$-mile length which, in conjunction with the start from Carlisle and the ascending gradient of 1 in 131, meant a headway of 9 to 10 min. between passenger trains, and longer if a passenger train was following a goods train.

South of Warrington the original Grand Junction line preceded the Manchester Ship Canal; and though it crossed the River Mersey and the Irwell & Mersey canal by a bridge at a height around 28/30 ft. the line was generally near ground level. When the Ship Canal came into being

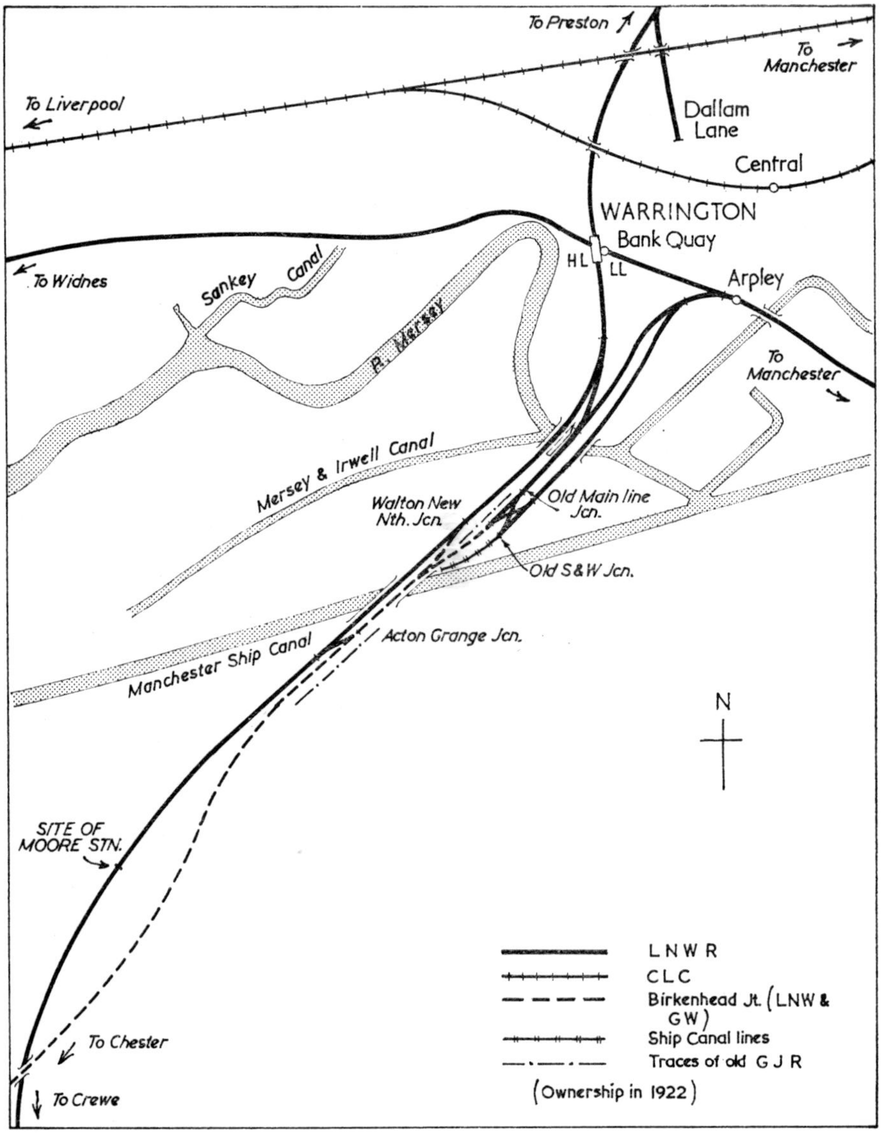

17 Layout around Warrington, 1922

the railway had to be raised considerably, and the present-day high-level girder bridge, a little to the west of the old G.J.R. bridge, is approached at each end by a gradient of 1 in 135. Some of the original formation of the G.J.R. can still be seen at a lower level, partly in cutting, below the present up main line (see Fig. 17); it came out of Warrington on the long, low Arpley embankment at a gradient of only 1 in 500. To communicate with Arpley, and with the extensive sidings north of the Mersey on Arpley 'meadows,' in a way to avoid reversal, a connection was put in between the Ship Canal bridge and the old two-arch stone bridge over the Mersey, which bridge can still be seen in service, and so has well fulfilled the stipulation of the G.J.R. Act of 1833 that it should be "firm and substantial." The gradient from the old bridge up to the high-level bridge would have been inconveniently severe for up trains starting from Warrington if it had been used also for the main line, and the curvature would probably have necessitated some speed restriction in the opposite direction; hence the newer 1 in 135 approach to the present main-line bridge. There is still the direct connection from Bank Quay to the old line to permit of freight and empty-stock movements; and the 'old-bridge new-bridge' route still is available and is sometimes used by main line trains to meet some local *contretemps*.

Warrington Bank Quay today has no traces of the original station nor of the enlargements made after the G.J.R. came north in 1837. The two-level Bank Quay was opened on November 16, 1868, giving passenger connection by stairs between the main line and the Widnes-Broadheath line. The low-level part of the station is now closed. South of the Ship Canal is the double-track line going off on the up side, and crossing over the main line near Norton to reach Frodsham. Over this line there was by the early 1850s a Manchester–Chester service of four trains a day each way, running via the L. & M. line between Manchester and Newton and so through Warrington. There was also an early Royal train trip over this line, in September 1853, when Queen Victoria, the Prince Consort and family travelled from Holyhead to Edinburgh via Chester, Warrington, Newton, Parkside and Carlisle, stopping at Carlisle for late luncheon. Probably on this occasion only has the Royal train ever been drawn by animal power, as from Holyhead jetty to Holyhead station the laden train was pulled by "six stout horses."

A few principal Anglo-Scottish expresses have always called at Wigan even down to the present day (e.g. the 16.05 ex Euston to Glasgow), but the station never attained an importance comparable to Preston on the Grand Trunk Route; it has been more a connecting and distributing point for passenger trains from various parts of Lancashire, and the area from the station south to Bamfurlong was for many years a great centre for marshalling coal trains. Though improvements were made from time to time in the old N.U. station, the present station with its two islands and one single platform came later, and the last real enlargements were in 1895. The principal occurrence in the old station was the derailment at speed on August 1, 1873, of the 20.00 'Tourist' express out of Euston, on that night a double-headed formation with no fewer than 25 vehicles. The last ten carriages left the rails, and eight of them were almost totally destroyed. Ten passengers were killed and 30 injured, but the cause of the accident was never firmly established.

Wigan's other claim to notice was the complex marshalling technique that so impressed Acworth in the 1880s. In his own words:

> "The newspaper train has another, though somewhat esoteric title to fame. It reaches Wigan at 10.10 a.m., bringing with it carriages

for Carlisle, and also two to be detached at Wigan. At this latter place it is joined by the 9.55 from Manchester, with through carriages for Edinburgh as well as Glasgow, also by the 9.35 from Liverpool, with carriages not only for Edinburgh and Glasgow, but for Blackburn and Perth in addition. Here is a piece of marshalling that for complexity is probably unequalled in the world. The train is timed to leave for the north after an interval of twenty minutes, and in the meanwhile a good deal of shunting has got to be done before it can start at 10.30 in the following order:

3 carriages from Crewe for Carlisle
2 ,, ,, Liverpool for Edinburgh
1 ,, ,, Manchester for Edinburgh
2 ,, ,, Manchester for Glasgow
2 ,, ,, Liverpool for Glasgow
1 ,, ,, London for Glasgow
3 ,, ,, Liverpool for Perth

"It is commonly said that every North Western official has been down to Wigan to see who can find the best solution of the puzzle. It is also whispered that no one is quite satisfied with any solution that has hitherto been offered."

Additional to being a centre of friction between the N.U. and the L. & P. and B. & P. as already recorded, the old Preston station was notorious for chaotic working and indiscipline. When the N.U. lease to the L.N.W.R./L.Y.R. combine took effect at the beginning of 1846 matters became worse, not better, for though James Chapman remained as local manager he no longer had the strong and instant backing of Theodore Rathbone, Hardman Earle and other firm N.U. directors, and had to work under a local committee. Chapman was able to frame clear and definite directions, but appears to have been too amiable for them to be obeyed without repetition, and he was inclined to be lenient before he took disciplinary action. In the earliest days much of the trouble was due to sheer inexperience, such as the disregard of time by engine-drivers, and this was particularly annoying at Parkside, as told in Chapter IV.

Though the offices of the N.U. management were at Preston station, all sections of the establishment there gave trouble. The platforms were only a few inches above rail-head level, and passengers developed the unchecked habit of crossing the tracks anywhere. The operating staff were more than once rebuked for crossing carriages via the small turntables from the east side of the station to the west when main-line traffic was about; to give more scope for these shunting movements a stationary pump had already been installed at Butler Street to obviate fouling movements by engines as they ran to and fro to fill their boilers by their own mechanically-driven pumps.

Booking clerks came negligently and carelessly on duty late in the mornings, until at least one of them had to go because of a cash deficiency in his till. The carrying department had to be reminded that no horse belonging to the company had to be sold or parted with on any pretence whatever without the written authority of the manager or the board. Officers and clerks at Preston had to be warned on February 3, 1844, that the L. & P. and L.C.C. were now friends of the N.U. and were using Butler Street station, and that none of those discriminatory practices in vogue up to January 1, 1842, had to be resumed. Despite previous chidings, when certain trains, particularly East Lancashire or Bolton-line trains, arrived there were often no porters to meet them, and on one such occasion the guard walked off without screwing on a brake, and the coaches began to move backward as the passengers detrained.

To cap it all, Chapman on September 30, 1847, was constrained to issue a notice to the staff: "Mr. Chapman is exceedingly surprised that any person in the company's employ should presume to put pigs into the Stables, and finding that the Head hostler has done so, desires that Mr. Robinson will instantly see that all pigs and fowls are cleared off the premises, the keeping of such being likely to lead to improper practices. The stable where the pigs now are is to be thoroughly cleaned and whitewashed, as no horse will live in it without, and any expense charged to the Hostler's wages."

Yes, indeed; from 1838 Preston could well be called the centre of the Crewe–Carlisle section: reasonably so geographically, and absolutely so for all happenings good, bad, indifferent and humorous. Lancaster might be the divisional headquarters; Preston was the headquarters of life. For many years all 'old soldiers' to be found on the railways in West Lancashire seemed to gravitate to Preston; and when their days were over increased tempo of station operation carried on the vitality. It must have been with a sigh of relief that after 25 years on the Wigan Branch, Preston & Wigan and N.U. Railways James Chapman wrote out his final order of the day on January 1, 1856: "Take notice that I have left the company's service, and that Mr. Dawlings is authorised to fill my place for the present."

Partly as a result of East Lancashire Railway opposition in 1855 to a Bill for a new and improved station layout, in which the L. & C. would have had a share, (but only as a result of its opposition to the original L.N.W.R. proposals), the N.U. station at Preston, despite some enlargements, retained many of its primitive features and poor accommodation for 42 years after it was opened. Not until 1880, in a major rebuilding sanctioned ten years earlier under Act 33 & 34 Vict., cap. 84, dated July 4, 1870, did the station assume anything like its present layout and form, and even then a pair of the old small turntables on platform tracks seem to have been retained for some years. This was the time when the great island platform 110 ft. wide, now Nos. 5 and 6, was put in and the large dining rooms on it opened. This made a wonderful difference to the 20-min. stop for late luncheon of all four Anglo-Scottish expresses. This stop for meals had been introduced first with regularity in March 1863, though spasmodic attempts had been made before. At that time the principal day train, the 10.00 ex Euston for Glasgow, instituted in June 1862, ran through Preston without stopping, running non-stop from Warrington (dep. 14.35) to Lancaster (arr. 16.07); but in the March of

1863 the Lancaster stop was eliminated and the train halted at Preston from 15.23 to 15.43—"time to dine" in the old call. Thus began the rough-and-ready period of the hot and perspiring woman.

In the early 1890s the 10.00 ex Euston to Edinburgh and Glasgow was due in at Preston at 14.20 and left at 14.40; the 10.30 ex Euston to Perth followed it into the present No. 5 platform at 14.50 and left at 15.10. Before this, in the up direction, the Glasgow–Euston express drew in alongside the other face of the island, No. 6 today, at 14.05 and left at 14.25, to be followed immediately by the up Perth. Thus in 65 min. four train loads had to be served with 'the Preston ordinary' at 2s. 6d. a head—but not by the hot and perspiring woman; the whole business had been more thoroughly organised, and passengers were served by waitresses who were "the pink of courtesy and overflowing with attention, and absolutely indifferent to tips" according to a writer of 65 years ago. From then on to the end of the 19th Century, when increasing use of dining cars did away with the 20 min. halt, was the hey-day of Preston station in a social sense, and one of its two hey-days in an operating sense.

It was the celebrated '2.00 p.m. corridor' out of Euston that started the rot. As a train, it began to run at the end of 1889; a first class diner was added in July 1891; but the appellation 'corridor' did not come until July 1893, when a second (third class) diner was added and two completely new 10-car trains vestibuled throughout were built specially for the service. Thereafter more trains quickly were given dining facilities, including the morning Glasgow and Perth pairs.

The 2.00 p.m. 'corridor' trains from Euston and Glasgow also led to the high noon of the first of the two operating heydays at Preston which quite put the Wigan efforts into the shade. The times varied a few minutes from year to year, but those of July 1895 are given. At 17.58 there arrived, at Preston from the north the 16.20 ex Windermere to Manchester, but marshalled behind the engine was a Whitehaven–London composite which had been picked up at Carnforth. At 18.08 arrived the up Perth express, marshalled in sequence Aberdeen–Euston, Edinburgh–Euston, Edinburgh–Liverpool, and Edinburgh–Manchester. At 18.15 the Windermere–Manchester train departed with the Edinburgh–Manchester coach in the rear; meantime the Crewe engine of the up Perth had collected the Whitehaven–Euston carriage. At 18.12 the up 2.00 p.m. 'corridor' from Glasgow arrived behind a Preston engine—or engines, as double-heading was the rule through the last ten years or so of the Webb *régime*; its coaches were marshalled in sequence for Euston, Liverpool, Manchester. The Crewe engine and Whitehaven coach, which had by that time picked up also the Aberdeen–Euston and Edinburgh–Euston carriages that had come in on the up Perth, then backed on to the Glasgow–Euston vehicles, and the train was away at 18.28, after a stop of 11 min. At 18.22 departed the Liverpool vehicles from Edinburgh and Glasgow off the two separate trains, but with one or two local Preston–Liverpool carriages added in front. Finally, at 18.34, the Glasgow–Manchester vehicles left in a train of their own. All these trains were handled at platforms 6 and 7 (present nos.) largely with the help of the scissors cross-over near the middle of

No. 6. With strict punctuality all went reasonably well; but of a December evening with trains running out of course it was chaos and old night.

During the last ten minutes of all this work the shouting and the tumult began to drift over to the other face of the big island, now No. 5, and to the adjacent face (now No. 4), where there had been monastic calm and urbanity. At 18.20 arrived the 17.30 ex Liverpool followed at 18.24 by the 17.40 ex Manchester, both of which had portions for Edinburgh and for Glasgow. At 18.30 the 2.00 p.m. 'corridor' out of Euston glided into No. 5. Within six minutes it had acquired the Glasgow carriages from both of the Lancashire cities, dropped coaches from Euston to Aberdeen and Whitehaven, and was off at 18.36. At 18.42 departed for the north a train with the Edinburgh coaches from Liverpool and Manchester, the Aberdeen coach from Euston, and the Euston–Whitehaven compo; and a stop of two minutes was made at Carnforth to detach the last-named vehicle.

There was at least one other marshalling puzzle that Preston sorted out daily around the turn of the century, but this was eased by being always in daylight hours. It was in connection with the 11.30 ex Euston. At 15.27 arrived from Manchester a train with carriages for Glasgow, Edinburgh and Keswick, followed in at 15.32 by a similar train from Liverpool with carriages for the same three places and also one for Whitehaven. 15.38 saw the arrival of the 11.30 ex Euston with vehicles for all four of the above-named places; and the three trains were then re-marshalled into a 15.47 departure for Glasgow and Edinburgh; another at 15.56 for Penrith and Keswick; and finally a 16.05 train for Whitehaven; but into the second and third trains were also put coaches from Manchester to Windermere and Whitehaven which had arrived in a separate train at 15.49, after the Anglo-Scottish express had left.

On July 13, 1896, the 20.00 sleeping-car express from Euston was derailed north of Preston station by running at too high a speed round the curves. The train was composed of six W.C.J.S. sleepers and one composite, all of them bogie vehicles, drawn by two 2–4–0 engines Nos. 275 *Vulcan* and 2159 *Shark*. *Vulcan* had put up the record time from Preston to Carlisle in the 1888 Race. An immediate result was deceleration, and an absolute veto against any resumption of the previous year's racing. Another result was that, as the station needed further enlargement, particularly to cope with the growing Blackpool and Fylde Coast traffic, a large amount of property to the west and north-west, including Charles Street, was bought, and this not only permitted the erection of a new island platform (now Nos. 1 and 2), but also enabled the sharp reverse curve to the north of the station to be eased considerably, though even now the left-hand curve of the main line is no more than about 330 yd. radius. The new island platform, and a dock for horse and similar traffic, were commissioned in 1903.

With the entry of the East Lancashire Railway into Preston in 1850 (under 10 & 11 Vict. cap. 289, of July 22, 1847, which Act authorised a separate station just south of Butler Street), and years later of the West Lancashire Railway to another station further down Fishergate, and the gradual growth of traffic, the layout of lines in the vicinity of Preston and the working of an intense train service became most complex. So much so that in the inter-war years, when traffic on summer Saturdays probably reached its peak, as many as 980 passenger trains were handled in 24 hr. at the main station. At such periods, the second of the two operating hey-days, trains from the north to Blackpool, and trains starting at Preston for the north, could be seen heading south over the Ribble out of the old Butler Street and East Lancashire portion of the station, and re-appearing northbound some 15 min. later through the newest platforms Nos. 1 and 2, the journey being effected via Preston junction, Lostock Hall junction, and the two Farington junctions, as shown in Fig. 18. All the curves shown except Farington East were in use before the turn of the century. By this means the main north and south platforms, Nos. 4, 5 and 6, and the approach lines, were kept clear for Anglo-Scottish traffic and for the trains from the south to Blackpool, and awkward reversals with attendant extra engine movements were obviated.

Lancaster's early importance as the connecting point with the Little

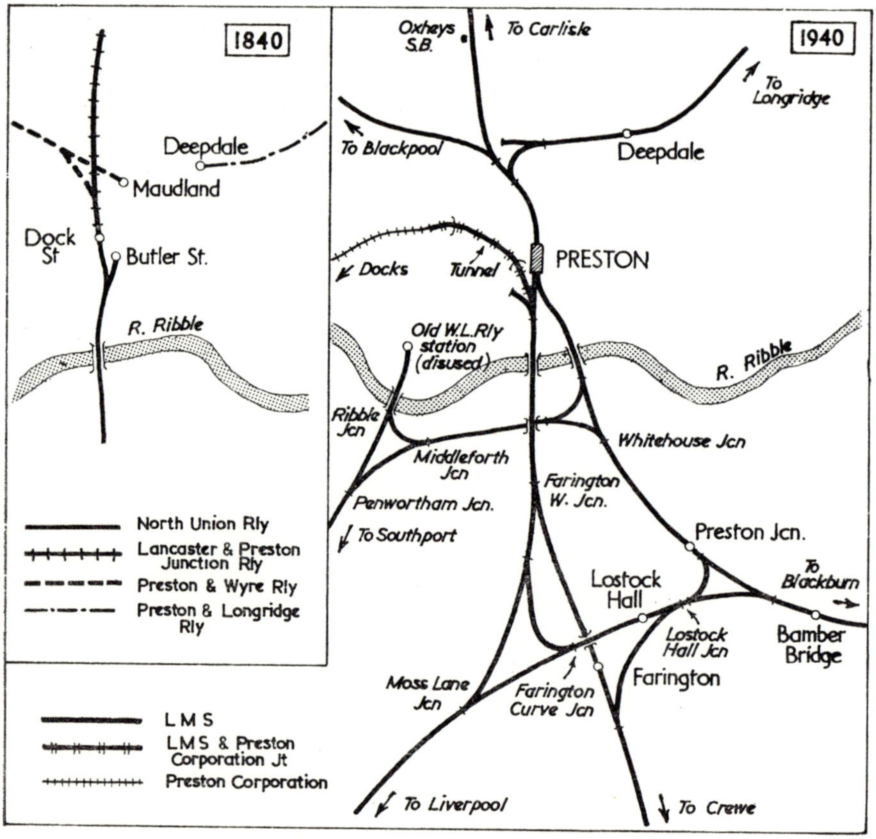

18 Layouts around Preston, 1840 and 1940

North Western Railway disappeared when the Wennington–Carnforth line was built; the junction point then became Carnforth, and as the Furness lines also came in there Carnforth soon grew far above its original wayside station level, though to this day it has no facilities for passenger-train remarshalling, so that trains which are to combine, such as the 8.20 up ex Carlisle and the 8.35 ex Barrow, must run at close headway on to Lancaster to combine.

The Lancaster shuttle service between the Little North Western station by the river bank at Green Ayre (called 'Green Area' in the early reports up to 1863) and Castle station began on December 19, 1849, but was suspended on October 31, 1876. It was resumed on February 1, 1881, and from then two or three goods trains a day also used the curve as well as three passenger trains in each direction. Years later, in 1908, this loop was electrified as part of the Heysham–Lancaster conversion. Years later again, an attenuated service by push-and-pull steam trains was introduced on February 12, 1951, while the line was being experimentally re-electrified at 50 cycles. Electric service began on August 17, 1953, over the whole Lancaster–Heysham route, but from September 1955 to March 1956 steam push-and-pull trains again worked these lines while the overhead structure was being renewed. Finally the loop was closed to all services on January 3, 1966, though the track has not yet (October 1968) been removed.

Lancaster Castle station retained much of its original or 1852 enlargement structure and layout, including very low platforms, until 1902, when the present station was completed after some four years' work. When the remodelling began in 1898 the old station still had only one up platform and one down platform, each with a bay at the north end, and there was an up and down goods loop round the back of the up platform. The two through fast lines between the main platforms date from 1902. The new layout was needed not only to deal with the great increase in the number of main-line trains passing through from the late 80s onwards, but also with the growth of Morecambe since the opening of the direct curve, and the need of handling the four or so trains a day in each direction on the Glasson Dock branch. One of the Glasson trains in each direction (the 8.00 ex Castle and the 17.30 ex Glasson) was a mixed passenger and goods. The amount of traffic at Castle in those days is scarcely realised. In the summer of 1903 there were 60 main-line passenger-train arrivals and 47 departures in the 24 hr., plus 20 Morecambe trains in each direction and the Glasson and Green Ayre locals. Considerable freight traffic also passed through the station.

The importance of the Morecambe traffic at Castle began only in 1888 when the direct double-track curve from Morecambe South junction to Bare Lane, and a new Morecambe station at Euston Road, were opened. Schedule time for Castle–Morecambe trains by this route was 9 min. compared with the Midland's 6 min. from Green Ayre. All 20 pairs of trains in the early years of the present century had to be dovetailed in with main-line passenger and freight trains over the first 1½ miles north of Castle. Out of Morecambe some of the trains went on past Lancaster to Preston or Manchester; but all up trains off the Morecambe branch going into the bay at Castle had to cross the down main line twice. Despite the 50 per cent longer travelling time, 9 min. as against 6 min., this service from Castle quickly captured much of the traffic from Green Ayre, because many of the trains on that route came from Hellifield or beyond, and the Midland was notoriously unpunctual.

This L.N.W.R. service succeeded what was perhaps the most extraordinary branch-line service ever to get itself off a main line. This also was an L.N.W.R. working, which 'served' Morecambe via the single-track curve from Hest Bank to Bare Lane. This was the original Morecambe branch promoted by the L. & C., and opened in 1864 as far as a very small station at Bare Lane by the junction with the Little North Western on the outskirts of Morecambe. Some of the early trains terminated here; others were taken on to the Little North Western terminus, then away up Northumberland Road. A count made by the L. & C. local committee of the L.N.W.R. while the branch was under construction in 1862 showed that 89 passengers in the day walked from Morecambe to Hest Bank to join main-line trains.

As recorded in an earlier chapter, this short line had been built double track. The L.N.W.R. soon singled it, but contrived until 1888 to run a service of six or seven trains each way a day, some of which came from and went to Lancaster and others Carnforth. The only link at Hest Bank with this branch was a trailing connection off the down main line. Through trains from Carnforth arriving at Hest Bank on the up main line had to back over a cross-over at the station's north end on to the down main then run forward wrong-direction on to the branch, and reverse once again into the tiny bay at the back of the down platform before they proceeded finally along the branch to Morecambe. The site of the bay is where the camping coaches now stand. Trains from Lancaster had an equally tedious procedure and occupation of the main lines, for the engine had to run round its train on the down main by means of cross-overs. But 'modernised' signalling was put in at once in 1864 to deal with these movements, in the form of a double-needle telegraph to communicate with the boxes on each side, and a single-needle instrument to communicate with the pointsman at the branch points. Direct facing access from the north on to the branch was not put in until July 1934! Of late years, with the closure of the Wennington–Lancaster line, the branch has got its regular service once more, with the Leeds–Carnforth–Morecambe diesel multiple-units. Around the turn of the century this branch was used also by the Furness Railway for its local Grange-over-Sands to Morecambe service.

Carnforth began its career as a junction, and changed its name from the original Carnforth-Yealand of the L. & C., when the Ulverston line arrived in 1857. Ten years later it increased in importance and complexity when the Furness & Midland Railways' joint line was opened over the 9½ miles from Wennington, and each of the three companies using the station had its own engine shed in the vicinity. The area then took on the layout it has today, and shown in Fig. 15, which indicates the pre-Grouping ownership of the lines. For many years up and down Barrow trains had to use a single curved platform; the second curved platform to accommodate down trains was not put in until 1938. Carnforth's main importance in the Anglo-Scottish chain was for years as a mail point, with a succession of postal trains stopping there between 21.00 and 4.30. The place was also a great postal distributing centre; and 65 years ago R. E. Charlewood recorded that a letter for Whitehaven posted at St. Bees went to Carnforth and back, making a 144-mile journey for a crow-flight of 4½ miles. The station has one other claim to transient fame—it was the scene of one of the best of films, *Brief Encounter*.

Oxenholme, the L. & C.'s first junction, has, like every intermediate station between Preston and Carlisle, lost much of its old interest, and it had much in the halcyon days of the L.N.W.R. At the time of writing (May 1968) a couple of steam bankers for assisting trains up to Grayrigg are still in service, but they will have disappeared ere the book is on sale. As there has been no shed at Oxenholme for some years, the bankers came south from the relics of Tebay depot, and when this was closed they came north from Carnforth. Oxenholme shed ended its life with the indignity of being razed completely; but it was less than two years old when it suffered its first indignity, that of a section of it being partitioned off to form the dwelling of one, Dorrington, as his home for the winter "as long as the alterations do not cost more than £50."

The Windermere branch is still open, but its service can be described only as moribund compared with the 12 to 14 trains each way on weekdays, plus three or four others between Kendal and Oxenholme, in the last decade of the 19th Century. Those were the days when a 2–4–0 Precedent normally took 180 to 200 tons unaided up the 1 in 80 out of Kendal on to the main line, and proceeded with its train to Preston if not beyond; and the locals comprised five or ten small six-wheelers with first, second and third class accommodation, hauled by a Webb 4 ft. 6 in. 2–4–2T. Oxenholme, as the point of junction between the L. & C. and K. & W., in later days came to have good accommodation for changing passengers, including a small, warm and happy refreshment room on the down platform that lasted until the end of the second world war. But being a point of junction it was also a point of friction when main line and branch were owned by separate companies; this culminated in the ejection of the K. & W. from the Oxenholme telegraph office of the L. & C. when higher authority found that room being used as the K. & W. booking office.

Tebay's importance apart from housing the Shap bankers was mainly to do with the traffic brought in and the empties taken away by the North Eastern Railway over the cross-country Barnard Castle line. The 13-mile section from Tebay to Oxenholme and the 3.65-mile length on to Hincaster Junction was the only part of the old L. & C. route north of Carnforth to have regular foreign engine and train workings apart from the N.E.R. engines and trains over the short distance from Clifton to Penrith, and the short-time operations off the Ingleton branch already described. For a time the Furness Railway ran passenger services with its own engines from Grange to Kendal, and sometimes to Windermere, and such workings lasted until 1914. During the early years of this century the N.E.R. worked a morning service from Kirkby Stephen through Tebay to Oxenholme and Kendal, and paid the L.N.W.R. 6d. a time for the use of the Oxenholme turntable.

Having got to Tebay something may be said about the Shap bankers, practice in regard to which blew hot and blew cold over the years. The L. & C. reckoned on a banker from the opening of the line, and erected a small shed, a siding and a water tank, known as Loups Fell, half-a-mile north of the present Tebay station, and with a water reservoir up on Loups Fell itself. When the train had passed, the banker came out of its siding, ran after the train and buffered up on the move with whatever skill the particular driver might have. This practice lasted for many years, until, according to G. P. Neele, due to a failure of the train engine at the critical moment far too heavy a bump at the rear end created a commotion, and running after the train was forbidden. In those days 'the sport of banking up Shap' was perhaps a more apt description than 'the practice of banking', for within a fortnight of opening day a traveller was recording in *The Railway Times* that his four-coach train had dashed up Shap at not less than 25 m.p.h. and that the banker was never able to catch up with the train; and a statement in connection with the derailment of a heavy goods train at Dillicar in July 1857 recorded: "Drivers here put on full power to make good headway up Tebay incline."

Loups Fell siding for the banker remained until near the end of 1862, when the locomotive department, such as it was at Tebay, moved to the south end of the new station; and at the request of John Ramsbottom a short siding for the banker was put in there, so that the assisting engine could come on to the train in the station instead of away up the hill by the Birk Beck. This saved the services of two signalmen. At some time the banking of passenger trains up Shap ceased altogether. This was certainly the case during the last decade of the 19th century and the first years of the 20th century, but at that time double-heading of main-line passenger trains was practically universal over the Crewe–Carlisle division. The down 'Tourist' involved in the so-called 'frozen vacuum brake accident' at Carlisle in 1890 had been given a pilot from Preston to Shap with a load = to 15. At the turn of the century the only banking permitted north of Preston was for single-headed up passenger trains that stopped at Lancaster; these were banked from Castle up the mile of 1 in 98 to No. 1 box.

In March 1906 banking was reintroduced from Tebay up to Shap summit, and straightway train drivers were permitted to run through Tebay station at slow speed, and the banker followed out the south siding and caught up the moving train. This reintroduction of banking followed the appearance of Whale's 'Experiment' class 4–6–0 engines, which did away with more double-heading of the principal trains; over the preceding couple of years the Whale 'Precursors' had reduced piloted mileage considerably. Despite their general design and 6 ft. 3 in. wheels the 'Experiments' were not particularly good pullers; they got up Shap all right, but not at any great speed. Unassisted they could manage 28/30 m.p.h. minimum with 230 tons and 25 m.p.h. with 300 tons; but with 350 tons behind 18/20 m.p.h. was often the rate when the Summit box was passed after four miles up at 1 in 75. On the other hand they were swift engines, and could gallop down either side of Shap at 80/83 m.p.h. In 1906 the five or six 'Experiments' on the L. & C. section were put more on to semi-fasts, and another four 'Precursors' were drafted to Preston and Carlisle for the more arduous duties; for a time piloting remained if the load was '17' or over, which in W.C.J.S. meant about 300 tons.

Another uphill change came in 1908 when banking of passenger trains up Shap was again terminated. Trains of a weight to need assistance were stopped at Oxenholme where a pilot, usually a 6 ft. or 6 ft. 6 in. 2–4–0, was put on and ran through to Carlisle. Southbound expresses were piloted in the same fashion, and a stop at Oxenholme was made to detach the assisting engine. The same pilot thus did duty on both Grayrigg and Shap in the northbound direction, but at the expense of a good deal of extra engine mileage.

Quite a lot of piloting was practised on freight trains in the early days of the L. & C., but usually with engines of the same Crewe type as the train engine. Ramsbottoms' 'Lady of the Lake' or 'Problem' class 2–2–2s were rarely seen north of Preston, whether as pilots or train engines; it was the Ramsbottom and Webb 2–4–0 classes that were the backbone of piloting for half a century, into L.M.S.R. days. But they did not look after all the piloting; and probably it was on these duties over the old Lancaster & Carlisle system that the Ramsbottom DX and Webb 'Cauliflower' 0–6–0 engines began to get their names as lightning runners.

Bibliography

As much of this book has been built up from the board minutes of the various railways that at one time made up the route from Crewe to Carlisle, frequent reference by individual footnotes has been avoided to improve readability. The board minutes consulted, and some of the other works to which reference was made, are given below.

Board Minutes and Associated Records	Wigan Branch Railway Preston & Wigan Railway North Union Railway Grand Junction Railway Liverpool & Manchester Railway Lancaster & Carlisle Railway Newcastle & Carlisle Railway London & North Western Railway (General Merchandise & Locomotive Committee)

The Finger Post, or Direct Road from John o' Groats to Land's End. (1825)

An Account of the Liverpool & Manchester Railway. Henry Booth. (July 1830)

A Description of the Liverpool & Manchester Railway. J. S. Walker. (1832)

Preston & Wyre Railway Prospectus. (1835)

Carlisle Journal. (August 22, 1835)

Report on the London & Glasgow Railway. (to the G.J.R. Board). Joseph Locke (1836)

The London & Glasgow Railway. Cornelius Nicholson (1837)

Cornelius Nicholson—A Well-Spent Life. Cornelia Nicholson (1890)

Report on Proposed Railway from Carlisle to Glasgow and Edinburgh by Annandale. Joseph Locke (1838)

Report to the Kendal Committee of the Lancaster, Kendal & Carlisle Railway. George Larmer (1840)

Railway Communication With Scotland; Report on Proposed Lancaster and Penrith Railway. Francis Whishaw (1840)

Report on the Formation of a Railway Between Lancaster and Carlisle. George Stephenson (1837)

Report on the Practicability of Embanking the Estuaries of Morecambe and Duddon. John Hague (1838)

Report on West Cumberland, Furness and Morecambe Bay Railway. By J.U. Rastrick (1838)

Reports of the Railway Commissioners on Communications With Scotland. (1840-41)

The Book of the Grand Junction Railway. Thomas Roscoe (1839)

Freeling's Grand Junction Railway Companion. (1837)

Drake's Road Book of the London & Birmingham and Grand Junction Railways. (1839)

Coghlan's Iron Road Book (to Liverpool, Manchester and Birmingham). (1839)

Mogg's Guide to the Grand Junction Railway. (1842)
Evidence on the Bill for Railway Regulation. (1841)
Kendal Mercury and *Westmorland Gazette.* (1837-47)
Steel's Guide to the Lancaster & Carlise Railway. (December 1846)
Scott & Benson's Guide & Handbook to the Lancaster & Carlisle Railway. (1847)
Railways; Their Rise, Progress and Construction. Robert Ritchie (1846)
Railways of the United Kingdom Statistically Considered. H. Scrivenor (1849-51)
Rides on Railways. Sam Sidney (1851)
Bradshaw's Guide. (September 1847)
The Octuple Agreement. (January 1, 1851)
English - Scottish Traffic Agreement. (January 1, 1856)
Life of Joseph Locke. J. Devey (1862)
Life of C. B. Vignoles. O. Vignoles (1889)
Railway Reminiscences. G. P. Neele (1904)
British Railways; Their Passenger Services. J. Pearson Pattinson (1893)
Board of Trade Report on Accident at Carlisle Station. (1890)
The Battle of Crown Street. G. O. Holt (*The Railway Magazine.* August 1963)
History of the London & North Western Railway. W. L. Steel. (1914)
L.M.S.R. Centenary Number; The Railway Gazette. (September 1938)
Carlisle Citadel Station Centenary Brochure. (1947)
Chronological List of the Railways in Lancashire. M. D. Greville (1953)
Lancaster & Preston Junction Railway. M. D. Greville and G. O. Holt (1960)
Lancaster Canal Tramroad. Gordon Biddle. (Jnl. of Railway & Canal Historical Society, Sept. & Nov., 1963)
R. B. Dockray's Diary. By Michael Robbins (Journal of Transport History, Nov. 1965)

Parliamentary Acts

Warrington & Newton Railway	10 Geo. 4, cap. 37, May 14, 1829 (Incorp.) 11 Geo. 4, cap. 57, May 29, 1830 (Branch, capital, locos.) 5 & 6 Wm. 4, cap. 8, June 12, 1835 (Purchased by G.J.R.) Extension Bill 1830 (Southward to Norton)
Wigan Branch Railway	11 Geo. 4, cap. 56, May 29, 1830 (Incorp.) 4 & 5 Wm. 4, cap. 25, May 22, 1834 (Absorption into N.U.)
Preston & Wigan Railway	1 Wm. 4, cap. 56, April 22, 1831 (Incorp.) 4 & 5 Wm. 4, cap. 25, May 22, 1834 (Absorption into N.U.)
North Union Railway	4 & 5 Wm. 4, cap. 25, May 22, 1834 (Incorp.) 3 & 4 Vict., cap. 5, March 23, 1840 (More capital) 7 & 8 Vict., cap. 2, May 10, 1844 (Amalgamation with B.&P.) 8 & 9 Vict., cap. 116, July 21, 1845 (Ribble Docks branch) 9 & 10 Vict., cap. 231, July 27, 1846 (Vesting in G.J.R. & M. & L.) 28 Vict., cap. 22, May 26, 1865 (L.N.W.R./L.Y.R. more capital for N.U. purposes) 51 & 52 Vict., cap. 176, August 7, 1888 (Dissolution)
Liverpool & Manchester Railway	8 & 9 Vict., cap. 123, July 21, 1845 (Parkside West curve)
Grand Junction Railway	3 & 4 Wm. 4, cap. 34, May 6, 1833 (Incorp.) 5 & 6 Wm. 4, cap. 8, June 12, 1835 (Purchase of W. & N.) 5 & 6 Wm. 4, cap. 9, June 12, 1835 (Alteration of lines) 8 & 9 Vict., cap. 198, July 1, 1845 (Consolidation of G.J.R., L.M.R., M. & B., B. & L., K. & L. Jct.) 9 & 10 Vict., cap. 231, July 27, 1846 (Lease of N.U. to M. & L./G.J.R.) 9 & 10 Vict., cap. 261, July 27, 1846 (New lines in Lancashire)
Chester & Crewe Railway	7 Wm. 4 & 1 Vict., cap. 63, June 30, 1837 (Incorp.) 3 & 4 Vict., cap. 69, May 19, 1840 (Take-over by G.J.R.)
Manchester & Birmingham Railway	7 Wm. 4 & 1 Vict., cap. 69, June 30, 1837 (Incorp.)
London & North Western Railway	9 & 10 Vict., cap. 204, July 16, 1846 (Incorp.) 9 & 10 Vict., cap. 294, July 22, 1847 (Various lines) 24 & 25 Vict., cap. 128, July 11, 1861 (Winwick cut-off, etc.) 33 & 34 Vict., cap. 84, July 4, 1870 (Preston station and lines) 41 & 42 Vict., cap. 182, July 22, 1878 (New lines and widenings including Glasson branch) 42 & 43 Vict., cap. 117, July 3, 1879 (New lines) 42 & 43 Vict., cap. 142, July 21, 1879 (Dissolution of L. & C. and K. & W., etc.) 51 & 52 Vict., cap. 176, August 7, 1888 (Dissolution of N.U. and P. & W.)
Preston & Wyre Railway	5 & 6 Wm. 4, cap. 58, July 3, 1835 (Incorp.) 7 Wm. 4, cap. 28, 1837 (Alter line and amend Act) 8 & 9 Vict., cap. 125, July 21, 1845 (Three branches) 9 & 10 Vict., cap. 306, March 1, 1847 (Lease to M. & L./L.Y.R.) 12 & 13 Vict., cap. 74, July 28, 1849 (Legalising L.N.W.R. participation in above lease) 28 Vict., cap. 22, May 26, 1865 (L.Y.R./L.N.W.R. more capital for P. & W. purposes) 34 & 35 Vict., cap. 64, June 29, 1871 (Amalgamation of B. & Lytham with P. & W.) 51 & 52 Vict., cap. 176, August 7, 1888 (Dissolution)

Manchester & Leeds Railway (Lancashire & Yorkshire Rly)	9 & 10 Vict., cap. 231, July 27, 1846 (Lease of N.U. jointly with G.J.R.) 10 & 11 Vict., cap. 163, July 9, 1847 (Change of name to L.Y.R.)
Bolton & Preston Railway	7 Wm. 4 & 1 Vict., cap. 121, July 15, 1837 (Incorp.) 1 & 2 Vict., cap. 56, July 4, 1838 (Euxton deviation) 7 & 8 Vict., cap. 2, May 10, 1844 (Amalgamation with N.U.)
Lancaster & Preston Jct. Railway	7 Wm. 4, cap. 22, May 5, 1837 (Incorp.) 3 & 4 Vict., cap. 4, March 1840 (More capital) 6 & 7 Vict., cap. 4, April 3, 1843 (Lease to L.C.C.) 12 & 13 Vict., cap. 87, August 1, 1849 (Transfer of management to L. & C.) 22 & 23 Vict., cap. 124, August 13, 1859 (Full absorption of L. & P. into L. & C.)
Preston & Longridge Railway	6 & 7 Wm. 4, cap. 122, July 14, 1836 (Incorp.)
Fleetwood, Preston & West Riding Jct. Railway	9 & 10 Vict., cap. 246, July 27, 1846 (Incorp.) 19 & 20 Vict., cap. 44, June 23, 1856 (Re-incorp. of Co.) 30 Vict., cap. 95, June 17, 1867 (Lease of F.P.W.R. to L.N.W.R./L.Y.R.)
East Lancashire Railway	10 & 11 Vict., cap. 289, July 12, 1847 (Incorp.)
Kendal & Windermere Railway	8 & 9 Vict., cap. 32, June 30, 1845 (Incorp.) 22 & 23 Vict., cap. 124, August 13, 1859 (Lease to L. & C.) 42 & 43 Vict., cap. 142, July 21, 1879 (Dissolution)
Lancaster & Carlisle Railway	7 & 8 Vict., cap. 37, June 6, 1844 (Incorp.) 8 & 9 Vict., cap. 83, June 21, 1845 (Lancaster deviation) 9 & 10 Vict., cap. 257, July 27, 1846 (Citadel station) 13 Vict., cap. 87, August 1, 1849 (Management of L. & P.) 20 & 21 Vict., cap. 151, August 25, 1857 (Ingleton branch) 21 & 22 Vict., cap. 128, July 23, 1858 (Low Gill deviation, and L. & P. matters) 22 & 23 Vict., cap. 124, August 13, 1859 (Consolidation of L. & C. Acts, Morecambe branch, full absorption of L. & P., lease of K. & W.) 42 & 43 Vict., cap. 142, July 21, 1879 (Full absorption of L. & C. into L.N.W.R.)
Citadel Station	9 & 10 Vict., cap. 257, July 27, 1846 (L. & C. to enlarge station) 24 & 25 Vict., cap. 166, July 22, 1861 (Enlargement, and regulation of management) 36 & 37 Vict., cap. 187, July 21, 1873 (Enlargement of station and construction of goods avoiding lines)
'Little' North Western Railway	9 & 10 Vict., cap. 92, June 30, 1846 (Incorp.)
Ulverstone & Lancaster Railway	14 & 15 Vict., cap. 102, July 24, 1851 (Incorp.)
Cockermouth, Keswick & Penrith Railway	24 & 25 Vict., cap. 203, August 1, 1861 (Incorp.)
Eden Valley Railway	21 & 22 Vict., cap. 14, 1858 (Railway Kirkby Stephen to Clifton)
Maryport & Carlisle Railway	1 Vict., cap. 111, July 12, 1837 (Incorp.)
Midland Railway	29 & 30 Vict., cap. 223, July 16, 1866 (Settle and Carlisle line)
Glasgow, Dumfries & Carlisle Railway	9 & 10 Vict., cap. 372, August 13, 1846 (Incorp.)
Caledonian Railway	8 & 9 Vict., cap. 162, July 31, 1845 (Incorp.) 9 & 10 Vict., cap. 249, July 27, 1846 (Deviation at Carlisle)

Index